CAESAR

CAESAR

Allan Massie

Carroll & Graf Publishers, Inc.
New York

Copyright © 1933 by Allan Massie

All rights reserved.

Published by arrangement with the author.

First published in Great Britain in 1993 by Hodder & Stoughton.

First Carroll & Graf edition 1994

Carroll & Graf Publishers, Inc.
260 Fifth Avenue
New York, NY 10001

Library of Congress Cataloging-in-Publication Data

Massie, Allan, 1938–
    Caesar / Allan Massie. — 1st Carroll & Graf ed.
      p.   cm.
    ISBN 0-7867-0121-8 : $20.00
    1. Caesar, Julius—Fiction. 2. Heads of state—
Rome—Fiction.
    3. Generals—Rome—Fiction. I. Title.
    PR6063.A79C34 1994
    823'.914—dc20   94-26430
                                    CIP

Manufactured in the United States of America

First, for Alison, as ever,
then, for Giles Gordon.

CHRONOLOGY

BC

100	Birth of Caesar.
81	Dictatorship of Sulla.
80	Military service in Asia. Alleged affair with King Nicomedes IV of Bithynia.
67–66	Forms alliance with Pompey and Crassus.
63	Pontifex Maximus. Consulship of Cicero. Conspiracy of Catiline.
60	First Triumvirate of Pompey, Crassus and Caesar.
59	Caesar's first consulship. Marriage to Calpurnia, daughter of L. Calpurnius Piso.
58	Proconsul of Cisalpine Gaul, Illyricum and, finally, Transalpine Gaul. Campaigns against the Helvetii and Ariovistus.
57	Campaign against the Belgae (Nervii).
56	Further campaigns in Brittany and Normandy. Renewal of First Triumvirate. Campaign against Veneti.
55	Proconsulship renewed for five years. Crossing of Rhine. First invasion of Britain.
54	Second invasion of Britain.
53	Second crossing of Rhine. Crassus defeated and killed by Parthians at Carrhae.
52	Revolt of Vercingetorix defeated at Alesia. Disturbances in Rome. Clodius murdered and Pompey elected sole consul.
51	Siege of Uxellodunum. End of Gallic War, and publication of Caesar's *Commentaries*. His Optimate opponents attempt to get him recalled to Rome.
50	Continued efforts by Caesar's enemies to bring him to trial.
49	Caesar ordered to dismiss his army. Pompey granted the

authority of a dictator. Civil war begins in January with crossing of Rubicon. Pompeian forces surrender in Spain. Caesar elected dictator.

48   Second consulship. Pompey defeats Caesar at Dyrrhachium but is defeated at Pharsalus and murdered in Egypt. Caesar occupies Alexandria.

47   Alexandrian War ends. Caesar defeats Pharnaces at Zela in Asia Minor.

46   Third consulship. Appointed dictator for ten years. Defeats Pompeians in Africa. Publication of Cicero's *Cato* and Caesar's *Anti-Cato*.

45   Pompeian army defeated at Battle of Munda. End of civil war. Fourth consulship.

44   Becomes Perpetual Dictator and is elected to fifth consulship. Attempts to crown Caesar as King in February. Preparations for Parthian campaign. Caesar murdered in March.

LIST OF PRINCIPAL CHARACTERS

(GAIUS) JULIUS CAESAR	Roman general, statesman and historian; Perpetual Dictator after his defeat of Pompey

His family and their relation to him:

CALPURNIA	fourth wife, daughter of Lucius Calpurnius Piso, ally of Pompey
JULIA	daughter, fourth wife of Pompey
JULIA	sister, mother of Octavius
GAIUS OCTAVIUS THURINUS	nephew and adoptive son, the future Augustus

His circle:

DECIMUS JUNIUS BRUTUS ALBINUS	Roman general and admiral; Caesar's closest friend and adviser, but also one of his assassins
LONGINA	Decimus Brutus' wife, daughter of
GAIUS LONGINUS CASSIUS	Roman general and praetor; a Pompeian who joined Caesar after the Battle of Pharsalus, but led the plot to assassinate him; brother-in-law of
MARCUS JUNIUS BRUTUS	cousin of Decimus Brutus and nephew of Caesar's enemy, Marcus Porcius Cato, whose daughter he marries; a supporter of Pompey who changed sides after Pharsalus, he was made Governor of Cisalpine Gaul and reluctantly drawn into the assassination plot
SERVILIA	Marcus Brutus' mother, half-sister of Cato, most favoured of Caesar's mistresses

PORCIA	Marcus Brutus' second wife, daughter of Marcus Cato and an accomplice in the assassination conspiracy
YOUNG CATO	Porcia's brother and one of Caesar's assassins
PUBLIUS SERVILIUS CASCA	cousin of Decimus Brutus, a tribune and loyal Caesarean although among Caesar's assassins
LUCIUS CORNELIUS CINNA	married to Pompey's daughter and one of Caesar's assassins
METELLUS CIMBER	civil war hero, the banishment of whose brother, Lucius Tillius Cimber, plays a significant part in the assassination of Caesar
GAIUS TREBONIUS	politician and tribune, who distinguishes himself in the Battle of Alesia; one of Caesar's assassins
MARCUS ANTONIUS (MARK ANTONY)	Roman general and consul, member of the Second Triumvirate
MARCUS TULLIUS CICERO	consul, orator and writer
GNAEUS CALPURNIUS PISO	son of L. Calpurnius Piso (brother-in-law of Caesar), a consul and later Governor of Syria

His rivals:

SEXTUS POMPEIANUS (POMPEY)	Roman general and statesman, known as 'the Great One'; fellow Triumvir and later enemy during the civil war; murdered in Egypt
GNAEUS AND SEXTUS POMPEIANUS	Pompey's sons, and successors as leaders of his party
MARCUS LICINIUS CRASSUS	Roman general, millionaire, fellow Triumvir and later rival, defeated and killed in Parthia
TITUS ATIUS LABIENUS	formerly Caesar's most trusted Roman general, later his enemy during the civil war, killed in the Battle of Munda
MARCUS PORCIUS CATO	Roman statesman, general and Stoic

philosopher; half-brother of Servilia, whom he idolised, and arch-enemy of Caesar

Others:

CLEOPATRA — daughter of King Ptolemy XII, who became Queen of Egypt on the death of her young husband-brother, Ptolemy XIII

THEODOTUS — Greek scholar and adviser to King Ptolemy XIV, formerly his tutor

PUBLIUS CLODIUS PULCHER — aristocratic gang-leader and tribune, friend of Decimus Brutus, murdered by Pompey

CLODIA — Clodius' notorious sister and lover

CAELIUS RUFUS — rejected lover of Clodia, against whom she brings a lawsuit, in the defence of which Cicero destroys her reputation

GAIUS VALERIUS CATULLUS — Roman lyric poet, also a friend of Decimus Brutus, whose heart is broken by Clodia

QUINTUS LIGARIUS — successfully defended by Cicero when prosecuted for bearing arms against Caesar, and one of his assassins

MARCUS AEMILIUS ·LEPIDUS — Caesar's principal deputy, Master of the Horse, and member of Second Triumvirate; married to a daughter of Caesar's mistress, Servilia

GAIUS CILNIUS MAECENAS — Roman statesman and patron of Horace and Virgil; Octavius' closest friend and, later, adviser

MARCUS VIPSANIUS AGRIPPA — friend and confidant of Octavius, later his greatest general

PUBLIUS CORNELIUS DOLABELLA — tribune and consul, married to Cicero's daughter, Tullia

C. SCRIBONIUS CURIO — a tribune and Caesar's agent, friend of Decimus Brutus, killed by King Juba in N. Africa

VERCINGETORIX — Gallic chieftain and hero, captured by

	Caesar after the Battle of Alesia and later murdered
ARTIXES	guard and companion of Decimus Brutus; the son of his captor, a cousin of Vercingetorix
AULUS GABINIUS	legate and Pompey's henchman who became Governor of Syria
APPIUS CLAUDIUS PULCHER	the son of Caesar's enemy and, briefly, the lover of Decimus Brutus' wife, Longina
SER SULPICIUS GALBA LUCIUS MINUCIUS BASILUS	conspirators in the plot to assassinate Caesar because of the grudges they bore against him
DIOSIPPUS AND NICANDER	Greek catamites and lovers of Casca.

CHAPTER

1

The river was no wider than a horse could leap. Beyond, on the farther bank, shepherds, angular figures wearing sheepskin cloaks, were gathering their flocks. Evening mist hid the sheep themselves from view; only the upper parts of the shepherds could be seen as the vapour rose from the marshy ground. It was cold. Rain began to fall. I turned away, and, my right knee throbbing – a legacy of our last campaign – hobbled the mile back to camp.

Casca was in his tent, drinking wine heated with nutmeg and cinnamon. He had removed his armour and stood by the table, slack-bellied in his tunic.

"Nothing to see. Nothing to report."

"Of course there isn't. Everything is arranged," he said.

"I wish I could be as confident. He's made mistakes before now, bad ones. Labienus used to say that 'impetuosity' was the General's greatest defect."

"Yes, and if he'd not been there to restrain him, we'd have been in the soup. Spare me the tune, old fruit. Well, old Lab isn't here now, and good riddance to him."

Labienus, the most experienced of the General's lieutenants, his companion since the first days of the Gallic War, disliked Casca, despised him even, deploring his predilection for boys and wine. Fair enough, if your chosen refrain was 'ancient Roman virtue'. But Casca was my cousin and my closest friend. I knew his weaknesses better than Labienus could, his strengths also. For all his self-indulgence and affectations, he had nerve. His soldiers adored him, finding amusement in the constant presence of Diosippus and Nicander, Greek catamites, scented curly headed effeminates, whom Casca professed to adore. This was nonsense. Casca cared for nobody but himself, with the possible exception of his fat old mother. We were friends, but he would have slit my throat if policy or his own interest required him to do so.

"I left Himself at table. He was pretending to drink deep, and flirting with the child-wife of some Ravenna cit. Rather a juicy piece, certainly a sweeter armful than Calpurnia. But she'll be disappointed, poor slut."

"Yes," I said, "orders are out. He has also issued a declaration that his intentions are honourable and his cause just."

"Spare me the Ciceronian balls. When we fight it will be for Caesar's career and Caesar's skin. And our own. If I can kill a few of my creditors, Rome will be a sweeter place. Do you know what my debts come to? Neither do I, I'm happy to say, though my mother wrote to me on the subject only last week. Not that there will be much action tomorrow. Crossing that ditch which for some reason you thought it necessary to inspect will be merely symbolic. He's already sent a detachment of troops to occupy Rimini. And Antony and Curio arrived there yesterday, having fled Rome disguised as slaves. I should have liked to have seen the gorgeous Antony in that part."

He blew a kiss.

"I suppose he's been waiting for them," I said. "I suppose that's been the cause of the delay."

"You suppose wrong as usual, cousin. The reason has been policy in part, to make the opposition commit itself so publicly to his destruction and disgrace that he can argue he has been forced to move in self-defence."

"And hasn't he?"

"Hasn't he? Perhaps he has. Who can tell, with Caesar, at what moment the play-actor removes his mask? But he has delayed also because he knows that this is the decisive moment of his career. He is a gambler who has staked all. There's no turning back. It's the first step that counts. Now he's got the dice in the box. 'Let them fly high,' he muttered to me this evening."

"Are you nervous?" I said. "They tell me Caesar dreamed last night that he lay with his mother."

"Caesar the dreamer," Casca said.

"Is there news of Pompey?"

Casca laughed. He thought the great General a great booby, an old woman, and laughed again when I reminded him that some old women like his own mother were very tough. Pompey had boasted that he had only to stamp his foot on the soil of Italy, and legions would spring from the ground. That report, some weeks back, had disturbed Caesar, till Casca said:

"We must cut the ground from under his feet, so that he stamps only the air."

"Are the omens favourable?"

"The omens, my dear, are favourable, as Caesar has commanded."

I retired to my own tent, and lay on my camp-bed, anxious. I knew myself incapable of my cousin's levity. Casca had played the part of the ruined man so long that he knew no other, was incapable of seriousness. My position was different. I was younger in spirit, had much to lose, was justified in dreading the future. In any case, civil war is terrible. For all I knew Pompey could make his boast good.

Night crept on. I was reluctant to extinguish the lamp. My grandfather's stories of the great proscriptions in the wars between Marius and Sulla came between me and sleep. What had Caesar's dream portended? The implication was evident, disturbing, inauspicious. If Rome was his mother, to lie with her was incest. I had nursed the broken head of my friend Clodius, murdered by a gang hired by Pompey. Cicero defended the murderer with his usual dishonest rhetoric. I was at one with Casca in my contempt for the great orator, the self-styled saviour of the city from Catiline, my mother's cousin, and perhaps lover.

I do not think I slept.

Before dawn, there was more than night movement – the ring of harness, the neighing of horses, the stamp of sentries, the susurration of a thousand legionaries. And then, far away, I heard the music, a thin and dancing pipe. I scrambled to my feet, and into my clothes, buckling on armour and seizing my sword. The mist was dense and clinging-wet, but the music drew me towards the river. Others pushed past me, hurrying towards it, soldiers moving in unaccustomed fashion, without orders or method. But for their eagerness, the sense of anticipation which enveloped us, you might have thought they were running away.

A splash told me we were approaching the bank. A horseman brushed past, the jolt of his horse causing me to stumble. But a path opened behind him, and then there was light. It came, like the music, from the further bank, a shaft of light, unnatural, unearthly. My chest heaved. I looked along that tunnel of light, and though I was gazing straight at it, was not blinded.

The piper sat on the far bank of the Rubicon, in Italy.

The music silenced the soldiers. They held back. A centurion near me shouted an order to advance into the stream. No one obeyed. The music floated towards us, and the mist swirled round the piper. Then a legionary cried: "It's the god Pan," and his shout was taken up, echoing along the wavering line, "Pan, Pan, Pan." The young man who had first cried the name threw himself on the ground. Others imitated his action. I kept my gaze on the piper who, without seeming to move, retired, fading into invisibility even as I tried to hold him in view. The music died away with him. There was a long grey silence. Shamefaced on account of their momentary terror, yet strangely exultant, the men scrambled to their feet, advanced on the stream, and crossed over into Italy.

"Some trick of the General's. You can count on that," Casca said. But was it? I have never known. When the incident was mentioned to Caesar, he smiled in that evasive, self-deprecating manner he had, that told you nothing, and yet hinted an enormity.

I remember that dinner in Rimini. Word had come to us that garrisons in the little towns nearby had surrendered, coming over to Caesar with protestations of loyalty. Caesar gathered his staff around him.

"This is not a time for feasting," he said, "but nevertheless I raise my cup of wine in token of my gratitude for your support, and to bear witness to my determination to succeed. We have taken an irrevocable step. When we crossed that stream this morning, we broke the laws of the Republic. You all know why I have done so. My enemies were determined to destroy me. I have acted in defence of my dignity, dearer to me than life itself. But do not allow yourselves to be deceived into thinking that this is a mere personal quarrel. I know indeed that you do not believe that. But I am also aware that in the weeks to come strenuous efforts will be made by friends, relatives and associates to persuade you that it is only that, and therefore unworthy of your support. So let me assert that I stand also in defence of the constitutional rights of the tribunes, and the liberties of the Roman people which my adversaries would subvert. Let me remind you that I offered to lay down my arms if Pompey would do the same. Let me remind you that I offered to surrender all my commands save Cisalpine Gaul and a single legion. Let me remind you that force was used against the tribunes who legitimately cast their veto against the Senate's decree that would have compelled me to disband my army without receiving any assurances of my personal safety. I did not seek this war. It was forced on me by my enemies. They wanted it, not I. I am only glad that it has provided me with the opportunity to number my friends. You here are chief among them, and I thank you with all my heart for your loyalty and courage. Our position is perilous, but we have known danger before. I trust in audacity, and in the justice of my cause."

Mark Antony led the cheering in which we all joined. There was relief that the period of uncertainty was over, that we had arrived at the moment when all was put to the test.

I confess that my own cheers were all the louder because of the fear I felt. It will be difficult for future generations to understand the awe which Pompey inspired. But it was natural. He had been the great man in Rome all my life. His achievements in Asia were unprecedented. Even Caesar's conquest of Gaul, in which I had been proud to participate, seemed a small thing in comparison. The Gauls were no better than brave barbarians, ignorant of the art of war. But Pompey had defeated great kingdoms and brought them under the yoke of Rome. Our Empire was his creation, rather than that of any other individual. For years he had overshadowed Caesar. I knew that when they first came together, Caesar was the least of the Triumvirate he formed with Pompey and Marcus Crassus. He lacked the former's reputation and the latter's wealth.

Our party had nothing to compare with Pompey's renown; it had nothing to compare with the wealth of his supporters. When I looked round that dinner-table, I saw few men whom the world had learned to respect, some – Casca, Antony, chief among them – whom it was accustomed to despise. I knew that many of

Caesar's adherents were as insolvent as Casca, desperate to repair their fortunes in the wreck of the State.

I was not among them; nor was I, like others, an adventurer of no breeding. I came from one of the greatest Patrician families; I could boast a dozen consuls among my ancestors. I was rich. My estates alone could support me in luxury, when I came to inherit them – and my father was old. I had nothing to gain, for I lacked neither wealth, reputation nor standing, and much to lose. Yet I held to Caesar.

If any ask why, I cannot well answer. When I read historians, I am amazed by the certainty with which they assure us of the motive of actions. It is curious that they know such things, when few could tell us with equal certainty why they fall in love with a woman or a boy. I was attached to Caesar's staff as a young officer in Gaul. It might be natural to suggest that this determined my allegiance. But Labienus, who was much closer to him, deserted his cause, though Caesar had never spoken of Labienus anything but warmly. Some said it was because he came from Picenum, Pompey's stronghold, and so owed a prior allegiance. I do not believe this. Something in Caesar's manner offended him. Was it perhaps the very same thing which held me to the General?

I perplex myself with these questions, now, when it can scarcely matter, when it may be that nothing matters. I do not believe I have long to live. I am kept here by the Gauls as a pawn, a bargaining-counter. I foresee an ignominious end. This morning I asked the youth who has been assigned to me, and who speaks tolerable Latin, if there was any news. I deduced the worst from his silence. But it may be he is only ignorant. After all, why should he be acquainted with affairs of State?

Yes, I confess. I am apprehensive. I do not fear death. No Roman nobleman does. I should like only to be certain that I may die in a manner worthy of my ancestors. It is my fear that this will not be permitted me. A knife in the dark is more likely; then my head sent to my enemies as token of a good deed. That was Pompey's fate. Caesar pretended to be disgusted; inwardly he was relieved. He wouldn't have known what to do with Pompey, who had not been a suitable subject for his famous clemency.

I run ahead of myself, here where I am held still.

*　　*　　*

Caesar's charm, Caesar's famous charm. He had a habit of putting his arm round you, and taking the lobe of your ear between his thumb and forefinger, and playing with it while he confided, or seemed to confide, his secrets to you. I wouldn't have tolerated this from any other man. When Caesar held me thus, I felt a thrill of pleasure. Does that admission demean me?

My perplexity is all the greater, because unlike Antony and Curio, I had no certainty of victory.

When Caesar retired that night, Antony stretched himself on the couch and called for the slaves to bring another flagon of wine.

He smiled at me.

"You'll stay and drink? You'll share this gaudy night, won't you?"

"The General suggested we should retire early. There's a war to be fought," I said, taking the next couch and reaching for the wine.

"There will be no fighting, not for a long time," Antony said. "It's a picnic, a holiday excursion."

"How can you be so sure?"

The smile that charmed and seduced men and women, that smile I so envied, spread across his face. There were always moments when Antony seemed like the god Apollo.

"They'll run like hares," he said. "You forget," he added, "I've just come from Rome. I know the calibre of our enemies. Nothing but wind. You heard I had to disguise myself as a slave? That meant that for a couple of days I congregated with slaves. Slaves talk among themselves in a way their masters never credit. Did you know that?"

He poured more wine, and waved the slaves who were in attendance away.

"Do you know what they said? They said that the Optimates — you know that's what Cicero calls the collection of elderly boobies arrayed against us? They said they were shit-scared. I could believe it."

"Pompey?" I said.

"Pompey is finished. He may have been a great man once. Now . . ." he turned his thumb down. "You've been in Gaul. Have you seen Pompey lately?"

"I was in Rome last winter. I saw him being carried in a litter through the Forum."

"In a litter ... The Great One is now a great lump of lard. He never knew much, except – I grant this – how to draw up an army. But in politics he was always a baby. He's been outmanoeuvred by Caesar's enemies, who were his enemies not so long ago, most of his life in fact. They've imprisoned him, and all he has left is his reputation. Reputation. I don't give a fiddler's fart for reputation. No, dear boy, the campaign before us will be like nothing you have seen in Gaul. They fight there. This time it will be a battle of flowers. And words. You can count on Cicero for words. What do you suppose the women are like in this town?"

So I accompanied Antony to a brothel, and went drunk and sated to bed as the sun rose. That was how I began the great Italian campaign.

CHAPTER

2

I t is not my intention to describe our campaign in Italy or the civil war that followed. For one thing, I do not know how much time I shall have to write this memoir; for another, I have too painful memories of the later wars so disastrously completed. Completed, that is, as far as I am concerned.

Some will see my detention here as justice. Ironic, or poetic, justice perhaps. How do I see it?

Well, let me say this. Caesar boasted of his clemency. He confined it to Roman citizens. He forgot clemency when it came to foreigners.

Take the case of the Gallic leader, Vercingetorix, for example. He was chief of the Arverni, a man of great beauty, courage and guile. I took part in that terrible campaign of Alesia. It was my first experience of total war. I rejoined the army while we were laying siege to the Gallic stronghold of Avaricum. It was winter. The snow lay knee-deep on the mountain roads. One of my fingernails fell off on account of the cold. Vercingetorix destroyed granaries and storehouses in an attempt to deny us food. Our legionaries were near despair. Caesar rallied them with insults and affection. We made a direct assault, and took the town. Caesar ordered or permitted – I have never been certain which – a general massacre.

"Why not?" Casca said. "There is food here for an army, but not for the civilian population." He was commanding a detachment sent to guard the corn-stores to prevent looting. Half the town was ablaze. The confusion was terrible. Women were raped before having their throats cut. Only a fortunate few were able to attach themselves to the army. Caesar gazed on the horror with equanimity. "The men have suffered much to achieve this," he said.

The Gauls did not despair. Vercingetorix threw himself into his citadel of Alesia. We laid siege to it. Soon we were ourselves besieged. A new Gallic army descended on us, invested our lines which were themselves investing the city. Only a commander of supreme rashness could have found himself in such a trap; only one of rare nerve and audacity could have saved us.

Caesar remained calm.

"Caesar is not destined to die in a barbarian land," he said, and touched his forehead.

One day, to our amazement, we saw the gates of the city open. We stood to arms, expecting an attack. It was not soldiers who began to descend the hill towards us, but a host of old men, women and children.

"So," Casca said, "supplies are running low there too."

They extended their hands towards us, pointed to their mouths, and cried out in their strange gibberish for food. Caesar gave orders that none was to be provided; neither should they be admitted to our lines: "Not even pretty girls or boys," he said. "It will do the garrison no harm to see their loved ones starving to death before their eyes."

For three days they kept up their wretched supplications. For three nights our sleep was disturbed by their piteous cries. Many of us were disgusted. A soldier does not cease to have tender feelings. But Caesar was adamant. When he found that one centurion had actually been rash enough to take possession of a lovely girl, he ordered him to be flogged, and demoted to the ranks. Then the girl was whipped out of our lines to resume her starvation.

Eventually the wretched people began to slink away. Where they went, whether any escaped, I have never known. Simply, after a few days, they had vanished. No doubt they crept into the woods to die.

By this time the relieving army had invested us. Caesar later claimed that there were eight thousand cavalry and a quarter of a million infantry. That is what he reported to the Senate, but it was sheer bravado. We had no means of knowing how many they were.

I am not going to recount the battle. It was like all battles, only worse than most. Truth to tell, accounts of battles rarely make sense. No, that is not true; they make too much sense. Historians give them a shape they don't possess. They credit commanders with a degree of control that is absent. I don't advise anyone to read Caesar's account of Alesia; talk to some of the legionaries who fought in the front line instead. As for me, I recall nothing of it. Trebonius later joked that I was as drunk as Antony, but that wasn't true. I might as well admit now that my memory has been obliterated by the fear I experienced. I had dreamed that I would die, and I very nearly did.

Eventually Vercingetorix led an attack from the town. I think he mistimed it. Half an hour earlier, before we had secured our position against the relieving army, he might have swept us away. Even so, we might have lost if the cavalry, disregarding an order from Caesar that they were to hold their ground, had not essayed an encircling movement. When the Gauls saw what was happening, many panicked and ran back into the city. It was that moment of terror which decided the day. We were able to move forward, a mass of metal, swords thrusting; we clambered over the bodies of our enemy and pursued those who still stood back into the citadel. When the gates closed against us, I knew Vercingetorix was doomed.

The next day he sent out a herald proposing terms. Caesar said he would discuss these only with Vercingetorix himself.

The Gallic leader rode out of the stronghold that had become his prison. He was mounted on a white horse. There was a sword-gash over his right eye, but he sat straight, proud as a bridegroom. When he dismounted he still stood a head higher than Caesar, who waited for him to make obeisance. The Gaul declined to do so.

He spoke in Latin, not very good Latin, but Latin all the same. He conceded victory, and asked for mercy for his troops and tribesmen. The stench of dead bodies and blood filled the air.

Without addressing his noble enemy, Caesar summoned two centurions and told them to load the Gallic chief with chains.

"Caesar does not debate with barbarians," he said, though during the years he spent in Gaul he had done so on many occasions.

Then he gave out orders. The two tribes of the Arverni and the Aedui would be spared; they should resume their position as friends of the Roman people. (This was clever: the Arverni were Vercingetorix's own tribe.)

"They have been led astray by evil counsel," Caesar said, still not deigning to address Vercingetorix himself or even to look him in the face.

All the other prisoners should be allotted to the legionaries. First, however, they should dig a pit for the dead.

Then he said to the centurions, "Take this man and keep him closely guarded."

He never spoke to Vercingetorix again. But he had a role for him. He was to be preserved to feature in Caesar's Triumph. That didn't happen for several years. Afterwards, as you know, Vercingetorix was strangled in the Mamertine prison. Vercingetorix received these insults that day with the utmost serenity. Caesar was the conqueror; but the day belonged to his defeated enemy. I felt ashamed of Caesar that night.

(Later: I gave this account to young Artixes, the son of my captor. He has spent some time in Rome, and reads Latin easily. He is a comely young man of some charm, and I believe he sincerely pities me. He is also, as it happens, on his mother's side, a cousin of Vercingetorix himself. I was interested to see how my account struck him.

Naturally some will say, reading this confession, that I wrote it in an attempt to curry favour with him. That would not have been unintelligent, but such was not my purpose. Actually I was surprised to discover while writing how strongly I felt. This is something I have noticed before, and it raises the philosophical question as to whether such writing actually alters one's feelings, whether it is not indeed an aid to insincerity. It is not a question I can answer. The truth is, as ever, complicated: we can never recapture our precise emotions, and brooding on past events is coloured by what has happened since.

"How could you follow such a man?" he said.

He has a peculiarly candid face, rather square under a shock of yellow hair.

"You never felt either his charm or his authority," I said. "Tell me, do you have any memories of your cousin?"

"Why should you care? You're a Roman, and an accomplice in his murder."

"You have read what I have written," I said. "That should explain my question.")

After the battle Caesar praised Antony and Trebonius. It did not concern me that he had no words for my own part in the action. I should have been embarrassed, to tell the truth, if he had said anything in my praise. I could see Labienus glower, however. He hated Antony whom he thought nothing but a debauchee. Perhaps it was at that moment that he began to separate himself from Caesar.

That night Antony came to my tent. He was drunk, as perhaps he had a right to be. I would have liked to have been drunk myself for another reason. I would rather not recall that visit, but for one thing he said.

"Caesar doesn't realise it yet, but Rome is now his."

I thought him absurd at the time.

He lay back on my couch, his tunic rucked up.

"Slaughter makes me randy," he said.

I suppose I smiled, as I tend to do when embarrassed.

"You look like a white mouse," he said, "a timid little white mouse."

I am naturally pale, but my hair was not white in those days, but straw-coloured. It amused Antony to make a play of words on my cognomen. Perhaps one of my ancestors was indeed an albino. I don't know. My features were always sharp, never handsome, and indeed as a child I was given the nickname "Mouse", which has remained with me. Well, Caesar means "hairy", but Caesar himself was bald, something which did embarrass him.

"Anyway," Antony said, "you don't need to worry. It's a woman I want."

He got to his feet, swaying a little, and yet, despite his drunkenness, moving with the languorous grace of a great cat. He put his hands on my shoulders as if to steady himself, and looked me hard in the face. His breath stank of wine. He leaned forward and kissed me on the lips.

"Little Mouse," he said, "little Decimus Junius Brutus Albinus Mouse. You don't need to look so frightened."

"I'm not frightened," I said. "I'm bored and disgusted."

"By me, Mouse?"

"Bored by you, and disgusted by what has happened today."

"Come," he said, "Vercingetorix played and lost. He's been the hell of a trouble to us. He knew the rules of the game. You can't blame Caesar for his triumph."

"I don't," I said, "I blame him for . . ."

I paused.

"Be careful, Mouse," Antony said. "Be careful not to speak against the General."

"Of course," I said, "one must never do that."

Caesar: warts and all. Was he ever sincere? We would have died for him, died for his smile. All those of us who were his generals and lieutenants in Gaul felt the wand of the enchanter. We all feared him also, even Antony, who pretended to fear of no man. But I have seen him reduced to stammering and blushes by a cold look from Caesar. Even Casca could be abashed by him.

The first time I saw Caesar he was emerging from my mother's bedroom. I was a child at the time, perhaps nine or ten. It was a summer morning and I had woken early, and being unable to sleep again, had turned towards my mother for comfort. And as I approached her door, it opened, and this young man, whom I didn't know to be Caesar, emerged, in a short tunic. He stopped and smiled, and touched my cheek with his forefinger and then took my ear between thumb and forefinger and held me at arm's length.

"So this is Mouse," he said, "little Mouse of whom I have heard such fine things. They tell me you love Greek poetry."

I nodded.

"So do I, boy. We must discourse on it at some future and more propitious moment."

Then he laughed, a laugh of pure merriment, and left me. I turned and followed him out of the house, watching him tip the porter, and my eyes lingered on him as he strolled away. Crossing the courtyard he tossed his folded toga over his shoulder. I had never seen a gentleman show himself in public in such a state of undress. I know now he took pleasure in advertising his conquests. I had no idea then why he had been in our house, and I did not understand that he was my mother's lover.

Of course he cared nothing for her. She, on the other hand,

adored him. When I went through to see her, it was as if I was looking on someone I had never met.

In those days Caesar had not yet won a military reputation. He was known only for his debauchery and debts. But that too I learned later. When I heard men speak of Caesar in those terms, I could not connect the man so described with the magnificent carelessness of his manner. At the age of ten I became his slave even as my mother was. It was a secret we shared and kept from everyone, especially my father: our adoration of Caesar.

Later, I overheard my uncle ask him why he had not divorced my mother.

"On account of Caesar?" my father said. "Dear boy, if every husband whom Caesar has cuckolded did that, Rome would be bereft of married couples. She is not likely to betray me with any other man. All us husbands make an exception of Caesar."

Perhaps you see now why his soldiers sang in his Triumph:

> Home we bring the bald whoremonger,
> Romans, lock your wives away,
> All his Gallic slaves and tribute,
> Went his Gallic whores to pay.

And not only Gallic whores, that's for sure. Of course on one celebrated, but never fully explained, occasion, Caesar was on the other side, as it were, of the fence.

As a young man, when serving as an aide-de-camp to Marcus Thermus, the proconsul of Asia, Caesar was despatched on a diplomatic mission to King Nicomedes of Bithynia. Nobody knows exactly what transpired there, but I have heard Cicero (admittedly an inveterate and unreliable gossip) declare that "Caesar was led by Nicomedes' attendants to the royal bedroom, where he lay on a golden couch, clad in a purple shift. Imagine that, my friends. Yes, indeed, that was how this descendant of Venus lost his virginity in Bithynia." That may be nonsense, is almost certainly embroidered. But it was widely believed. The versifier Licinius Calvus published a little squib about

> The riches of Bithynia's King
> Who Caesar on his bed abused.

And once when Caesar was arguing in the Senate in defence of Nicomedes' daughter Nysa, and listing his own obligations to the King, Cicero, again, shouted out in his excitable provincial manner: "Enough of that, if you please. We all know what he gave you, and what you surrendered to him in return."

And it is true that there were certain Roman merchants in Bithynia at the time, who doubtless recounted what happened there; there is no good reason to suppose that their version was all lies.

Anyway, these things were widely bruited in Rome even when I was a boy, and that made Caesar appear in a curious fashion still more dazzling. Any other man would have been over-whelmed by the shame of it. Any other man would have hid his face and shunned public life. Not Caesar. He carried it off with the same swagger with which he could confront the son of the woman from whose bed he had risen. But I have often wondered whether he set himself to achieve the reputation he did win as a ladies' man precisely because of this stain on his honour. After all, nobody objects to a man who chooses to make love to boys, but to submit to the embraces of a man older than yourself is considered dishonourable in an adult. We call such a man a pathic, and generally despise him. That's true even of the Greeks, as you can read in Plato. Incidentally, Bibulus, who shared a consulship with Caesar in 59, actually described him in an edict as "The Queen of Bithynia who once wanted to sleep with a monarch, but now wants to be one."

Well, that comes closer to the point, of course.

What I am saying may appear evasive to any reader of this memoir – if I survive to finish it, and if it survives to find a reader – but I do not think the events in which I was concerned can begin to be understood if Caesar himself, in his manifold variety, is not at least offered for understanding.

Which leaves me with the question I can't answer: was there any other reason why the disgraceful episode with King Nicomedes did him so little lasting damage?

I once, years later, asked my mother if she believed Caesar had ever really loved her. She laughed.

"Of course not, darling," she said. "I adored him, but that was quite different. I couldn't even deceive myself at the time. I knew for instance that he was carrying on another affair simultaneously, with Postumia Sulpicius – a very silly woman by the way. No, Caesar wasn't like Pompey, who, it may surprise you to know, really adored the women with whom he was engaged. Of course, there was another difference. Pompey as a young man was really beautiful. You won't believe that, looking at him now; but he was so beautiful we used to say that every woman just wanted to bite him. Caesar was, I suppose, handsome, in a cold sneering sort of way, but it wasn't his looks that won him his successes, which, by the way, included Pompey's second wife, Mucia – or was she his third, I can't remember. Anyway she was the mother of three of his children, and Pompey thought she was absolutely secure. And so she was, till Caesar came along. He used to call Caesar 'Aegisthus', you know."

"Aegisthus?"

"Oh, you are slow, Mouse. Aegisthus, the lover of Clytemnestra. Mind you, this didn't stop Pompey from marrying Caesar's daughter, years later. But you know that, of course. Poor girl."

"Poor girl?"

"Well, Pompey was impotent by then, Mouse, besides being usually drunk by bedtime, they say. No, if you ask me there was only one woman that Caesar ever came close to loving, and I've never understood why."

"Who was that?"

"Servilia. Your cousin Marcus' mother."

"Servilia, that dragon?"

"She may seem a dragon to you, Mouse, but she's a very clever woman. She knew how to hold Caesar. He kept returning to her."

"Well, I knew of course that they were allies, and that they'd had an affair. That was no secret. We used to make Markie weep about it when we were children. But all the same, that bore, with her constant talk about virtue and her relationship to the Gracchi. You really think he loved her?"

"Yes," my mother said, "which didn't stop her from prostituting your cousin Tertia for Caesar's delight."

Tertia was a sweet little thing, not like her mother at all. She took to drink and died young. Perhaps my mother was right after all.

And of course Cicero, I remember, uttered one of his *bons mots* on the subject. When Caesar arranged two or three years ago to have some confiscated estates knocked down cheap to Servilia at what was supposed to be a public auction, Cicero said:

"It was even cheaper than you think, because a third (*tertia*) part had been discounted."

It was rumoured, of course, that Marcus Brutus was Caesar's son. When he was a small boy, this accusation would also reduce him to tears of shame and fury. Later, he rather encouraged the notion, while professing that it was impossible. Like all people who parade their virtue, my cousin Markie is a twister, Janus-faced.

Young Artixes said to me: "You talked of his charm and authority. But all I see is a scoundrel. And I am still amazed that you could follow such a man. It was clear to us Gauls that he was a destructive force. Couldn't you feel that yourself?"

"Artixes," I said, "I don't know if you have heard what Marcus Cato said."

"I don't even know who Cato was."

"You're fortunate. Anyway, he said: 'Caesar was the only sober man who ever tried to wreck the Constitution.'"

"I don't understand what you mean by that."

"Never mind."

"Come," I said to Artixes, seeing disappointment in his face, "let us take a stroll in the evening air, and I'll try to explain."

(The circumstances of my arrest are not, you see, at present either arduous or oppressive. I am rather well treated, in fact, and I am having to revise my notions about Gallic civilisation. It is true that such wine as they have is abominable, but my comforts are considered, and the food is tolerable. Best of all, I have a sort of wild garden in which I am permitted to walk — under supervision, of course. It descends to a river, and there are mountains across the plain. It is pleasant in the evening under the chestnut trees, with the scent of ilex in the air. And young Artixes is a charming companion; I have really grown quite fond of him.)

The evening air was soft. Birds sang. A dog barked in the

village below. The laughter of girls rose towards us, and Artixes said, "What do you mean by the Constitution? This is a word I have heard Romans speak before and it always puzzles me."

"It puzzles us too," I said. "That is part of the problem. You must understand, Artixes, that years ago Rome was ruled, as your tribes are, by kings."

"Well," he said, "that's only natural. Everyone has kings, surely."

"Not exactly. Some states are what we call republics. No, don't ask me to explain, you will understand what a republic is when I have finished. But if I explain every word then we'll never get anywhere. Now the Romans were dissatisfied with their kings."

"Why?"

"Well, first, they were foreigners."

"I call that feeble, to take foreigners for kings."

"Perhaps it was, I don't know, it was a long time ago. Then the son of the King was a bad man."

"What did he do?"

"Raped a girl."

He looked at me with what I took to be dismay, lost again.

"But he was the King's son," he said. "Surely she should have been honoured to do his bidding."

"You might think so, but she wasn't, and her father and brothers were very angry. They rose up against the King and drove him out of the city."

"Yes," he said, "I understand that. So they made themselves kings."

"Not exactly. The Romans then decided kings were a bad idea. Don't ask me why. They just did. So they decided to have a new, different form of government. Instead of one man being king for life, they would divide the government between two men who would be equal to each other, and who would only hold power for a year. They weren't called kings, but consuls."

"Were they killed at the end of the year?"

"No."

"Then how did they persuade them to give up power?"

"They just did. Those were the rules."

"And this still happens?"

"We still have consuls. I should have been consul myself next year."

"And now you're not. You're here instead."

"Yes. Only nowadays the consuls don't have much real power."

"I understand. This way of doing things doesn't work."

"It worked well for a long time. Very well. Too well perhaps. Rome became great and powerful. You know that, you have felt our power. We conquered other countries and tribes and extended our Empire."

"Yes, you kill people and call it peace."

"If you say so, but that's not how we see it. Anyway the Empire became so big that generals had to command armies and provinces for a long time, and in the end the generals became more powerful than the consuls."

"So the generals became kings."

"Not exactly."

Sometimes I wonder if Artixes is quite as ingenuous as he seems to be. He has after all lived in Rome, admittedly in a species of detention. He must know more about Roman politics than he pretends. But when he looks at me with his blue eyes wide open, and smiles in that frank admiring fashion, I can't think him other than innocent.

And yet . . . I put my arm round his shoulder.

"Artixes, you know all this, I think."

He smiled again.

"Well, some of it," he said.

"So it's a game."

"It's interesting to hear how you explain it. And I do want to know about Caesar, and why you followed him until . . . And these women. I've heard of the Queen of Egypt. Men say she's ravishingly beautiful."

"Cleopatra? No, she's not that. She's more interesting than that."

"Tell me about her."

CHAPTER

3

Most Romans loathe Egypt and the Egyptians. There is something about the place that disturbs us. It is, I think, on account of the ever-present consciousness of magic. Everything seems to come from the primeval slime of the Nile. The Egyptians worship animal gods, and one cult, I have been informed, expresses devotion for a dung-beetle. A stench of corruption pervades the country, and few Romans manage to get through a day without looking nervously over their shoulder or seeking reassurance that some witch has not cast a spell on them. It is foolishness, but it is infectious foolishness. Even Mark Antony was affected. He displayed a nervous anxiety which was foreign to his nature.

It is something to do with the landscape. Even though Rome is so great a city, we Romans are by instinct and inheritance country-dwellers. We are comforted by trees, mountains, rivers, lakes, and the sea. Our rivers are friendly things compared to the brooding presence of the Nile. We are happiest, and most at ease, in our country villas. The gods of our country districts are friendly beings; every grove and spring has its tutelary spirit, and it is easy to live in harmony with such beings: easy and pleasant. There is no country, no landscape, in Egypt: instead, a waste of sands interrupted only by monuments to the dead. We Romans have a proper reverence for our ancestors, and proudly display the masks of those who have achieved renown in the service of the Republic. The Egyptians, intoxicated by the idea of death, abase themselves before the wary spirits of their dead. The land is in thrall to the idea of death.

Of course, Alexandria is a great city, the most wonderful in the world. Alexandria, being Greek in its foundation, is not characteristic of Egypt: with its libraries, law-courts, miles of warehouses, harbours busy with the shipping of all nations of the civilised world, there is much to delight, little – it might seem – to dismay the visitor. Yet, even Alexandria has been infected by the poison of Egypt. There was an old woman in the market-place who was said to be two hundred years old; she sold magic potions to ensure longevity. My cousin Marcus Brutus wished her to be prosecuted for fraud; Caesar only laughed. "She does no harm," he said; erroneously.

Our arrival was horrid.

After the victory at Pharsalus, where Pompey's chief army was utterly destroyed, the Great One had fled to Egypt. The country is of course nominally independent, but Roman influence has long been considerable there, and Pompey had formerly championed the cause of King Ptolemy when he was driven out of his country by rebels. Ptolemy had come to Rome, where Pompey had spoken for him in the Senate, and the King had employed lavish bribery to win still more support; he had further contrived to assassinate various members of the opposing party who had also come to Rome to plead their case. No Egyptian thinks anything of assassination, and it was said that the King's success in this enterprise regained much of the respect which he had lost. Even so, he was not successful in his main endeavour, for at that time Pompey had many enemies himself in the Senate, who feared that the restoration of Ptolemy by Roman arms would only add to Pompey's power, since Ptolemy, understanding little about our Constitution, would feel indebted to the Great One rather than to the Senate. So nothing was done on his behalf, until, as a result of the famous meeting between Pompey, Caesar and the millionaire booby Marcus Crassus at Lucca, the three of them formed what Cicero (in private) described as "a criminal conspiracy to share sovereignty and dominate the Republic". Then, as a result of their new ascendancy, Pompey's policy was put into practice, and Gabinius was ordered to lead his army from Syria and restore King Ptolemy. This he did, for he was an efficient officer, despite being also a habitual drunkard; and in any case the Egyptian army was no match for Roman legions. King Ptolemy was now dead, but had been succeeded by his two children, a boy also called Ptolemy, and a daughter Cleopatra.

In the Egyptian fashion, these were married to each other. It is very strange. As you may know, the Egyptian royal family is really Greek, the first Ptolemy having been one of Alexander the Great's generals, but they have so far adapted themselves to the base customs of the country they rule as to be quite happy to practise incest. Normally Greeks, however degenerate, are as averse to incest as we Romans are. The prohibition of incest is apparently of great antiquity, and I would have thought it innate in mankind; and yet the Egyptians appear to find it natural. Certainly they take no exception to it.

Marriage did not, however, appear to exclude the rivalry which one generally finds when there are two contenders to a throne – you know how common such rivalry is in Gaul, Artixes – and the young Ptolemy and Cleopatra were said to be on such bad terms with each other (no doubt fomented by partisans) that there were even rumours of civil war.

At any rate Pompey fled to Egypt confident that the heir of Ptolemy would show gratitude to the man who had re-established his father on the throne. Perhaps he forgot that the Ptolemies were now Orientals, and therefore unacquainted with that noble sentiment.

Caesar was slow in pursuit, for reasons which I could not fathom and which he did not trouble himself to explain. Instead of following Pompey directly, he delayed, and made a diversion to Troy. I was among those whom he chose to invite to accompany him.

Naturally, even though I was alarmed by his procrastination, which I feared would allow Pompey to reassemble an army and thus prolong the civil war, even perhaps reverse its course (perhaps Caesar had information which he denied me), I was honoured to be chosen, and delighted to have the opportunity to see Troy. My mother had instilled a love of Homer in me from my earliest boyhood, and of the two great epics, it has always been the *Iliad* to which I responded most warmly.

My first feeling was of disappointment. Little remains of the proud towers and mighty ramparts. The scene is melancholy, the famed Scamander sluggish. Mount Ida was invisible, veiled in mist. A chill wind blew from the sea. There were mud-flats and rushes where the Greeks had camped.

"Ten years to capture this," Trebonius said. "Homer's Greeks must have been rare incompetents."

Trebonius always had a habit of looking down his nose at the world. Now he sneered, "And Agamemnon, Ajax and Achilles rare boobies."

"You think so?" Caesar said.

"Well, don't you, General? When you think of what you yourself achieved at Avaricum and Alesia, Troy looks small beer, a wretched place that wouldn't detain us seven days."

"You are right of course, Trebonius." I could see that Caesar was annoyed. He was flexing his fingers as was his habit when he strove to control his irritation. "With command of the sea, with modern siege weapons and a trained army, we would have made short work of these poor Trojans. Is that your opinion also, Mouse?"

Unlike Trebonius, I was responsive to Caesar's moods. I remembered how he loved to boast of his descent from Venus; I recalled that it was in those groves of oak and chestnut above Troy that she had coupled with Anchises, and given birth to the hero Aeneas, who later, guided by his mother and the other gods, escaped the burning city and sailed by slow and arduous stages to Italy, taking with him his little son Iulus, from whom Caesar claimed direct descent, though all true Romans are the children of Aeneas. And so I said:

"It is a mistake, surely, to judge antiquity by the standards of our own age. Certainly one cannot believe that either the Greeks or the Trojans would have long withstood our legions. Nevertheless, it is barbarous to laugh at them. If men ever cease to be moved by Homer, that will be the time to despair of humanity. Then we will be right to abandon all dreams of greatness. In Homer we see greatness yoked to strange infirmity, honour wrestling with dishonour in a single breast; we see all that is great and ennobling in war, and all that is terrible and abominable too. Is it not a mark of Homer's transcendent power that we weep for both Hector and Achilles? Is it not eternally true – the picture that he offers – of the unending struggle between men's will and the pressing weight of necessity? Yes, Trebonius is right: a modern army would make short work of Troy. On the other hand, what poet of today is capable of moving us as Homer does? For that reason we should venerate the sad remains of Ilium. For that reason, we come here to weep and to pay homage to the glorious dead."

"Bravo, Mouse," Caesar said, and pinched my ear.

And yet, though I knew I had spoken as he wished me to speak, and said the words that he desired to hear, I could not escape the certainty that he was laughing at me, even as he applauded.

"You are becoming quite a little master of rhetoric," Casca said to me that evening.

He sprawled in his tent, with a goblet of wine in his hand. His face was ruddy with drink. Diosippus knelt beside him, between his open knees, massaging his fleshy thighs, while Casca's left hand played with the boy's curls. Nicander stood behind his master, oiling his neck and shoulders, and scowling at Diosippus.

"You have learned how to flatter Caesar," Casca said.

I felt myself flush and looked away.

"But I meant all I said, cousin. I cannot endure to hear Trebonius sneer at Homer. If we abandon trust in poetry, why, then we become . . ." I paused, searching for words.

"We become sensible men," Casca said. He leaned forward and kissed Diosippus on the mouth. "There is more honey in a boy's lips than in all the words of Homer. But you are wise to flatter Caesar: for your own sake. I only ask you to remember the old proverb: whom the gods wish to destroy, they first make mad."

"What do you mean?"

He stood up, letting the towel that covered his midriff fall to the ground. His belly sagged. He waddled to the couch and lay face down. The boys followed him and resumed their massage. He turned his face towards me:

"Has Caesar spoken of his plans for a new Troy, a new Rome?"

"No, he has said nothing about that. What do you mean?"

"What does he mean? That is the question. Now bugger off, Mouse. You too, Dio. Leave me with Nicky."

He stretched out his hand and thrust it between Nicander's shapely legs, pulling the boy towards him.

*　　*　　*

We sat on deck under a starry sky. It had been rough and was now calm. My nausea had abated. Caesar was in relaxed and friendly mood. He sipped wine mixed with water and talked of literature, and then idly of philosophy.

Our enterprise was audacious. It had been confirmed that Pompey was in Egypt. Our own force was small. We had perhaps four thousand legionaries and eight hundred cavalry. The islanders of Rhodes had been constrained to furnish us with ten warships. Our intelligence was defective. It was rumoured that Pompey had a considerable fleet, the remnants of those legions which had survived Pharsalus, and some two or three thousand armed slaves. But we couldn't know for sure. He might have had three times that force. Yet Caesar did not appear concerned. He spoke of the effect of the prestige won by Pharsalus. "It is worth two legions," he said.

"I was pleased, Mouse, to hear you speak of Homer as you did. I have never trusted the man who is deaf to poetry."

"Trebonius is a good officer and devoted to your service."

"I would trust him in the field, certainly. But he is a mean fellow, a lean fellow, a crabbit soul. Look at the stars, Mouse, look at the stars. Keep your gaze fixed on them. That is a golden rule of life and politics. The man who forgets the stars is no favourite of Destiny. He is doomed to petty struggles, capable of taking only a short view of things. The stars are my friend, Mouse. Whenever I feel the temptation to despair, I have only to gaze upward on such a night as this to recover my even and confident tenor of mind. Serenity..." his voice drifted away. We sat in silence, only the waves lapping against the prow.

"What is Rome?" Caesar said. "A city, an idea ... has it ever occurred to you to wonder why we Romans have been so favoured by Fortune? Have you considered that all history leads to this moment when Rome is the mistress of the world, and I am Rome's master?"

"Pompey still lives, Caesar, and he has sons with armies."

"Poor Pompey. I was fond of him, you know, Mouse. I truly thought of him as my friend, my last friend ... and he betrayed my faith."

"Caesar has many friends."

"Caesar has no friends, for, with Pompey eclipsed, he has no equals, and friendship is possible only between equals. Does that seem very arrogant to you, Mouse?"

There was no land in sight, merely the limitless sea, dark purple shading into dense night, but the stars clear above.

"Answer me, Mouse. Does that seem very arrogant to you?"

But I could not answer. I saw the truth of what he said, and I hated it, and would not acknowledge it.

"Marcus Crassus thought he was my friend, because I owed him so much money. He was only my creditor. You know the story of his death."

Of course I did. Everyone knew it and had been horrified by it, even though at the same time we were ashamed.

Crassus had led his army against Parthia across the great desert of Arabia. Somewhere in the sands, his intelligence faulty, he had found himself surrounded by the horse archers of the enemy. Keeping out of range of our weapons, they had teased Crassus' mighty army like boys baiting a bear tied to a stake. The Romans pressed together. Many fell exhausted by the heat and the congestion. At last, Crassus, never famous for courage, roared (they say) like a wounded bull and led a mad charge. He was stopped by an arrow in the throat. His body was stripped and left for the fowls of the air, the dark birds that cast their shadows over the sands. But his head was cut off and carried to the camp of the Parthian king, who was, as it happened, watching a performance of *The Bacchae*. (Thus do barbarian kings imitate the practice of civilised men.) When the head of King Pentheus is brought on to the stage, some vile but ingenious actor substituted the head of old Crassus.

Carrhae was the greatest disaster Roman arms had suffered since Hannibal's victory at Cannae almost two hundred years ago. It was strange that Caesar should brood on it now.

"One day," he said, "I shall avenge Crassus."

My mother used to speak with horror of Crassus' campaign against the leader of the slaves' revolt, Spartacus, of how, when he had defeated the slaves, he had six thousand of them crucified along the Appian Way. They lined the road from Capua to Rome. The sight and stench of the bodies, rotting in attitudes that indicated the nature of their agony, disgusted her, she used to say; for eighteen months she had been unable to bring herself to revisit our estates in the south on account of the horror that she would be compelled to see.

Why did I think of this now?

"My conquest of Gaul was glorious," Caesar said, "and yet what is Gaul, compared to the splendour of the East? Alexander never thought to carry his conquests to the West. Some day Rome must dominate Parthia. I thought, when we were at Troy, of a new Rome, born from a colony planted there on the site where our race was nurtured. From such a base. After all, Rome cannot be the centre of the world. Things come full circle, Mouse. It may be that my Destiny is to retrace the path taken by my ancestor Aeneas, and then . . . but I am already twenty years older than Alexander when he died . . . still, Destiny . . . It is a paradox, Mouse, which you have understood in Homer. We act by reason of the force of our will, and yet Destiny governs all. What shall I do with Pompey when I take him, Mouse?"

That was another question I found hard. With what crime could Pompey be charged? Though we were sure that Caesar's decision to invade Italy was justified, nevertheless Pompey had opposed us by the will, the explicit order, of the Senate. I could not conceive of any legal action that could be brought against him, and I could not believe that Caesar would willingly order any Roman citizen – least of all Pompey, who had once been married to his daughter Julia – to be put to death without trial. Besides, how often had I heard Caesar deplore the conduct of Sulla who had restored order to Rome after an earlier civil war by murdering his enemies.

I said: "I cannot believe that Pompey will choose to survive his disgrace."

"You don't know Pompey, Mouse. He will not feel disgraced. He will feel he was betrayed. He will be full of resentment, not shame. Resentful men do not fall on their sword. How calm the night is, a night for talk of love, not death. Have you broken with Clodia, Mouse?"

I had not imagined that Caesar knew of my passion for the lady. I did not reply.

"She will bring you nothing but harm," Caesar said. "Besides, she's old enough to be your mother."

I wonder if he thought then of that morning when I had

seen him emerge from my mother's room. Perhaps not; great conquerors can't be expected to recall their every conquest.

We sighted Alexandria early on a bright morning. It was late summer and not yet hot. The city shone before us. I had not imagined so many white and sparkling palaces or the beautiful curves of coast and harbour. Gardens of villas brilliant with flowers, ran down to the water.

Then a galley put out from the port to meet us. Caesar smiled. He was sure that it contained a deputation of notables come to honour him. He was (as usual) right. They boarded our ship, some of the older ones finding the transition difficult, and being forced into ludicrous positions. A bald man, with deep brown eyes and sagging jowls, advanced towards Caesar. He introduced himself as their spokesman, by name Theodotus, a Greek who had won some celebrity, as I learned subsequently, as a professional lecturer; his counsel was now said to be valued by the young King Ptolemy, whose tutor he had formerly been.

"And more than tutor, I'll wager," Casca said.

Now Theodotus extended his left arm in one of those exaggerated gestures which are the stock-in-trade of the professional rhetorician, beings never far divorced from the world of the actor.

Two Nubian slaves, tall glistening fellows, naked but for loincloths and elaborate head-dresses, responded. The taller of them dived into a basket and withdrew an object wrapped in cloth. There was clearly going to be some sort of presentation. The second Nubian spread a carpet before Caesar and remained kneeling, while his companion also knelt and began to unwrap the parcel. He removed a succession of cotton cloths. The first two were crimson, the third white with a brownish stain.

"Now," Theodotus cried, his voice commanding.

It was years since I had seen Pompey in the flesh, and at first I was not certain it was the flesh. I thought they had toppled a statue and removed the head as an earnest of their benevolent intentions towards Caesar.

But Caesar stepped back, threw his hands up, covered his face as a widow does. The Nubian adjusted the position of the severed head. I was standing at an angle and it seemed as if Pompey was smiling. But that must have been some optical delusion.

Trebonius stepped forward, and, twitching a cloth from the Nubian, covered Pompey's head.

Theodotus was speaking. I think he was claiming credit for himself in the organisation of the assassination of Caesar's enemy. He stretched out his hand towards the General, opening it to reveal a ring. Caesar, as if he acted without thought, took the ring, held it up for a moment, and passed it to me: the engraving showed a lion holding a sword between his paws.

Theodotus said: "He was endeavouring to form an army, to maintain the prosecution of this terrible war which has been so grievous to all lovers of Rome, of peace and of Caesar. He had partisans in the city, adherents of the King's sister who has set herself up against His Majesty. It was necessary to act. We did so for the safety of Egypt and out of friendship for Caesar." He bowed low. "Dead men don't bite, General," he said.

We were all horrified by what we had seen; yet we stood there and listened as this well-larded man, whom I had at once marked as a consummate hypocrite, argued that it was greatly to Caesar's advantage both that Pompey should be dead, and that he himself should have played no part in the execution of his rival. "You may consider, Caesar, that in our zeal to do you service, we have acted, with uncommon dexterity and good judgment, as a species of *deus ex machina*."

And Caesar, though he stood there weeping, could not hide the truth of these words from himself.

"When Caesar has had time to reflect, he will understand that our gift to him is priceless. Now he may indulge in grief for his dead rival, his former friend, but when he retires tonight, his heart will swell with the knowledge that we have done for him what he would have had done, and that he is yet innocent of Pompey's blood."

He then invited Caesar to take up residence in the royal palace as the guest of his absent majesty.

"It seems to me," Artixes said, "that Caesar was at least as great a hypocrite as this Greek whom you revile, for he must have been pleased just as the Greek assured him he would be."

"Of course," I said, "but his tears were genuine none the less. You have heard what he said about Pompey. You must understand the solitude he knew when he saw that Pompey was no more."

And then I recited to the boy that great passage in which Homer tells how the aged Priam came to the Greeks' camp to beg the body of his slaughtered son, the hero Hector. I forgot in my emotion that Artixes does not understand Greek, but he listened intently. I suppose the music captivated him. Besides, barbarians are accustomed to long paeans of praise for dead heroes, and I don't suppose they listen carefully to the words.

I did not tell him that that evening Caesar said to me:

"First Crassus, then Pompey. Their heads looked well set on their shoulders back at Lucca."

"I saw how deeply you were moved, General."

"Cruel necessity, Mouse. Never lose the capacity to weep. Nothing unmans a man so surely as the refusal or inability to cry at appropriate moments."

It was soon evident that, despite the murder of Pompey, our situation in Alexandria was full of danger. As I have said, Caesar had rashly brought only a small force with him. The Egyptian army, though probably contemptible, was large. There were also troops composed of Roman veterans, old soldiers of Gabinius, who had remained in the country, and had now been re-formed in the semblance of an army. No one could be sure whom they obeyed. Most dangerous of all was the Alexandria mob. Trained legionaries may have no fear of regular troops, but they hate street-fighting against an enemy that is hard to identify, that comes and goes, that resorts to murder in back alleys, that profits from its own irregular nature.

Caesar was aware of these dangers, yet seemed careless of them. When news came that Pothinus, a palace eunuch, had summoned troops from Pelusium, and given command to Achillas, the officer who, we believed, had murdered Pompey, Caesar was strangely indolent. He remained in the palace near the harbour working on his memoirs of the Gallic War. I urged him to action; he merely smiled. "Time enough," he said. I could not understand his lassitude.

There were riots in the streets. I took it upon myself to order that the legionaries be confined to our camp by the harbour. Then word was brought that an Egyptian fleet, perhaps that which had been sent to Greece in aid of Pompey, was anchored in the inner basin. Our escape to the sea was blocked. Still, Caesar did nothing but dictate to his secretaries.

What was to be done? The chief officers held a council of war in his absence.

"What is the General doing?" someone – I cannot at this distance recall who – enquired.

"Playing with fire," Casca said. "He is bored by success."

This was nonsense. Caesar was stricken by one of those unaccountable spells of lassitude which in the past had preceded some of his greatest victories.

"He is waiting for a sign."

It was time to provide one. I again assumed responsibility, and commanded the docks to be set alight. The fire spread to the Egyptian ships in the inner basin. Some were burned; others fled seawards. For the moment our position was eased. Following up this success – slight though it was – I despatched two centuries to seize the Pharos and the mole which connected it with the town. There was some brisk fighting, but the enterprise was happy. We were now able to construct a line of defence. Admittedly our position was still dangerous, but it seemed to me that it would require a frontal attack to dislodge us, and I did not believe the Egyptians capable of that.

The young King Ptolemy was our hostage. I set little store by that, for I could not believe that the Egyptians would not happily sacrifice him, since they are by nature incapable of loyalty. Unlike Romans they set no store by promises, but will promise whatever they think may secure an immediate advantage. Anyone who has dealings with them knows, however, that their word is not worth a docken.

I reported to Caesar the measures I had taken. He approved them, but absently.

"I have always known I could rely on you, Mouse," he said.

"To the death," I replied.

He smiled and pinched my ear.

I hoped we would now be able to embark on a discussion of strategy, but at that moment we were interrupted by a knock on the door. A centurion entered, followed by slaves bearing a rolled-up carpet on their shoulders. They laid it on the marble floor, very gently, and stepped back.

"So?" Caesar said.

"A gift to my lord from the Queen of Egypt," one said.

"Well," Caesar said, "let us see what the Queen has sent us."

"Be careful, Caesar. It may be a trap."

"You are too cautious, Mouse."

The carpet had been placed some fifteen paces to Caesar's right, and was unrolled towards him. It was obvious that it contained an object. For a moment I suspected that the macabre and disgusting taste of the Egyptians had contrived to present us with another corpse: which of our friends might be revealed cruelly murdered?

I was wrong. A girl lay there, in a short purple shift, rucked up to display plump but shapely legs. She sprang to her feet, not apparently stiff as a result of her surely uncomfortable journey within the carpet. She looked Caesar in the eye and then threw herself on the marble pavement, stretching out her arms to embrace his ankles. He bent down, put his hand in the thick tresses of auburn hair and raised her up. Caesar was not a tall man, but she reached only to his chest. She smiled, showing white, even teeth. Her mouth was rather large, and her eyes sparkled.

"Do you know who this is, Mouse?"

"No, of course not."

"I rather suspect the Queen of Egypt has delivered herself to me. You must be dusty, madam," he said to the girl. "I will give orders that a bath be prepared."

Two hours later, Caesar emerged from his bedchamber.

"Now I have truly tasted Egypt," he said.

Many have said that Cleopatra bewitched him. But that is nonsense. Nobody ever bewitched Caesar, certainly no woman. She delighted him, but that is not the same thing at all. She was little more than a schoolgirl, fifteen years of age, and though her body was a woman's, and her breasts beautiful as pomegranates, her nature was childish. He called her "Kitten", and in her grace, impulsiveness and cruelty, she was indeed feline. Of course he made jokes about this, at my expense, Kitten and Mouse – there is no need to repeat them. Caesar too had an adolescent streak.

There is no doubt, however, that, even though she didn't bewitch him, from that first hour she determined his Egyptian policy. Before her arrival, he had been considering how best to use his possession of young Ptolemy. Now he was ready to discard him just as one spits out a melon seed. It was clear that Cleopatra was to be established as the ruler of Egypt, under Caesar's control. You may think this was an absurd ambition considering that we were beleaguered. But Caesar cared nothing for such considerations. Cleopatra sat on his knee and stroked his cheeks and begged for stories, and expressed wonder at his exploits; Caesar played with the rich tresses and kissed those luscious breasts, and ran his finger along those cherry-red lips, and feasted on her dark almond-shaped eyes, that seemed some-times black, sometimes a deep purply blue; and had formed his determination.

One thing should be said. Cleopatra cured him of that lassi-tude which had afflicted him ever since he held Pompey's ring with the lion supporting a sword in its paws. If he spent half the day, and all the night with her, in the other hours he recaptured his wonted energy.

Cleopatra didn't love him, of course, being capable of passion but not love, quite different emotions as I know to my cost; and that might have been grief to him, but wasn't, he being too vain to feel what wasn't there, or the pain of its absence. Instead he took great pleasure in recounting his exploits to her, believing that she was as deeply impressed as she pretended. The light in Alexandria towards evening is violet-coloured, as cranes fly black overhead; and that is how I see them, on the terrace, the Queen sitting on his knee as he talked and talked and she stroked his cheek, her profile hard against the darkening light over the sea. Her nose, I thought, would be too large when her features were fully formed. She listened and purred. She knew when to laugh too, and this pleased him, for Caesar had no great sense of humour, but considered himself a wit.

And he exerted himself, hoping she would be as amazed by what he did now as she pretended to be by what he recounted. To please her, he had her brother murdered in the prison where he had been confined, and even yielded to her request that they should view the unfortunate boy's corpse. Then she nuzzled

Caesar and he squeezed her breasts. "I'm so glad he's dead," she whispered.

Otherwise his renewed exertion was to our common benefit. It relieved me of much anxiety. Though our restored position owed more to what I had undertaken during his weeks of lassitude, yet the evidence of the General's new-found vigour pleased and comforted the soldiers, making them bolder. Whatever one says against Caesar – and, as I intend to demonstrate, there is much that can be said – no one can deny his possession of an extraordinary gift: there never was (I believe) a general so capable of inspiring the ordinary legionary. How he did it, performing what miracle, I do not know. Perhaps it was simply that he conveyed to them his certainty of his own Destiny. But other generals have been equally certain that they were favourites of the gods, and yet their soldiers have run away.

I felt exhilaration at our restored fortunes, and pride also, on account of the part I had played, and I did not yet experience any of the doubts and fears I came later to entertain. This was short-sighted. Looking back, I see so clearly how the Egyptian interlude fed his inordinate appetite.

I had only one encounter alone with Cleopatra. She set herself to charm me. She was little more than a child but she couldn't be with a man, alone, for even a few minutes without setting herself to make him her slave, desperate to be in bed with her. It wasn't what she said – that was commonplace – or even how she said it. She spoke Greek, of course, very fluently, but full of mistakes; and, do you know, I found that charming. She giggled when I said:

"Don't you know that in your language a neuter plural subject takes a singular verb?"

"Grammar," she giggled, "my tutors were always on at me about grammar. It matters awfully, I don't think."

"You do know Caesar will have to leave Egypt, don't you? Will you be all right when we go?"

She scratched the top of her plump thigh.

"I've got an itch. What was that you were saying?"

"I was asking if you'll be all right when we leave Egypt."

My words sounded silly.

"Why does he call you 'Mouse'?" she said.

"It's a childhood nickname."

"It suits you. Of course I'll be all right. I'm the Queen."

"I think sometimes you can't wait for us to go."

"Doesn't everybody think like that about Romans?"

(You'll agree with her, Artixes, won't you? I wish your father would let me go.)

"Does Caesar know you feel like that?"

"I wouldn't tell him."

"But you tell me."

"Mmm."

She pulled up her skirt, and pointed her finger at a round red spot, on the inside of her thigh, near the top.

"Look, that's why I'm itching. It's a bite. I think saliva would be good for it. Would you like to lick, Mouse?"

It was the hour when there are no shadows, but it was cool and dark in the great chamber, and I knelt on the marble, which had ingathered the heat of the dry season, with my head between the legs of the Queen who was also a girl less than half my age, and did as she bid. My tongue rippled over that red spot, and her fingers twined in my hair, and then she drew my head back, and thrust the fingers of her other hand between my lips.

"Now taste my cunty fingers."

Delight suffused me. I swivelled, pressing myself between her legs and my hands kneading the flesh. The Greek word "ecstasy" means in its root standing outside oneself, and I knew ecstasy then, seeing the picture we made and living it at the same time.

"I shall make Caesar give me a child, I think," she said. Her legs held me tight, and she withdrew her hand and bent down and kissed my mouth, thrusting her tongue where her fingers had been a moment before.

Caesar said: "There is no reason why I should not divorce Calpurnia and marry Cleopatra. It would be a fine thing. Even Alexander did not achieve such a marriage. To take possession of Egypt is to hold the East . . . the East, of which Pompey boasted himself master."

He must have known it was impossible, and since Cleopatra was not a Roman citizen, also illegal. Even the appearance of such a marriage would destroy his position in Rome. I could imagine what a meal Cicero would make of it, and I couldn't believe Caesar did not understand this himself. And yet, at that moment, I encouraged him.

"Bring the Queen to Rome," I said.

CHAPTER

4

Each time I return to Rome, the city seems less itself. There are new buildings and new people, and what used to be familiar has lost its old proportions. (I write in this present-perfect tense, though it is improbable I shall have again this experience of a return home that is like an arrival somewhere unknown.)

On this occasion my mother had even moved house. The noise on the Esquiline, she said, had become insupportable, and so she was now living in a property inherited from her mother, which stood on the Aventine. It was peaceful there, with black-birds and siskins in the garden, and, she assured me, a night-ingale when darkness fell. It felt wrong, that absence of bustle.

"The truth is," she said, "you hear more Greek spoken than Latin where we were. Now tell me all about Caesar, darling Mouse. Is he well? Is it true that he is having an affair with the Queen of Egypt? And did you simply adore Egypt, or hate it? People always do one or the other, mostly the latter. Dear Pompey claimed he adored the place, and look at what it did for him. But you haven't answered my questions."

"You haven't given me time, and so I've forgotten now what they were . . ."

"Don't be a tease."

"Very well, Mother. In reverse order: I neither loathed Egypt nor loved it; the Queen of Egypt is having an affair with Caesar, but neither heart will be broken. As for the General, Caesar is Caesar: I'm sure you must have heard him say so."

"He wrote to me, you know, by the last post, to say how well you had done, and how I should be so very proud of you."

"Caesar excels at graciousness. You know that too, Mother."

"I've asked Calpurnia to supper. I hope you don't mind. She is desperate to have word of her hero-husband."

"What word should I give her? He has sent her presents by me. That's something, I suppose."

"I leave it to you to decide. There's no doubt, by the way, that she knows all about the Queen."

"Nobody, Mother, does that."

I withdrew, sacrificed to our family gods (as it is proper to do after a journey, to honour them and express gratitude for one's safe arrival) and retired to the chamber which had been prepared for me. I could not sleep. My mind was troubled, as it had been for weeks now, by images of Cleopatra. It amused me that my mother had arranged that Calpurnia should be with us; it showed that her capacity for demure mischief-making was not exhausted.

Calpurnia is more of a puzzle to me than Cleopatra. Of course it's well known that Caesar married her for political reasons – her father, Calpurnius Piso, was consul in 58 and a trusted ally of Pompey's when Caesar and Pompey first came together in friendship. But he remained married long after the political value of the union had expired, and he did so even though Calpurnia was notably lacking in charm or beauty. Thin, angular, with a voice like an Ostia fishwife, and a temper to match, she frequently embarrassed Caesar at dinner-parties. She had the absurd habit of disputing people's observations on matters of which she could not be other than ignorant. Moreover, she didn't hesitate to contradict Caesar himself. I remember once when the talk turned on the question of the transmigration of souls – a theory that had long attracted Caesar – and he spoke of how, visiting Athens for the first time, he had found his way to the house which he was seeking without enquiring directions from any passer-by, but travelling with certainty as if he had already made that journey many times, perhaps even daily, in another life, she interrupted to suggest that he was probably drunk, because it's well-known that drunk men are favoured by fortune . . .

"Besides," she said, "I expect it was a brothel you were seeking, and I've never heard of a pig that couldn't find its way to a sty."

Caesar tried to laugh it off – and indeed Calpurnia made this last comment with a bray like a she-ass, inviting us to share the joke – but he wasn't pleased. I wondered then if he was frightened of Calpurnia.

It sounds absurd. We all know that Caesar was fearless. He made a point often enough of telling us so. Yet, as my friend Gaius Valerius Catullus was wont to say, "The most mysterious silence in the world is that which surrounds a man and woman when they are alone together."

Now, naturally enough, she questioned me narrowly concerning Cleopatra – Calpurnia was the sort of woman who always knew the stories that were going the rounds. She didn't trouble to hide her conviction that Caesar was again being unfaithful to her. Most women would conceal such knowledge, on account of their pride. But Calpurnia's pride was of a different order; she delighted in presenting herself to the world as a wronged woman.

"She's of an age to be his granddaughter," she said.

"Not quite."

"I've done my calculations. She would be under marriageable age if she was a Roman. What does he see in her?"

"She amuses him. There's nothing more to it. Except this: the relationship is political. The importance of Egypt is well-recognised. Therefore it's a good thing to be on friendly terms with its Queen."

"Friendly terms! But you men always stick together. The only thing that surprises me is that he preferred her to her brother. He had him put to death, didn't he? Was he very ugly?"

"I've no idea."

"You're a rotten liar. You're blushing, your face gives you away."

I tried to turn the conversation to more general questions. But she kept returning to the matter of Cleopatra.

At last she said: "He'll have to come home in a couple of months. His dictatorship expires, doesn't it? Will he ask for it to be renewed, or will he be content with more ordinary honours?"

"How can I answer a question if his wife is ignorant of the matter?"

Then, to divert her, I sent a slave to fetch the presents which Caesar had entrusted to me.

"There's something inescapably vulgar about all Oriental workmanship," she said.

Nevertheless she took them with her when she left, though I later heard that, when Caesar eventually came home, he found that some of the jewels which he had had his quartermaster so carefully select had been passed on to Calpurnia's favoured freedwomen. As a loan, of course; if she dismissed a servant she took care to retrieve anything she had lent her.

When Calpurnia left, I said good night to my mother, and went out into the streets, saying I required fresh air, to blow away memories of Calpurnia's spite.

"You won't find that in Rome, nothing but filth. Behave yourself," and she held out her cheek for me to kiss.

I felt, as I knew I would, the excitement of return, the strange sense of liberation that the city's nocturnal life offered. I passed through the Suburra, stopping to admire the filthy shows outside the brothels. My ears were assailed by the babble of countless tongues, as if all the languages of the world sought to express their vices in the stew of Rome. My poor dead friend Catullus had often insisted that filth and beauty were two sides of the same coin. And, thinking of Catullus, I admitted where I was heading, in a roundabout fashion.

He had loved Clodia to distraction; I myself only knew him after he had broken away, with tears and in trembling. His voice shook when he spoke of her. He could escape neither the memory of her love – the beauty of those great dark ox-eyes – nor the horror with which she had filled him. "We are drawn to what terrifies and disgusts us," he said. "She demands adoration, like the goddess Cybele, and then slays her admirers. Her lusts are insatiable. She exhausts her lovers, and unmans them. I trust, Mouse, that you will never find yourself in the clutches of so terrible a woman."

That was the warning he gave me, and since then, Clodia's reputation had been utterly destroyed. Who does not remember the lawsuit she brought against Caelius Rufus, himself a close friend of Catullus? (They were the same age – I am some years younger.) When Caelius left her, she accused him of all sorts of crimes: he had tried to poison her, he had defrauded her of money she had lent him, he had plotted the assassination of an Egyptian diplomat, he had tried to raise a riot in Naples; and so on. It was a collection of absurdities. Men said the woman had taken leave of her senses.

Caelius got Cicero to defend him. I was in court. It would be, people promised, better than the gladiators. "Cicero hates Clodia, on account of the way her brother persecuted him. You know, of course, she was her brother's lover. Fact." That was the way people talked.

Cicero's speech was masterly. Whatever doubts – generally well-founded – people have expressed about his character, no one has ever denied his genius for forensic oratory. And I doubt if he has ever displayed it to more effect than in his defence of Caelius.

He began quietly, in subdued fashion, remarking that the case against Caelius scarcely needed a defence. It was enough to draw attention to the beauties of his friend's character and the honourable nature of his career. It would be a pity, he observed, as if in an aside, if such a career should be besmirched "by the influence of a prostitute". Surely, he asked, the wantonness of women ought to be controlled?

This appeal to the solidarity of our sex had the court nodding in approval.

Then he turned on Clodia, though without even glancing in her direction. He would hesitate, he said, to mention a Roman lady, the mother of a family, in a law-court, without due respect,· if she had not herself launched such an attack on his worthy friend Caelius. There was another reason for him to hold back; he couldn't confess to be unprejudiced, not only on account of his friendship with Caelius, but also because "I have in the past had grave personal disagreements with the lady's husband – I beg your pardon, I mean of course her brother – I always make that mistake."

And he turned to the jury, spreading his hands wide in simulated apology, while, behind him, Caelius and his friends, who may have known the gibe was coming, rocked with laughter.

Cicero knew, however, that he had to walk warily. Clodia belonged to one of our greatest families, while he himself was a new man from the unimportant town of Arpinum. So, rather than attack Clodia directly in his own person, he summoned up the memory of her greatest ancestor, Appius Claudius the Censor. He had his imaginary figure (for all reconstructions of dead men must be only imaginary) describe his own achievements, praise the virtue of the great ladies of the Claudian family, and then deplore the manner in which Clodia had disgraced them: her choice of a plebeian form of the family name was itself disgraceful, and yet her conduct disgraced even the plebeians.

The woman, Cicero suggested, was not only bad. She was also silly. She was frivolous, without any sense of dignity. She behaved like a woman in a comedy; she might have been created by Terence or Plautus. Since we all knew that the women in these comedies were heartless and impudent tarts, Clodia shrivelled before our eyes. She had, Cicero implied, the morals and manners of a whore, whose word cannot even be weighed.

Finally, he turned to the charge of poisoning which Clodia had laid against Caelius, and laughed it out of court, exposing its improbability, even impossibility. It was the product of nothing but spite. "This is not the final scene of a comedy," he said, "it is the end of a farce"; and which of us, hearing these words, did not glance at the ox-eyed beauty and see her aristocratic splendour fall away to reveal the naked showgirls who prance, cavort and gesture obscenely in these degraded spectacles. "You will not convict a virtuous nobleman on the word of a vile trollop"; that was his message.

Clodia did not move during this terrible attack. If she felt the faces of the crowd turn towards her, she gave no sign. If she was aware that the young men who had accompanied her to court were drawing away from her, dissociating themselves from her disgrace, she paid no heed. And at that moment something appalling happened. I fell hopelessly, overwhelmingly in love. I was seized with the most intense desire.

Even as I trembled, I asked myself why this should be. "Know thyself" – that is the sum of wisdom offered by the philosophers, and few of us know ourselves but slightly. Perhaps that is the greater wisdom. For, in this revelation now vouchsafed me of the form of union I desired, I knew, even as I throbbed with impatient lust, that I was surrendering to a part of myself, perhaps my profoundest nature, which would render me an object of scorn and contempt to all virtuous men. I was horrified by what I learned of my own character, and yet it was inescapable that, with loins aching, I presented myself at her house that evening.

She was alone. I could not believe that she had passed an evening alone in her life. The great saloon into which a stammering slave ushered me was cold as a winter morning. I waited a long time. I wanted to run away. Reason prompted me to make my escape while there was still time. I remembered the awful words Catullus had spoken. I remembered how he had told me that she would sleep with a squinting Spaniard who polished his cheeks with his own urine, how he himself had waited in her antechamber while she pleasured herself with ignoble wretches she had picked up in filthy taverns or sleazy streets.

I recalled his lines:

> Give her my goodbye, her and all her lovers,
> Whom she hugs so close to her in their hundreds,
> Loving not one, yet with her constant lusting,
> Leaving their loins limp . . .

I remembered the poem written on the myth of Cybele and Attis. (Do you know the myth, Artixes? Let me tell it you.) Attis loved the goddess Cybele, with passionate terror, such as the old gods demand. Either in obedience to her will, or to keep himself pure for her service (there are different versions of the story), he castrated himself with a stone knife, and lived as her worshipper, far from cities, in the forest, with a group of other youths who had submitted in like fashion to the goddess. Well, my friend Catullus took this story, and translated it to the present day. The voice in his poem is that of a Greek youth who has joined her cult, abiding in the wild region where alone she reigns now, and has mutilated himself to do her pleasure and honour. But then, in the poem, he recovers from his madness, and looks back with bitter pain and sorrow on all that he has lost. Learning of his remorse, the goddess lets lions loose on him, so that he flees, in terror and renewed madness, to the heart of the forest darkness.

And when Catullus read these verses to me, he laid his hand on my shoulder and said, "I pray, Mouse, that you never know the like."

"Have you come in mockery or in pity?"

She was standing before me, and, immersed in these memories, I had not seen her approach. Her hair hung loose, and she wore a white gown, like a virgin. It was very simple and fell in folds to the ground. How did I know at once that it was all she wore? Her huge dark eyes were even darker, being in shadow from the candle which she held in a golden holder in her right hand, raised aloft.

"I wish neither, Decimus Brutus."

"I was in court today."

"With all Rome."

Her left hand was laid on my cheek, cool, dry and with a tender touch.

"And you thought . . . what?"

I could not speak.

Perhaps my silence maddened her, for she tore her nails the length of my cheek, and the blood ran.

"How many men were there, ranged against one woman? And you were among them and you have the impertinence to come here. Was it to see if I feel shame?"

I sat still, like a dog that has been whipped, and fears to move, lest he invite more trouble.

Then she gave way to rage. She threw the candlestick across the room. (Fortunately, it fell in such a way as to extinguish the flame.) She delivered a tirade that would have inflamed the mob. She cursed Cicero in words that a lady is not supposed to know, let alone utter. She reviled the male sex, hypocrites, brutes, and deceivers. She denounced Caelius as an invert incapable of pleasing a woman; she had found better lovers among slaves and freedmen. She returned to Cicero. Did I know she had years before had him in thrall? He had adored her, sworn he would leave his wife and marry her, and she had laughed at him. That was why he hated her so. It was not his sense of morality that had been outraged – "Cicero's sense of morality, the man who defended the murderer of my brother – what claim has that sack of dung to morality?" – No, today he had taken the revenge which his own wounded vanity had demanded and long nursed the desire to achieve.

She paused.

"Your cheek's bleeding."

She rang a bell, sent the slave for water mixed with myrrh and hyssop, and bathed my wound.

"You will have had worse wounds in battle."

"None sharper."

"It was a shame to make a pretty boy like you a surrogate for that old impotent lecher. He couldn't do it, you know. Not like Caesar. Or you, I'm sure."

She let her robe fall away, and drew me down on top of her on a gold rug made from lionskins. Her tongue licked the last blood that still seeped from my cheek. That was how it began.

It could not finish. It has never been able to finish. It was like nothing else I have known. Like everyone I have had many lovers – the first indeed was her brother Publius Clodius Pulcher, whom Cicero derided as "the pretty boy". He was even more beautiful than his sister, and it was no wonder, I have often thought, that they should have had an incestuous relationship, as everyone asserts, for in both the sexes were strangely mixed. The Roman people adored Clodius as if he had been a lovely girl, and many feared Clodia as a virile destroyer. In bed with her, I discovered more of myself than I had ever imagined, and yet remained confused. She felt no tenderness, except for the memory of her brother, and yet no one, at certain moments and in certain moods, so filled one with tenderness. She terrified me, and I adored her.

She was ill that evening when I left my mother's house and made my way to hers on the Palatine. The house was dark. For a moment I thought it deserted, and knew both relief and heartache. I never approached her chamber without trepidation, dreading to learn who or what I might discover there. But this night again she was alone, as that first time. She had been suffering from fever. Her beauty, so well preserved by art, was disturbed by nature. She looked her age.

When we had made love, performed our sexual acts, achieved

a short-lived escape from the desert into which we were abruptly returned, she told me she was dying.

I wept, I remember that; yet even as I did so, felt my heart lift at the prospect of escape. It was an illusion; I have never escaped, any more than poor Catullus did. The only persons who were unaffected by her – the only ones who enjoyed her and maintained equanimity – were her brother, who as a child of Eros knew delight without the sense of waste, and Caesar.

She was fascinated by Caesar for that reason. He had escaped her, and yet she felt no anger against him. This puzzled her.

"When he first told me – in this very bed – that he was a god, I laughed at him. I thought he was inviting me to share a joke. But he meant it. He is descended as everyone knows from Venus, but he believes he is also inhabited by the goddess. They tell me he fucks the Queen of Egypt now. Is she as beautiful as they say?"

"She does not compare with you, Clodia."

"But . . ."

"She is a child, an adolescent. What fascinates Caesar is that she is no more capable of love than he is."

"Then they are well-matched. Does Caesar know you fucked her?"

"He would not care. Clodia, I have served Caesar for years. He is the most wonderful and remarkable man I am ever likely to know. Naturally, we laugh at his little vanities, and we often find him exasperating, but our mockery is exercised in self-defence. It is an attempt to pretend that Caesar is a man like ourselves."

"He is not so different," Clodia said.

"But he is."

"He is only different in having no heart, and let me tell you, Decimus Brutus, that there are many men like that."

"And women, Clodia?"

"You mean me, of course. Well, I am not angry to hear you say so, as I would once have been. I told you I am dying. I shall not linger here to waste away. I shall simply remove myself. So there is no need to tell lies any more. I know what people say about me. That brute Cicero slandered me to the world, and the world believed him."

She laid her hand on my sleeve, and the bones stood out clear.

"I said I would not lie, but I still say they were slanders. You don't understand, Decimus Brutus, what it is to be a woman, how a woman is thwarted, perpetually thwarted, how her rage rises to see what is permitted to men and denied her. Well, very early, when I was still a child, my brother and I made a vow. We mingled our blood to seal it."

She paused, and took up the candle and examined her face in the glass, as if seeking the child she had been. And as she did so, I could envisage them, the boy-girl and the girl-boy, each of a beauty such as no sculptor could hope to seize, pressing against each other, lips yoked, their very blood commingling as they strove to unite two souls in a single body and achieve that perfect unity which the philosophers insist we once possessed and must now forever seek in vain.

"That we would be utterly ourselves, denying nothing, yielding to our every desire, fulfilling nature, hearkening and obeying every prompting of the senses, so that we might achieve the freedom of the gods, that freedom which consists of being absolutely oneself, untrammelled by conventions or the morality which the timid have constructed to ensnare the brave. You have known both of us, you more than any other have loved both of us, for what we are rather than for some imagined picture of what we might be, or be thought to be – and yet, my dear, even your love has fallen short of the perfect love we felt for each other, each being the other and the other each. Now I see that we aimed too high, exceeded our powers. Publius is dead. I am dying, a slave to lusts I no longer find delight in. My reputation – since Cicero – could not be worse. No decent woman in Rome will receive me in her house. I have always despised such women, and what they call decency, and once I would have laughed at my exclusion. Now, I do not know. The cold grey fingers of death have touched me, and what will I find when I descend to the Shades? Will the gods be angered at my presumption? Will Cybele, whom Catullus said I aped, turn on me with terrible wrath? We cannot play gods, I have learned that, my dear, too late, and yet, even as I come to this conclusion, which terrifies me and makes a mockery of my life, I see that there is an exception: Caesar, descended from gods, inhabited by Venus. Do you understand, Decimus Brutus, little Decimus Brutus, Caesar believes himself to be what my brother and I aspired to be? And in time, I will wager, the Roman people will find themselves in agreement. The Senate – that assembly of timid and greedy goats – will fall down and worship him. They will decree that Caesar is indeed a god: 'Divus Julius', they will chant, 'divus Julius'. Temples will be consecrated to him; and what will you do then, little Decimus Brutus? I will tell you your choice. You must acquiesce in the murder of liberty in Rome, or you must kill Caesar."

"Kill Caesar?"

"Kill Caesar. It is Caesar or Rome, and as a patriot, you will choose Rome. Kill Caesar. Now go, my dear, and do not return. You have meant something to me, and that is what no living man, except Caesar, can boast. I shall embrace my brother for you, and Gaius Valerius also, if he does not shrink in terror when we encounter each other in the Vale of Shadows."

CHAPTER

5

Caesar returned to Rome before the end of the year, in order to ensure that the prolongation of his dictatorship be effected without difficulty. That was achieved. Opposition in Rome was muted, though many of course still sympathised with our enemies. Despite Pompey's defeat and death, these were still numerous. They held North Africa and Spain. The leaders were now Pompey's sons, the renegade Labienus, and Marcus Porcius Cato, the one man whom Caesar utterly hated. In general, hatred was an emotion Caesar despised. He called it "wasteful". No doubt that was his opinion, but the cause of his inability to feel hatred went deeper. To hate someone was to admit him as an equal, and Caesar recognised no equals. This made his hatred of Cato all the stranger, for there was no respect in which Cato could be thought to match Caesar. He was an incompetent general, whose legionaries loathed him, because his pride (or perhaps his secret suspicion of his own incapacity) made him treat them abominably. Caesar could always be free-and-easy with the common soldier for he had no doubt of his superiority, and knew that he could quell insolence or disaffection with a frown or a single biting sentence. Cato was stiff and bullying and a savage disciplinarian; and perhaps it was because inwardly he feared the men he was so eager to dominate. Besides, Cato was a bore with no sense of humour. I have remarked before that Caesar had no fundamental humour, but he was always capable of the sort of quip that pleases the legionaries. And they would follow him eagerly anywhere, into all sorts of danger, confident in his genius; whereas those who served with Cato tell me that he took the precaution of assigning some of his bodyguards to protect his back from his own men. I would find this hard to believe of any other Roman general.

Moreover, Cato was a wooden orator, and a man of lamentable judgment. He was a drunkard, of the heavy sullen type. There was no joy in him. Caesar once described him to me as "the coldest dullest piece of base metal you will ever meet". And yet it wasn't enough for him to despise Cato, as I did; he was consumed with hatred.

Why? Obvious reasons may be advanced. Cato once threatened to bring a prosecution against Caesar on account of atrocities committed in the conquest of Gaul. That threat certainly disturbed Caesar's vanity. No one, after all, was ever more careful of his reputation than Caesar. But of course he knew that the threat was empty. What happened in Gaul, horrible though it frequently was (I'm sorry, Artixes), was no worse than any other conquest. It is easy for people who never leave Rome or their country estates to preach morality; but you cannot subdue a proud people, and win Empire and glory for Rome, without harsh measures. Caesar was never afraid to take such measures, and on the whole his methods were justified. After all, even you must admit, Artixes, that Gaul was pacified, whatever has happened subsequently. Even that won't, I am certain, alter the fact that all Gaul is now incorporated within the Roman Empire, which Gauls themselves will eventually confess to be to their benefit. Civilisation cannot be spread amongst barbarians by the methods which appease the consciences of civilised men. To subdue barbarians inevitably requires a degree of barbarity.

Besides, it was absurd of Cato to try to arraign Caesar on such a count. He never tired, after all, of talking about his great ancestor, Cato the Censor, and everyone knows the part he played in the spread of Empire. It was that model of Republican virtue who concluded every speech in the Senate, no matter what the ostensible subject of the debate, with the words: "and in my opinion Carthage must be destroyed". He didn't rest till that was done, not a stone left standing, and the people either massacred or sold into slavery. And yet his admiring grandson would have charged Caesar with war crimes. No wonder it gave Caesar such pleasure – malicious pleasure, I grant you – to found the city of Carthage anew.

Cato's assumption of superior virtue infuriated Caesar, all the more because so many people accepted it unquestioningly. He thought him a hypocrite. He also considered that Cato not only failed to understand what Caesar called "the predicament of the Republic", but was an obstacle to others' comprehension.

And then a personal element sharpened the hatred each felt for the other. Cato's half-sister was Servilia, who was, as I've remarked before, in my mother's opinion at least, the only woman Caesar ever really loved. When they were young Servilia is said to have dominated Cato who revered her as the very model of Roman womanhood. And then she submitted to the dissolute Caesar, with his dangerous Popular political attachments, and his connection with Gaius Marius – for an aunt of Caesar's had actually married the old brute. This was too much for Cato; he went about saying that his sister had been bewitched and also that it was a great mistake on the part of Sulla, when dictator, to allow himself to be persuaded to remove Caesar's name from the list of proscribed persons. He liked to quote Sulla's remark as he reluctantly spared Caesar: "In that young man I see many Mariuses." "Just so," Cato would say, as if this judgment represented the sum of political wisdom. So Cato hated Caesar on account of his debauchment of Servilia.

There's actually rather a good story about this triangular relationship. During the debates in the Senate concerning the conspiracy of Catiline, Caesar and Cato were of course on different sides – indeed, you may remember that Caesar was actually suspected of involvement. Well, a note was passed to Caesar, and Cato leapt up and accused him of receiving messages from the enemies of the State. "I assure you, Conscript Fathers," Caesar said, "this note relates to a purely private matter." "Why should we accept the word of a liar who sympathises with Catiline?" Cato shouted. "I urge that Caesar be commanded to produce the note that we may all see what treasonable business he is engaged in." "Very well," Caesar said, "if Cato insists I shall let him see the note, but I protest that it should go no further." "I shall decide that," Cato replied. So Caesar passed him the note, which was a love-letter from Servilia, couched in extremely explicit terms.

I have often heard Caesar tell that story.

Then the matter of Servilia's son, my cousin Marcus Junius Brutus, also came between them. This seems strange when you consider how dull Markie is, but Caesar and Cato competed to exercise influence over him, each affecting to think him the coming great man, a model of virtue. It was absurd; nevertheless that was how they felt. Of course there have always been rumours that Markie was Caesar's son, and I know that sometimes at least Caesar liked to think that this was so. Absolute nonsense, as my mother assured me: Markie was the very image of his extremely dull father. Cato of course was horrified at the suggestion. It seemed to me that he half-believed it, however, and was convinced that if he could attach Markie to himself, this would disprove the story. Be that as it may, it was quite a comedy to see the pair strive for the boring young man's approval and devotion. As for Markie, he took the competition for granted; even as a youth he was so puffed up with conceit that it appeared perfectly natural to him that two of the great men in the State should vie for his confidence and approval. Can you imagine anything more ridiculous?

He inclined towards his uncle who appealed to his dull taste and his antiquated notions of Republican virtue. If you ask me, he was always a little afraid of Caesar, partly because his pedestrian intelligence found it difficult to follow the leaps of Caesar's conversation; and he was of course shocked by the audacity of Caesar's speculations. Besides, he was ashamed of his mother's affair with Caesar, and not even Markie could convince himself, despite the rare ability he has always had to believe exactly what he chooses, that they were only good friends. On the other hand, like most people, he couldn't resist Caesar's famous charm, and even Markie couldn't fail to find Caesar a much more agreeable companion than Cato. So he succumbed to Caesar whenever he was present and rebelled against him in his absence.

Cato worked hard to persuade him that Caesar was fundamentally evil, as well as being a danger to the Constitution which they both adored. So at the beginning of the civil war, Markie attached himself to the respectable party and followed Pompey to Greece. No doubt he thought Pompey would win; that, after all, was the received opinion among those who underestimated the magnitude of what Caesar had achieved in Gaul. Markie's decision to join Pompey was clear evidence of Cato's influence, for Servilia detested the Great One, because he had been responsible for the death of her first husband, Markie's father.

He didn't distinguish himself during the campaign which ended at Pharsalus; Markie has no more notion of soldiering than I have of rope-dancing. Indeed, though Pompey had proclaimed himself delighted to receive such a virtuous young man, he had taken care to give him no responsibility. Pompey may have been in decline, but he still knew better than that.

Caesar of course was delighted to make Markie one of the most conspicuous objects of his clemency. He even ordered us to save him by all means, and if he refused to surrender, to let him escape. In fact he was one of the first to run away, and spent a couple of days skulking among the reeds at the edge of a marsh. Then he got to Larissa whence he wrote to Caesar in the most friendly terms. Caesar at once invited him to join us.

I was in Caesar's tent with Casca when he arrived, and we found the whole thing nauseating. First, Caesar dissolved in tears, saying again and again that his one fear during the battle had been that the noble Brutus might be slain.

("Fat chance of that," Casca whispered. "I bet he was safe in the rear." And indeed, I later heard that he had spent the day of the battle writing an essay in his tent, till slaves brought him the news of defeat and he ran away.)

Then Caesar kissed Markie, and wept some more, and Markie wept too, and begged Caesar's pardon, and excused himself by saying that he had been under his uncle's influence. It was a ludicrous scene. I have attended many such, but I can't recall one more absurd.

The upshot of it all was that Caesar soon appointed Markie Governor of Cisalpine Gaul. Casca remarked that while Caesar might be besotted, his judgment hadn't entirely deserted him. Cisalpine Gaul was then one province where we could be sure there would be no fighting. Markie at once set himself to win popularity with the people under his jurisdiction, but he took care to remind them that all their blessings were obtained as a result of the goodness of Caesar.

Caesar was now eager to proceed with the African campaign.

"It gives me a chance to settle Cato's hash for good," he said. "That is essential, for you see, Mouse, as long as he is at liberty, opposition will continue. He is a festering boil, which must be lanced."

I agreed with him entirely.

Despite his desire for speed, certain matters held him in Rome.

The first, and most grievous, was a mutiny by his favourite Tenth Legion, then stationed at Capua. They had grounds for complaint. Their pay was even further in arrears than is usual in armies. Some, whose term of service had expired, had been denied demobilisation. Land promised to veterans had not yet been assigned. So both their present state and their future prospects were unsatisfactory, and now they learned that they would be required to embark for Africa. Agitators, recruited in my opinion by Caesar's enemies in the Senate, infiltrated the camp and found the tinder dry. Accordingly a committee was formed – as committees always are in such circumstances. The officers were arrested and bound in chains, as officers always are unless they have the wit to run away; and the men talked about marching on Rome, determined to lay their grievances before Caesar and demand redress. It was a nasty moment. It was clear to me that if Caesar should fail to suppress this mutiny, everything for which we had worked, fought and suffered would be destroyed. I am told that when the news of the mutiny reached Cato in Africa, he not only ordered that it should be published throughout his camp (in itself an act of extraordinary folly, since mutiny is as contagious as an outbreak of rioting in a city), but went happily drunk to bed, and stayed drunk for two days. He deserved to have his throat cut for being such a blockhead. However, he got away with it for the time being.

Caesar, as I have said, was at his best and most masterful in the hour of crisis. Calm weather did not suit him; storms aroused and stimulated his genius. He tried to temporise with the mutineers, sending young Sallust, an officer whom he held in more respect than I did, to the camp near Capua, with authority to promise substantial sums of extra pay. Sallust wasn't even accorded a hearing, being met with a volley of stones and insults, which persuaded him that his life was in danger. He therefore fled back to Rome.

It was soon after this that the legionaries themselves moved north. Other troops had been attached to their unworthy cause, and the danger was indeed very great. The excitement in Rome was immense, especially among our enemies who went about promising each other that Pompey was going to be avenged, and that it would soon be possible to restore what they described as "Republican normalcy". Their excitement wasn't even allayed by the news that the mutineers had sacked properties on their march and murdered two men of praetorian rank. The ordinary citizens took a different view, and a more sensible one. They were frankly terrified and looked to Caesar to protect them.

Caesar called his chief lieutenants together to consider how the matter should be handled. Incidentally, since I have often heard people who knew nothing of his working methods declare that he acted always on his own judgment, paying no heed to the opinions of those around him, I must point out that this wasn't the case. Quite the contrary indeed; he invariably paid close attention to what others thought, even if he also liked to make it seem that the eventual decision was entirely his. That was his nature, and that was how he liked to work.

On this occasion Antony's advice was clear. (I don't know why I say "on this occasion", since Antony never lacked confidence in his own opinion – at least till Caesar challenged it, when he would backtrack with the speed of cavalry in flight.)

"Caesar," he said, "we have no shortage of loyal troops still under discipline. We should march out of Rome and confront the buggers. Make it clear you won't stand for any nonsense, but are ready to fight them if need be. That will sort them out. We can all be certain that they won't engage in battle against you yourself."

That advice was typical of Antony: vigorous, flattering to Caesar, and thoughtless. I looked round the table and noticed several heads nod in agreement. They weren't heads I would have trusted to plan an excursion to the country.

Caesar gave no sign whether he approved this plan or not.

Caius Cassius, a recent adherent to our party (he had fought in the Pompeian army at Pharsalus) looked grave. Some may have been surprised that he had been invited to attend this council, but it was Caesar's policy to bind reconciled enemies as tightly as possible to his cause and person. Now Cassius spoke, anxious, as was natural enough, to make an impression.

"I have no doubt that my friend Antony has considered the matter carefully," he said. "He knows these legions, and may have judged wisely. Yet it occurs to me that he may have overlooked what I would call the political aspect. There is reason to believe, is there not, that this mutiny has been fomented by agitators?"

"For myself, I detect the hand of Labienus," Caesar said.

"Thank you, Caesar. I am grateful to have my suspicions confirmed. Now what do I mean by the political aspect? Simply this: if we march out against them, Caesar's enemies will take heart. They will say that his legions are divided against each other. They will say his party is split. They will therefore attract new adherents."

"Bugger new adherents," Casca said. "I'll tell you something more dangerous still. If we march against them, they won't stand their ground, but they won't surrender either. Antony is right in saying they won't dare to face you in person, Caesar. But they will withdraw in good order, they're soldiers dammit, whom we have trained. We know what manner of men they are. We know their pride. And what then? They will believe that their cause can only be saved – their lives even – if they retire and ally themselves to our enemies. It's too great a risk, Caesar."

"So what should we do, Casca, if you reject our dear Antony's proposal?"

"Buggered if I know," Casca said.

"Well, Mouse?" Caesar turned to me. "Have you words of wisdom to offer?"

"I should hesitate to call my opinion wisdom, but it seems to me that you should do nothing which might suggest to them that you recognise that they are not under your orders."

"By Hercules," Antony shouted, "what sort of nonsense is this? They've mutinied, Mouse, in case you haven't noticed. That means that they have defied orders, rejected orders. Or don't you know what the word 'mutiny' means?"

"Oh yes," I said, "I think I do. And if you will allow me to repeat what I said, and this time listen carefully, Antony, I suggested that Caesar should not act in such a manner as to let the mutineers believe that he recognises that they are not under his orders. I mean by that, Caesar, that you take the initiative, not by confronting them, but by issuing the sort of order which they will find quite easy to obey . . ."

"I'm still lost," Antony said.

"Never mind, dear," Casca said. "Mouse is right, Caesar."

I have recounted this conversation in some detail because in the subsequent report which Caesar gave to the Senate, he allowed it to be understood that the plan by which the mutiny was quelled originated with him. I owe it to my dignity to draw the attention of posterity to my part in its defeat. Indeed, though I don't deny that Caesar delivered the final masterstroke, everyone who attended that council knows very well that the grand design was my work.

So word was sent to the mutineers that they could enter the city, and camp in the Field of Mars, so long as they first laid down their arms. (The gates of the city were of course well-guarded by loyal troops.) They obeyed this instruction to the extent that I had thought probable; that is to say, they carried only their swords with them. That terrified the citizens – no bad thing in itself, I thought.

Caesar was angry when I collected him from his house. Fortunately, his anger was controlled. He explained to me that he was revolted by the disloyalty, self-will and stupidity of the men.

"We have been through so much together," he said. "We are part of the same body. Don't they understand that, if they are to command and I am to fall in with their wishes, the whole nature of the bond between us will be tarnished, even destroyed? I have no patience with their greed and insolence."

"Very well, Caesar," I said, "but when you address them, be cold, not warm."

"I shall be cold as a night in the mountains of Helvetia," he replied.

We arrived in the Field of Mars and made our way to the dais which had been erected. Caesar took his seat. For a few minutes he paid no attention to the men swarming beneath us, but spoke only to me and a few others around him. I took stock of the situation. Now that my plan was approaching fruition, I felt nervous for the first time. It was after all possible that it would not work, and in that case things could turn very nasty indeed. There might even be a general massacre.

When Caesar at last lifted his head, looked at the troops and spoke, his voice was bored. He asked to hear their complaints. He spoke as if he had never previously seen these men with whom he had fought throughout Gaul and at Pharsalus. It was,

I must confess, a marvellous piece of theatre: and it disconcerted them.

Nevertheless, after a pause, while they waited to see who would have the courage to speak first, the complaints came fast and thick. Speech tumbled over speech as they told of their wounds, their hardships, what they had suffered in his cause, the great deeds they had accomplished, the friends they had lost, the rewards they had expected and been denied, their desire to be demobilised.

The speeches went on too long. The mood was growing more restive. Still Caesar gave no sign that he had heard.

Someone shouted: "We've torn our guts out for you, Caesar."

One legionary pushed forward, clambered halfway up the platform before he was stopped. He tore a patch off his left eye, revealing a horrid vacancy.

"I lost this at Alesia, and still they wouldn't give me my discharge. What do you say to that, Caesar?"

Caesar looked up. He raised a hand. There was silence.

"Very well," his voice seemed unconcerned, an actor's voice. "I have understood what you want. You can all be demobilised immediately. Leave your swords with the guards as you disperse. As for money, you all know Caesar. You can rely on me for every penny you are due and every penny you have been promised. Give your names and the amount you claim to the quartermaster. You'll have to wait, though, till I return from Africa to get settlement in full. I'd counted on you for that campaign. Now it'll have to be fought with other legions. They'll be the ones which will take part in my Triumph when I return. I think that's everything."

Nobody broke the silence. They were utterly taken aback. Either they hadn't expected this easy agreement, or they were disappointed by it. The ringleaders of course had been cheated of the fight they had been paid to foment, but that wasn't the main cause of the strange change of mood. No, it was, first, that reminder of the Triumph he was due, and the realisation that they would have no share in it, even though so many of them were veterans of the battles which had secured the honour for their General. And yet there was, I realised, a still more bitter thought: their discovery that Caesar believed he could do perfectly well without them.

So nobody moved or uttered a word. It was like a funeral before the lamentation begins.

"Citizens," Caesar said, and was rewarded by a howl of pain and grief. He had never addressed them as anything but "soldiers" or "comrades", and now he was calling them "citizens" as if they were no more important than voters whose support he might be trying to elicit.

They broke ranks, crowding round him, tugging at his sleeve, begging him to forgive them, take them back into his service, punish the ringleaders who had led them so grievously astray. It was a ludicrous scene; grizzled veterans were sobbing like women. One centurion of the Tenth even shouted, "Punish us, Caesar, punish us as you think fit, decimate us even, so long as you take the rest of us back and let us accompany you to Africa."

At dinner that evening Caesar glowed with pride. He talked at length about the art of controlling men.

"Touch their pride and they are yours," he said.

He seemed to forget that it was as a result of my advice that the day had turned out so satisfactorily. I didn't hold that against him, of course. My task was to advise, his to execute. Nevertheless it would have been more gracious if he had acknowledged the debt he owed me.

CHAPTER

I was not disappointed when Caesar informed me that he would not require me to accompany him to Africa, though it was naturally irritating to learn that many were muttering that I had fallen out of the Dictator's favour. That wasn't, of course, the case. Caesar made it clear that he was expecting me to supervise his political interests at home.

"I would rather have those whom I don't trust with me, under my eye, and leave behind those whom I trust absolutely," he said.

I acquiesced proudly, though I extracted from him the promise that I should rejoin the army as soon as he felt my services were not absolutely necessary in Rome. After all, I am a soldier first and foremost, and no old warhorse is happy to be out of hearing of the trumpet.

Apart altogether from my public duties, I had other reasons for being content to remain in the city. My knee was still troubling me, and the Greek doctor whom I consulted advised that prolonged rest and regular anointing with a compound of almonds and crocodile oil would be the best treatment.

"If you don't give it time to recover, my lord, you will be a hopeless cripple in ten years," he warned.

Then my father's health was declining, and it was natural that I should wish to attend his deathbed. We had never been close, for he was a man of old-fashioned rigour and considerable stupidity, who had never understood my more audacious flights or had any sympathy with my eagerness to taste life to the full. But I honoured him and was satisfied that I had never failed in my duty towards him. My mother too was pleased to have me at home, finding my presence a great comfort, as my poor father grew ever more capricious and absurdly demanding. Indeed it was fortunate that I was there, since I was able to thwart a scheme he had devised to leave almost half of his property to "the common good of the Roman people". The deluded old man believed that this would secure him the fame which he had not achieved in life – as if this could possibly matter to him when he was dead, while it would have been a serious inconvenience to us (or so it seemed then, Artixes) to be deprived of our rightful inheritance.

Finally, Clodia having departed into the dark chamber of her own death-journey, I was agreeably engaged in an affair with a young Phrygian dancer, a creature of unquenchable gaiety and acrobatic inventiveness in the art of love. I would certainly have been loth to leave Rome before I had exhausted this young person's considerable charms, which seemed to me to combine the ardour of Clodius with the seductive sluttishness of Cleopatra.

So it was with equanimity that I said "Farewell" to Caesar, and it was in truth a relief to be free of his overpowering and demanding presence.

Rather to my surprise I found myself being cultivated by Cicero. I have mentioned him several times in this memoir, Artixes, and generally, I think, disparagingly. Well, there was good reason for that, but it occurs to me that I may have conveyed an inadequate impression of this remarkable man. For he was remarkable: one of the few men in Rome to have achieved the highest position in the State without the advantage of either birth or great wealth (though he acquired the latter, of course).

He was now, I suppose, about sixty. (I have, of course, no works of reference to hand and must rely on my memory and my impressions.) His great days were behind him. It was almost twenty years since he had had his finest hour, when, as consul, he exposed and destroyed Catiline's conspiracy. He had bored everyone ever since with his accounts of how he had saved the State. It was indeed one of those triumphs which had ill consequences for their author. Cicero had put Roman citizens to death without trial, and this crime pursued him all the rest of his days. That was what his enemies – and his sharp tongue had won him many – recalled when he boasted of his achievement. It had won him the fierce enmity of my adored Clodius, and so, as a young man, I never heard good of Cicero. But I have already recounted what Clodia said about the man who defended the murderer of her brother and our lover.

Nevertheless no one has ever denied Cicero's intellect, and few his charm. When he set himself to please, he usually succeeded. Even Caesar, who distrusted him on account of his vanity and indecision, delighted in his company. And I confess that, despite all that I knew and all that lay horridly between us, I was flattered to be invited to his dinner-table.

He alternated that spring between excitement and depression. He knew that he had blundered at the commencement of the civil wars when, as a result of his vanity and poor judgment, he had attached himself to Pompey and the conservatives in the Senate.

"I risked life and property for their cause," he said, "and yet, you know, I was never appreciated by them. I was excluded from Pompey's council, though I had greater and deeper experience than any who surrounded him. Of course Pompey was ever easily influenced. All the same you would not have thought he could be such a fool as to ignore the value of my advice. But there it is. He was a great man, but limited. He was always conscious of his intellectual inferiority to me, and, I suppose, also to Caesar."

He often spoke in this vein. It was clear, too, that he still believed he had a political future. I could have disillusioned him, but it seemed more polite, and perhaps more useful, to listen to his speculations.

"Caesar has achieved much," he said. "The question is what does he intend to do with the power he has accumulated. I realise naturally that this matter cannot be resolved till these wretched wars have been brought to a successful conclusion. But that can't be long now. I have a great respect for Cato, but" – he poured wine and sniggered – "only someone with as little self-knowledge as that dear man could suppose him to be a match for Caesar on the field of battle. So Cato will lose in Africa, and then Caesar will turn on Gnaeus Pompey, who, between you and me, my dear, is little more than a brigand, and drive him out of his Spanish fastness, and then . . . and then, where shall we be?"

"Who can tell?" I said, knowing I was not supposed to supply an answer.

"The first essential is that the Republic should be reconstituted. I am sure Caesar understands this, aren't you? After all, what else can he do? Rome will not tolerate a Perpetual Dictator, the government of a single person. I realise that he may wish to be granted the dictatorship for an indefinite period, that's natural enough, but equally, it must be largely an honorific, at most supervisory, title. If we are to have the government of a single person, what should we call him? A king? We Romans will never tolerate monarchy. Caesar would have to be mad to suppose we might. And one thing we all know about Caesar is that he is not mad. Or is he, young Brutus?"

"You have already answered that question, sir," I replied.

"Quite so. But we must consider that these terrible wars have deprived us of many able men, and torn the heart out of many noble families. The list of the illustrious dead is long and melancholy. Moreover discord, resentment, and the desire for revenge govern many of their heirs. How are the parties to be reconciled? Where shall we find the means of establishing a new concord of the different orders in the State? How shall we reconcile the demands of the victorious soldiery with the rights of landed proprietors? What steps are necessary to re-establish the authority of the consuls? How do we govern this great Empire which we have won? These are all matters which will perplex us during the period of arduous reconstruction which must follow the end of the wars. You, Decimus Brutus, are deservedly deep in Caesar's confidence. What does he plan? How does he propose to set about this reconstruction? For my part, I cannot see how it can be achieved unless he is prepared to surrender power and authority back to those bodies which properly exercise them. You cannot, it seems to me, perpetuate a system evolved to answer a crisis when that crisis has itself disappeared."

"No doubt Caesar has given consideration to these matters," I said. "They are what must be discussed. I do not think I am at liberty to expatiate further."

The position was delicate, you see. The questions Cicero raised were proper and must indeed have occurred to anyone who had reflected on the situation. I knew, however, that Caesar shied away from exploring them. He preferred always to act according to the promptings of instinct. He was fond of remarking that "Decisions are best made when they force themselves upon you; that is, when the hour is ripe."

But it would have been impolitic to hint in this gathering that we (Caesar's friends, that is) had really no idea of how the Constitution should be reformed post-bellum.

"The question surely is whether, or to what extent, something which has been shattered can ever be repaired?"

The speaker was scarcely more than a boy, an adolescent, whose chin seemed innocent of the razor. He was slight, but compactly made. He had clear grey eyes, sweetly curving lips, and light hair which flopped over his left eye. He spoke in a cool voice, and did not look at the company but seemed to be examining his finely formed and shapely arm which rested on the back of the couch on which he lay. I had arrived late that evening, having been detained on a matter of urgent business, and had not been introduced to him; Cicero, like many egotists, was often careless in his observation of elementary good manners. The boy had looked at me two or three times in the course of our supper, through long eyelashes, smiling as if he knew me and we had an understanding denied to the others present. I wondered who he was, and found myself interested.

Cicero was surprised by his interjection.

"What do you mean?" he said.

The boy hesitated. His tongue stroked his lower lip and he kept his eyes fixed on his arm (golden-brown, shadow-dappled, smooth as alabaster).

"It's presumptuous of me, I know. I've so little experience. But if it was the demands of Empire which broke the traditional structure of the Republic, then I don't see how that can be restored, unless we were to abandon Empire, which is unthinkable."

Cicero pressed the tips of his fingers together, moved them apart, brought them together two or three times, elevated his chin, held the attention of all.

"Hmm," he said, "those are deep thoughts for one so young, and not unintelligent, not unintelligent by any means, no. Let me see now . . . Yes. I think I see where you are at error – error which is, as you sagely suggest yourself, perhaps inescapable on account of your inexperience. (And let me say in passing that I commend you for admitting your inexperience, which is a fault to which the young rarely confess, though we might all agree that it vitiates any opinion they might express on any subject.) So, my dear boy, your error consists, in my opinion, for what it is worth," he lowered his chin and smiled on us, "not an inconsiderable worth, I am perhaps entitled to believe on account of the encomia which have been lavished on me during my long and not unproductive career – very well then, your error consists in taking a purely mechanistic view of public affairs. You concentrate on the structure of the Constitution, and observe how it came under strain. But in doing so, you neglect to consider the far more important and significant question, which is not 'How?' but 'Why?' And they are not, give me leave to assure you, by any means the same thing. We can easily see how things fall apart; but why? That goes deeper, and perhaps it requires the wisdom which only age can bring even to commence to offer an answer. So, I must say that in my view we are concerned principally with a question of morality. Yes, morality, not mechanics. The sickness of the Republic lies not in its institutions – institutions which have so gloriously stood the test of time – but in the men who inhabit them. Selfishness now reigns where zeal for the public good used to flourish. We are suffering, that is to say, from what I shall call 'individualism'. What do I mean by that? Simply this: the readiness of men to respond to any public matter with the question, 'What's in it for me? Where may I find personal advantage?' rather than the question that so nobly informed the minds of our forefathers, 'What does Rome require of me?'"

He paused, looked round the table, fixing his gaze on each of us and holding it, till the other turned away, perhaps in embarrassment. Even I found myself lowering my eyes, but when I looked up I saw that the youth who had raised the matter was returning Cicero's scrutiny with a calm and candid look. A smile played around his lips, and he appeared eager to hear what the veteran orator had to impart. There was no insolence in his smile, and I do not believe that even Cicero felt any, but it was Cicero who broke off the exchange and, with an air of urgency, resumed his discourse.

"What does Rome require of me? That is the question I have

put to myself throughout my long and not inglorious career. It was in full consciousness of the import of that question that I confronted the information brought to me concerning the foul conspiracy of Catiline. If each of us asks himself that question, we shall know how we should conduct ourselves. This vice, which I call 'individualism', is in my view Greek, not Roman. Let us extirpate it from our public life, and then we shall resume our antique Roman virtue. Individualism is the curse of our age and the occasion of our present discontents . . ."

His hand shook as he raised his goblet of wine, and he wiped first his lips, then his temples, with a napkin.

For my part, it seemed that he had spoken more dangerously and more rashly than he knew. This term, "individualism", which he had coined: who incarnated it but Caesar?

The party broke up. I contrived to attach myself to the youth who had aroused my interest on account of his demeanour and intelligence.

"I should know who you are," I said, as we stepped into a summer night that was now cool. "But I am sorry to say I don't."

"That's natural," he said. "I was a child when we last met, and of course I have changed. Since then, I have been away. But I know you, and have heard my uncle speak warmly of your talents and character."

"Your uncle?"

"Caesar. I am Gaius Octavius Thurinus. My mother is Caesar's sister."

"But of course," I said. "Forgive me, but you were indeed a child, if an attractive one, when I last saw you, and now you are a youth – and even more attractive."

"Oh," he said, not resisting when I took his arm, "it is kind of you to say so. I have been cultivating Cicero. This term he uses, 'individualism'. I find that interesting."

"Cicero takes a Romantic idea of the past," I said. "In my opinion men have always been quick to fight for what they see as their own personal interests."

"Oh yes, I understand that, but nevertheless I think he may be right when he says that the pursuit of self-interest dominates public life, to a greater extent than it used to."

"Perhaps, but you are to remember that the competition for

honour and glory has always dominated men's minds. Which of us does not seek personal glory?"

"I am sure you are right," he said, "and yet there must be a means surely of harnessing this desire to the public good; and may not Cicero be correct in saying that our ancestors found such a means, and we have lost it?"

Over the next weeks I saw much of young Octavius. I could not see enough indeed. It is not too much to say that I fell in love with him. I was charmed in equal measure by his beauty and his intelligence. Yet it was something beyond these qualities which so attracted me; even at his most affectionate, I was aware of the distance which he kept between himself and the rest of mankind – even a lover. It was a distance I longed to bridge, and my failure to do so intensified my passion. Even as I kissed his lips and felt his arms steal round my neck and his smooth limbs intertwine with mine, I was conscious that something of him stood apart, that he never surrendered himself even to the pleasures in which he delighted, that he was always observing all that we did, and exercising judgment in his uncanny detachment. It was this quality which so inflamed me. In love we always seek possession, and yet the closer I held him to me, the less I was able to take possession of his essential being.

At one moment he seemed only a boy delighting in his beauty, and in the admiration which he aroused in me. Certainly, he sought admiration. He would lie naked, inviting me to stroke his shapely thighs (which he shaved and oiled with great attentiveness), murmuring as my lips moved over his flat smooth belly, caressing my neck and shoulders and running his fingers down the line of my back. His joy was real as mine, and yet he remained aloof, superior, remote, as if he observed all at a great distance. Even Clodia could not surpass his ability to tantalise a lover.

The philosophers declare that the love between a man and a youth may be the noblest of emotions. They assert that the mature lover schools his friend in wisdom and virtue. I know the theory well. But it was not like that with Octavius, and I believe it rarely is. I was enthralled, and, being enthralled, diminished. If I were to approach Artixes (to whom I shall of course not read these pages of my memoir) as I approached

Octavius, then I might indeed enjoy what philosophers promise. But Octavius, though a youth, seemed older and wiser than I. I was for those weeks his slave, as I had been Clodia's.

I neglected my wife for his sake. Longina was the daughter of Caius Longinus Cassius. I had married her a few months previously at Caesar's urging, to cement, as he put it, Cassius' reconciliation to our party. She was not much more than a child, charming, vivacious, ignorant, and, I thought then, vicious. She had little to offer one who had enjoyed the embraces of Clodia, and I soon found she bored me. She adored dice and gossip, and she had a circle of dissolute boys of her own age, who had, as my mother would have put it, more money than sense. I was soon convinced that she betrayed me with more than one of them. I suppose it is fair to admit that I bored her also. She could be a charming companion, and she was certainly very pretty, but she never, at that period, said anything that remained in my mind for longer than the time she took to utter it.

Nevertheless one good thing came out of my marriage: I learned to know my new father-in-law, Cassius. Cassius had always been an object of some suspicion to us Caesarians. We respected his military record, of course; it was Cassius who, as praetor, had extracted the remnant of Crassus' army from the disaster of Carrhae. That was no mean achievement. We knew too that, if Pompey had followed his advice, our campaign in Greece would have been even more perilous and difficult than was the case. But few trusted him; his sardonic tongue wounded easily, and, it seemed, with pleasure. Even Caesar was not comfortable in his presence, complaining of his "lean and hungry look". He tried to laugh off the unease Cassius occasioned. "Let me have men about me that are fat."

Now Cassius said to me:

"Has it occurred to you that the State is out of balance? I yield to none in my admiration for Caesar's genius, and I know that you, Decimus, are his most loyal adherent. But . . . I belong to the Epicurean persuasion, you know, and we believe that there must be a measure in all things; nothing to excess. Isn't Caesar's preponderance in the State somewhat excessive? His glory outshines all others. The splendour of his sun casts all others into the shadows. How long do you suppose Roman noblemen, reared, as we all are, in a tradition which lays such great stress on virtue and personal achievement, will be content to lie in obscurity as a result of the light that is concentrated on Caesar?"

"These are dangerous thoughts."

"But they are only thoughts, words taking the air, philosophical speculations, no more than that."

He poured wine.

"Cicero," I said, "has been talking of the dangers of what he terms 'individualism'. Are you saying the same thing?"

"Cicero, let us agree, is an old windbag. We have always striven to excel, and what is that strife but the individualism he has now discovered? But formerly, the contest was one in which any man of noble birth might hope to triumph. It was agreed that that triumph should not be enduring; that others must have their turn in the limelight, while men of outstanding merit rested in the background ready to resume their labours if the State required their service. But now? Things are different, aren't they? Caesar's pre-eminence is such that we find ourselves asking whether we serve Rome or Caesar."

"Young Octavius" – to my annoyance I felt myself blushing as I pronounced his name – "suggested to me that our ancestors found a means of harnessing the desire to excel to the public good, which we, in our generation, have lost."

"That young man would be wise not to let his uncle hear him speak in that vein. But he is right. The question is: what should be done? Do you think, Decimus, that it might be possible to persuade Caesar to retire from public life? There is, after all, the example of Sulla."

"Sulla is not a name to mention to Caesar, especially not as a pattern he might follow."

"I understand that. I am not speaking idly, Decimus, as Cicero now speaks. Caesar is heading for trouble. The more he separates himself from his natural peers, the more he stands alone in his glory, the more surely he breeds discontent. The last public service Caesar could do would be to withdraw, to devote his talents to the practice of literature perhaps. After all, he often says that that is his chief joy in life. I don't believe him, of course; everyone knows he prefers women and war. But that is no reason why he shouldn't be taken at his word. I was never worried by Pompey's pre-eminence because I always knew that

Pompey was more show than substance. But Caesar is a different matter. His pre-eminence is real. That is why it is dangerous: for him and for Rome."

"What do you mean, Cassius?"

"He will return victorious from Africa. He will then go to Spain and extirpate the last remnants of armed opposition. What will he do then? There are those who say he wishes to call himself King."

Dusk was falling. We were in Cassius' villa in the Alban Hills. A fierce winter wind threw red-tinted clouds across the sky. The tops of the pine trees bent before it. Far below one could see the wind troubling the waters of the lake. Cassius threw another log of beech-wood on the fire. It spat and crackled; sparks of light danced and died away.

"A new year," Cassius said. "What will it bring?"

"Caesar would never accept a crown," I said.

"No? You think not? I wish I could be as certain. Cicero says that Caesar will throw off the mask of clemency when he has finally disposed of all his enemies in arms. Do you believe that?"

"No," I said, "I don't. Caesar's clemency is not assumed as a disguise or as a necessary policy. Say what you will against Caesar, censure his pride; nevertheless recognise that his impulse to clemency is innate. He is clement by nature."

"He is clement," Cassius said, "because he feels so great a sense of his own superiority. It is a means of registering that superiority. To revenge himself on his enemies would be, in his eyes, to lower himself to their level. Yes, I understand that."

"That may be so. But I also know that this impulse was fortified by his own youthful experiences in the days of Sulla's proscriptions. I have often heard him say that history proves that by practising cruelty, you earn nothing but hatred. 'Nobody,' he says, 'ever achieved an enduring victory by such means except Sulla, and Sulla is a man I do not propose to imitate.'"

(If I read this passage to Artixes, he will certainly answer that Caesar practised abominable cruelties in Gaul.)

"All right," Cassius said, "I accept that. But do you know what Cicero is also saying: that it is a disgrace to live under Caesar's rule. He has even been heard to mutter that he wished Caesar would persecute him, so that he might regain his self-respect."

"In my opinion, Cicero would in the last resort abandon his self-respect more readily than his comfort and security."

"You are right there, Decimus. Indeed he has already done so, which accounts for his grumpiness. Well, we shall not settle these matters this afternoon, but remember: I do not think things can continue as they are. I fear we are to be confronted with the choice between tyranny and anarchy, and I do not know which is the more to be feared. I have heard Caesar quote Euripides: 'Is crime consonant with nobility? Then noblest is the crime of tyranny.' It is a temptation which I fear he will find irresistible. And then where shall we be? Meanwhile, let's to supper. I trust my daughter is conducting herself to your satisfaction. She needs a husband's discipline, having been spared a father's on account of my long absences. And, Decimus, keep a tight hold of young Octavius. That friendship you have established may serve us well."

If only he knew, I thought. Perhaps he did, and did not care.

Word came the next month that Caesar had destroyed his enemies in Africa. Even those who were hostile to Caesar rejoiced, since Cato and the other commanders had allied themselves to King Juba of Numidia and even gone so far as to propose to surrender an imperial province to the barbarian King. Cato, either fearing Caesar's vengeance or disdaining the clemency which he would have received as an insult, fell on his sword. I could not regard this as other than a satisfactory conclusion to a foolish life. Ironically, many received it rather as proof of Cato's superior and antique virtue. For my part, I have never admired suicides, though I know this is an unfashionable opinion. It pleased me, however, that Octavius was of my mind.

"I can't see why people praise suicides. It's living that takes courage. Not to give up. I shall never never give up."

I believed him. I still do, now when the temptation of suicide is . powerful. So easy, I think, to despise and resist that temptation, to condemn the act, from a position of security and comfort. But now . . . to choose my own way, rather than to expose myself to the humiliation of whatever death is determined for me? And yet . . . I see Octavius touch his upper lip with his tongue in that perhaps nervous gesture of his, and hear his cold,

clear voice: "... not to give up. I shall never never give up."
We discussed it further, I recall. He suggested that it was time
we put away what he called "the dramatic affectations of the
old Republic. A man is but a man," he said. "He should not see
himself as a tragic figure. Keep such gestures for the stage. Life
is not a play or drama."

Can he really, so young, pretty and untried, have said all that,
brooded on such matters?

Are his words a comfort to me now or a reproach?

CHAPTER

7

Caesar returned from Africa and celebrated four Triumphs in a single month to commemorate his victories in Gaul, Egypt, Pontus and Africa. This was a statement of his unprecedented glory. Of course, the first three should have been celebrated long before, if the exigencies of civil war had not prevented it. But he was pleased to group them together in this way. The month of holiday delighted the people and confirmed them in their belief that Caesar was like no other man who had ever lived. After all, Triumphs are rare. A single Triumph has conventionally been regarded as the apogee of the most illustrious career. This concatenation of Triumphs emphasised, as nothing else could – not even the dictatorship for life which he was soon to be voted – his extraordinary pre-eminence.

Naturally, as one of his chief and trusted lieutenants, my own part was conspicuous. Caesar was too wise and cautious to deny his generals their share in his glory. I rode immediately behind him in the first Triumph, which celebrated his conquest of Gaul. Indeed, I played my part in mitigating the effects of an unfortunate accident, which, had I not been at hand, might have turned into the sort of catastrophe which would have set the superstitious muttering about evil omens.

It happened like this. As Caesar rode through the Velabrum, serene amidst the cheering crowd, the axle of his triumphal chariot broke. The cart lurched to the left. Caesar was thrown sideways and would have toppled to the ground had I not spurred my horse forward and seized his shoulder, arresting his fall. The horses were reined in, and carpenters or wheelwrights (I am vague about tradesmen) hurried forward to repair the damage. The procession was halted for perhaps half an hour, to the consternation of those behind. Naturally Caesar thanked me for my help, but there was a note in his voice which I interpreted as resentful. It was as if my intervention had somehow detracted from his glory on this day of days, even though a moment's calm reflection should have told him that his glory would have been considerably more tarnished if he had taken a toss.

Nevertheless, that evening Casca remarked:

"Poor Mouse, haven't you yet understood that Caesar finds it easier to forgive his enemies than to thank his friends? But don't take it too seriously. I hear you have a charming little affair in train. Dangerous of course, but that adds to the charm."

After that unfortunate incident, which at least gave Caesar a good chance to hear some of the bawdy songs his legionaries were singing in his honour, he ascended to the Capitol between two lines of elephants, forty in number, which served as torch-bearers. The populace is always delighted by the sight of elephants, and there was certainly on this occasion something agreeably grotesque in seeing these great beasts lining the ascent with flaming flambeaux rising above their mighty shoulders. Generally, I am bored by elephants, partly perhaps because I know how ridiculously useless they are in war, when they are more likely to disrupt their own side than the enemy. But I have a theory that the populace's attachment to them is connected with the terror which the Carthaginian elephants reputedly inspired in our legions when first encountered; it satisfies the people to see a force which so alarmed their ancestors now tame and domesticated. I suppose that is fair enough; it is, you might say, a symbol of Rome's mastery of the world.

As I have already mentioned, the Gallic Triumph saw the end of Vercingetorix. I was sorry about that, and had indeed urged Caesar to consider breaking with tradition in order to spare his defeated but never dishonoured foe.

"It will do us credit in Gaul," I said, "and reconcile many to our rule. Moreover, Vercingetorix is a man of such courage and character that I really believe we could find a use for him. I know that you have been considering broadening the Senate to include provincials, even Gauls, among its members. Don't you think there is a case for making Vercingetorix one of them? He has, after all, now been held for several years here in the city, and though I haven't had conversation with him myself, I am told by those who have that he has divested himself of his barbarian habits of thought and behaviour, and come to appreciate something of the majesty of Rome. You have shown notable clemency to those Romans who viciously and without good reason set themselves against you. Mightn't it be a good idea to show the same generosity towards one who has claims to be regarded as the most formidable enemy you have defeated? After all, our concept of Empire is going to have to change, you've suggested as much yourself. Sooner or later, we shall find it necessary – and indeed desirable – to regard the conquered peoples as partners rather than subjected enemies."

I may say that I had got this idea from young Octavius, but I saw no reason to attribute it to him at that moment. If Caesar assented, then I would remark that my suggestion was the fruit of conversations I had had with his nephew; if he declined my proposal, then it would have been unfair to lay the responsibility at Octavius' door. Besides, I didn't want Caesar to suppose that I was capable of being influenced by one whom he thought of as a mere boy. He might have started to enquire more closely into the relations between us, and I had no fancy that he should do so.

"I had never thought of you as a political theorist, Mouse," he said. "Perhaps there is something in what you say, and it is certainly true that I intend to reform the Senate, though I don't remember discussing the matter with you. But your immediate proposition is absurd. Vercingetorix conducted a vicious and unprincipled war against us. Thousands of my soldiers lost friends and comrades as a result of his obduracy and treachery. I will not cheat them of the death they have a right to expect. Nor will I put other Roman lives at risk by doing anything which may encourage barbarian chieftains to think they can oppose our arms, and not suffer as a consequence. To spare Vercingetorix would be a terrible precedent, which would let loose a tide of bloodshed throughout the Empire. Do you not realise, you fool" – yes, that is how he addressed me, and it was at that moment that I understood the cold anger I had provoked – "do you not realise what holds the Empire together? I will tell you in one word, and that word is 'fear'. Perhaps a time may come when moods will have changed, and when the subject peoples will look on Rome as a Father. But not yet; now the most we can hope is that they will respect and fear us as their master. And even if that moment of which I speak arrives, is it not true that there is always something of fear even in the love which a son may feel for his father? Mouse, Mouse, two emotions rule the world and govern the ordinary man: fear and greed."

"What of love of virtue and glory? You cannot discount them."

"I spoke of ordinary men, not of the exceptional man. Yes, I myself . . ." he paused, drummed his fingers on the table and looked, for a long silence, into the distance as if great armies ranged themselves before him and he gazed on twilight battle-fields disturbed only by the cries of the wounded and the circling of those birds of prey that feed on the dead. "Yes, Caesar may be driven by the loves you speak of, the desire for fame and glory, for that supreme virtue that stands aloof from the common run of curs, but they, snarling and cringing in the mire, what can they know of such things? No, fear and greed are the passions that make men what they are . . . There are moments also, at owl-light, when it seems to me that even Caesar's search for glory is but another, more rarefied expression of greed. It may be a form of fear also; for what would Caesar be without such glory — something which even he dare not contemplate? No, Mouse, Vercingetorix must die the death prepared and ordained for him. Besides," his voice lightened and he bestowed on me that smile which of all smiles could most surely charm men, "the mob might turn against me if I spared him. They like death and executions, haven't you noticed?"

He stood up, took my arm and led me to the window whence we could gaze down on the Forum, busy in preparation for tomorrow's Triumph. He pinched my ear.

"Mouse, there have been moments when I have hoped that you at least understood me. But it seems not. So let me speak plainly. You compare my determination that Vercingetorix should die with my clemency towards those senators and others who have opposed me in our terrible civil wars, and you confess yourself baffled. But consider that clemency: does it abate the fear I arouse in such men? Not at all. Almost the reverse. A Roman nobleman who owes his life to my clemency feels himself forever my inferior. He knows my greatness, because he can never forget that for one terrible long hour I held his life, his neck, between my thumb and forefinger. He has faced extinction at my hands. And he is made conscious of his inferiority by the action of my grace. But a barbarian cannot think like that. He is incapable of it, because his sense of honour is quite different from ours. He would merely think I had in some way gone soft, that Rome could therefore be opposed with impunity. The Roman senator, whom I spare, feels on the other hand in Caesar's clemency Caesar's strength. He stands rebuked by Caesar's refusal to punish him. Besides, Mouse, you must think of this. It is against the law to put Roman citizens to death without trial, and Cicero has never been forgiven for his decision to do so in the case of those who joined with Catiline. But it is different with barbarians, and so Vercingetorix must die."

They say he did so with great courage.

Was it further to mark out his pre-eminence that, in the Pontic Triumph which followed, Caesar ordered that one of the decorated wagons should bear, instead of the customary stage-set representing scenes from the war, merely the legend:

"I came, I saw, I conquered."

The simplicity of the sentiment struck awe and dread in the hearts of all.

I was exhausted when the month of Triumphs was over, for I had been entrusted with many onerous duties and grave responsibilities. These included the organisation of the Troy Game, that sham fight which is one of the oldest and most hallowed of our rituals. It was founded, we believe, by the Father of the Roman People, Aeneas himself, and only youths of noble birth are permitted to take part. There is naturally much competition for selection and this itself would impose a considerable burden on the Master of the Game, for there is no end to the attempts made by parents of candidates of dubious eligibility to persuade him that their son should qualify. I can tell you, I could have had my pick of more than a couple of dozen matrons in the week of selection. Even when the two troops have been chosen, the management of this mimic war is no easy task. It is amazing how even well-bred youths will cheat shamelessly to gain an advantage.

I am proud to be able to say that my mastership of the Troy Game was regarded as exemplary.

I was given one other task of a surprising nature in the weeks that followed the Triumphs. It was a time when Caesar was much occupied with administrative reforms (some of them ill-thought-out) and with the reform of the calendar which Alexandrian Greeks had persuaded him to be desirable. This had taken possession of his mind and was one of the few occasions when he risked unpopularity with the mob, which always hates change of this sort.

While Caesar was involved with these matters, Cicero took it upon himself to publish a eulogistic biography of Cato. I do not think this was intended as a deliberate act of provocation, though no one can be certain of the motives of a man as complicated as Cicero. On the one hand his relations with Caesar were friendly. They dined together, and Cicero rejoiced in the evident delight which Caesar took in his conversation, which, if you discounted the strain of persistent egotism (itself indeed at times almost endearing) was witty, agreeably malicious and superbly wide-ranging. It would indeed have been a dull man who resisted the charm of his historical and philosophical speculations. Of course there were many such dull men, who agreed with Mark Antony that the old man was a prosy bore; but Caesar was not one of them, and neither was I.

Moreover Caesar carried his admiration further. When Quintus Ligarius was prosecuted for bearing arms against Caesar (this prosecution being a notable exception to Caesar's rule of general clemency), he invited Cicero to defend him. "Invited" is too weak an expression; he implored him to do so in terms that could not fail to flatter a man with half Cicero's allotment of vanity. Nevertheless Cicero hesitated, being, as I supposed, fearful of how Caesar would view his intervention. Caesar, however, remarked: "Why may we not give ourselves a pleasure we have not enjoyed for such a long time: of hearing Cicero plead a cause? Especially since I have already determined what I think of Ligarius, who is clearly a bad man as well as my enemy." When these sentiments were relayed to Cicero, he felt it was safe to accept the brief. He spoke with all his old eloquence. Young men who had not previously had the opportunity to hear him in action were amazed. Some were even moved to tears, such was the pathos he evoked. The charm of his delivery, the fertility of his argument, the copiousness of his illustrative examples, combined to render him irresistible. Men reared in camps, who had spent ten years in grim warfare, felt perhaps for the first time the power of oratory. No doubt in the great days of the Republic, they said, such experiences were common; but they came as a revelation in the new world of the dictatorship.

All eyes turned to Caesar as he sat in judgment. It was seen that he grew pale. He could not sit still. It was evident that his mind was torn with conflicting passions. At last, when Cicero summoned up the terrible memory of the battle at Pharsalus, describing it in terms worthy of Homer, representing Caesar as Achilles and Pompey as Hector (a dangerous comparison, in my opinion, since we Romans are the heirs of Troy) Caesar was seen to tremble – I wondered if he was on the brink of one of those epileptic fits of which he was so ashamed – he let the documents in the case slip to the floor, raised his right hand, and cried:

"Enough. Caesar conquered Pompey, but Cicero has conquered Caesar by his eloquence. I order that the prosecution be abandoned."

Then he signalled to me to help him from the court. His whole frame trembled as he leaned on my arm.

Perhaps it was on account of this triumph that Cicero felt bold enough to publish his *Cato*. That was itself an extraordinary performance. Of course he had reason to feel gratitude to the dead man, because it was Cato who, many years before, when a tribune, had proposed that Cicero be accorded the honorific title of "Father of his Country". At the same time, while Cicero's respect for Cato's obstinate adherence to the old, unreformed Republic was certainly genuine, he was far too intelligent and civilised to have taken any pleasure in Cato's boorishness, xenophobia, and contempt for intellectuals. The eulogy was therefore an act of will; it was also – it could not fail to be – the most coherent and persuasive criticism of Caesar's dictatorship. The language was of course coded; Cicero was far too cautious and timid to offer overt criticism of Caesar. But he was a master of all the rhetorical skills, and no one could read his *Cato* without feeling the force of his implicit thesis: that government by a single person was contrary to both the traditions and interests of Rome. The Republic, he insinuated, had served Rome well, and secured our liberties. Republican institutions had been sufficiently flexible to endure for centuries and to enable Rome to withstand a succession and variety of crises. Was it right to cast our inheritance aside either to gratify the ambition of a single person, however noble and virtuous, or to resolve a temporary difficulty?

"The science of constructing a commonwealth," I had heard Cicero declare, "or renovating it, or reforming it, is like any experimental science, not to be taught *a priori*. Nor is it a short experience – the experience, let us say, of a single generation – that can instruct us in that practical science, because the consequences of moral causes are rarely immediate; and that which now appears desirable, even speciously necessary, may be prejudicial in its remoter operations."

Holding court at his dinner-table, reclining on his couch, with his eagle head quivering, his scraggy neck extended (as if inviting the sword), he spoke with a lucidity inspired by his passionate commitment to what he saw as truth. (That was how it impressed me at the time; in retrospect I wondered if this was not yet another extraordinary piece of advocacy. How do you gauge the sincerity of a master of language?)

"Man's nature is intricate, and the objects of society are of the greatest conceivable complexity. It follows therefore that no simple disposition of power within a State can be suitable either to man's nature or to the quality of his affairs. The government of a single person is simplicity indeed, better suited to barbarian tribes than to Roman citizens. When I hear men like Antony boast of the simplicity of contrivance aimed at, and achieved, in any reformed Constitution, then I stand amazed by such a display of ignorance of the complexities of political science. Simple governments are fundamentally defective. When ancient opinions and rules of life inherited from our illustrious forefathers are taken away, the loss cannot be estimated.

"Men talk," he said, "of the necessity of the moment. That is easy talk, superficially cogent. A man like Antony" – and when he said Antony, did he use the name, I wondered even then, as a code for Caesar? – "men like Antony, incapable of reflection, devoid of the impulse of veneration, an impulse which should defend us against rash speculation, talk of the need for innovation. Well, it is true, I admit, that a state without the means of reform is without the means of its own preservation. But, my friends, but – and it is a great and powerful but – we should remember this: a spirit of innovation is generally the result of a selfish temper and confined views. Men will not look forward intelligently to posterity, who never look backward, with admiration and affection, to their ancestors. I have talked to you before of the dangers of what I term individualism. Why? Because, my friends, I am afraid – we should all be afraid – to put men to live and trade each on his own private stock of reason; for that stock can only be petty and narrow in its foundation. We would do better to avail ourselves of the general bank and capital of wisdom and experience which we have inherited from the generations that made Rome what it is.

"I am told," he continued, "that the times are out of joint. It may be so. Indeed it is only too evident that in certain respects they are so. But seek the reason, my friends. Do not be satisfied with easy answers. Is it not apparent that men like Antony" – and, as his lip curled and his voice trembled, I could have no doubt that, if he had dared, he would have substituted the name of Caesar – "such men have no respect for the wisdom of others, no respect for tradition, no respect for our inheritance? But they pay it off by a very full confidence in their own wisdom. I would be more comfortable if I could find myself in agreement with them; more comfortable and more foolish . . .

"So the times are out of joint? Very well. Be it so. Our age is unhappy, riven by civil war, disputes, selfish ambition. But even that is not the sum of our misfortunes. It is the true misfortune of our time, of this decadent age, that everything we have inherited has become the topic of debate, that the Constitution of Rome, constructed with care, intelligence and patriotic fervour across the centuries, has become a subject for altercation rather than enjoyment. If we continue to follow this course, we shall have no fundamental law, no strict convention, no respected custom, to restrain absolute power. Instead of finding ourselves obliged, and comfortably and properly obliged, to conform to a fixed constitution, we shall find ourselves subject to a few men of power – dynasts, to use the Greek term – who will make for themselves a new Constitution that will conform only to their own designs and selfish ambitions."

He dared not speak so openly in his *Cato* as he did to guests at his dinner-table, but such were the arguments – what the Greeks call "the sub-text" – which underlay the biography. Cato had become less a man than a symbol. Well, that was fair enough. He was a better and more effective symbol than he had been a man, throughout his blundering and stupid life.

Caesar was disturbed by the *Cato*. I think he was angry also, partly because his admiration of Cicero was genuine (as far as any such emotion in Caesar could be called genuine), partly because he hoped that Cicero would reciprocate the feeling. And of course in a sense Cicero did; he admired Caesar even while he condemned his course. He liked Caesar too. He sometimes suggested that Caesar was the only man with whom he could talk on terms that approached equality.

But Caesar's disturbance went deeper, unsettled him in a way in which he had thought he could no longer be unsettled. Cicero challenged his understanding of himself. For a moment he opened Caesar's mind to the suspicion that his own star-ordained course might be misguided. Naturally he thrust that suspicion behind him.

"The trouble with Cicero," he said, "is that he clings to certainties that the winds of the world have swept away."

I think that, in his own view, he personified these winds.

"This *Cato* must be answered," he said. "We cannot allow it to be supposed that Cicero has produced an argument that daunts us. Unfortunately, occupied as I am with practical matters, I have no time to do it. Mouse, you write well. I have always found your reports models of lucidity and good sense. Did you know, by the way, that I have had the report you delivered me in Africa on political feeling here in Rome copied and distributed to senior officers as an example of how these things should be done? Moreover, I admire your power of sarcasm, your ability to cut through cant. And Cato, you'll agree, was all cant. Yes, Mouse, you must compose an *Anti-Cato* for me. You must show him up for the obstinate and malicious fool he was. Twenty thousand words should be enough. I give you a week. You can manage that? Good. It is essential that we undercut Cicero's argument, and the best way of doing so is to

demonstrate that his hero was a buffoon who had no understanding of the way the world is going. It will be published
under my name. I think that's necessary. It will attract more
attention that way. That's settled then."

So that was how I came to compose what, though I say it
myself, was the most effective political tract to be published in
Rome in my lifetime. I destroyed Cato's inflated reputation. I
made it clear that, if Cicero took such a man as his hero and
exemplar, his own arguments couldn't be worth a bowl of piss.
I enjoyed writing it; it was brutal, sarcastic and witty. Rome
laughed over it for weeks. Cicero immediately retired to his villa
in Campania, for he couldn't tolerate the mirth which I had
aroused at his expense. Men said that his *Cato* had all the gaiety
of an old woman who had eschewed sex, while my response
was as delightful as a nubile girl. And of course Cicero dared
not make any reply, or criticism of what I had done, because he
believed Caesar was the author.

Only two considerations disturbed my pleasure in my achievement. The first was Caesar's response. Naturally, he was lavish
in praise, for it was a principle of his always to commend good
work done by those whom he considered his subordinates, and
in this case he recognised that my squib had achieved exactly
the effect which he desired. It had lanced what he feared might
prove a festering sore. Besides, he couldn't help but be amused
and pleased by Cicero's evident discomfiture . . .

And yet he broke off his expressions of satisfaction to say:
"It's no criticism of you, Mouse, to say that I wish I had had
time to write the thing myself. I'm not questioning what you
have done, which is indeed admirable, when I remark that you
have not risen to the full measure of the argument. You have a
rare talent for sarcasm as I have remarked before, but you lack
the fundamental scepticism of true greatness. There is a lack of
strength and freedom in your argument. There is a lack, too, of
exuberance. But then how could it be otherwise? You are a good
chap, and a skilful writer, and I am fond of you and grateful to
you. But you are not Caesar. You have not cast yourself free of
the chains formed in the prison of conviction."

Considering that the *Anti-Cato* – of which, I repeat, I am the
sole author, for Caesar did not add a line, did not even revise
the tract, whatever some people may assert – has a freshness

and life that is absolutely missing from his own, frequently tur-
gid account of his Gallic War, I thought this not only poor
criticism, but a piece of what, coming from anyone but Caesar,
I would have termed "impertinence". Of course I did not say
so, but accepted his observations without comment.

But the other consideration was still more disturbing. I could
not clear my mind of Cicero's sub-text. I found myself wondering if he might not be right.

CHAPTER

Fortunately, I had not long to brood on these matters. Affairs in Spain demanded Caesar's personal attention, and this time, to my great pleasure, he required me by his side.

"It will be the most formidable campaign since Pharsalus," he said, "and I need those generals whom I trust most. There is no immediate work for you in Rome, in any case, Mouse, and you are not yet due to take up the governorship of Cisalpine Gaul. Besides, I propose that young Octavius should also accompany me, and I can think of no officer better fitted to introduce him to the arts of war than you. Except myself, of course, but I shall be too occupied to give the lad as much attention as I could wish. Between us, however, we shall see to his schooling. Besides, I am afraid that if you were not with us, he would fall under the influence of Antony. I say nothing against Antony, of course. I know his loyalty and his capacity. I recognise his charm and attractiveness as I applaud his courage. Nevertheless, I can't pretend that I think he is the best influence on the young, and certainly not for my nephew who is also my heir."

And so it happened that I travelled with Caesar and Octavius. On account of the lateness of the season – it was the second half of November when we were at last able to leave the city – we chose the land route, and journeyed by carriage through Cisalpine Gaul and along the northern coast of the Mediterranean, entering Spain by that narrow pass between the mountains and the sea.

Caesar's conversation on this long journey had all its accustomed charm and interest. He delighted in instructing Octavius in history, politics, and military affairs. He loved to let his talk range wide, especially in the evenings after supper, when he would discourse on philosophy and literature. I confess that I myself have learned more from Caesar than from any other man, and it was clear that Octavius derived much benefit from this extended intercourse with his uncle. Nevertheless, he was too shrewd to accept everything that even Caesar told him, and on more than one occasion irritated the General by the pertinacity of his questioning.

I would have found the journey delightful but for two things. The first was that even before we set out, Octavius made it clear to me that our relationship had changed.

"I shall always be fond of you, Mouse," he said, "and remember our little affair with tender affection. But I am no longer a boy to be stroked and petted. I regard this campaign as the beginning of my career in public life, and I don't choose to expose myself to scandal and contempt by giving any suggestion that I am a pathic. I'm sure you will understand my reasons, and sympathise with my decision. I know you will, because I believe your love for me is based on respect and not merely on lust. Besides, any hint that our relationship remained as it was while my uncle was in Africa would endanger us both. I am fairly certain that Caesar knows about what had been between us, for my friend Maecenas has established that Caesar has set spies on me, no doubt to determine whether I am suited to be his heir. I know you don't like Maecenas, but I assure you that in such matters he is completely reliable."

He was correct. I detested and despised Maecenas, a young nobleman who claimed to be descended from Etruscan kings. He was a dandy, aesthete, and scented epicene, and I was quite sure that he was in love with Octavius himself. I also feared that he would lead him into vicious practices. The only consolation was that Maecenas was not to accompany us, but had left to study rhetoric and philosophy in Greece, where I had no doubt he would find many less respectable diversions.

I did not argue with Octavius, or try to persuade him to change his mind, for, as he supposed, I understood the good sense of his decision. That didn't make it easier to bear; and indeed the last six months had seen him grow more beautiful and desirable than ever. But I have always had a high regard for virtue, and the chief virtue, after courage, is self-respect. Without self-respect, indeed, neither wisdom nor virtue is possible. So I acquiesced.

Nevertheless, the constant presence of Octavius, while he denied himself to me, was bitter-sweet. On the one hand, I could not fail to delight in the charm of his person, his smile (which he still bestowed as freely as ever on me) and his conversation; I was still warmed by the affection he continued to show me and by the evident pleasure he took in my company. On the other hand, I was tormented by desire. I found myself repeating lines which my poor Catullus had addressed to Clodia.

And then Antony made matters worse. He had conceived a strong dislike of Octavius: "the white-headed boy", as he called him. (Actually his hair was pale-gold in colour.) Antony has never been able to guard his tongue, especially in his cups. One night he was angered when, in a discussion at supper, Octavius exposed the inadequacy of his arguments, and Caesar laughed and nodded in appreciation.

"The boy has you there, Antony," he said. "Your shoulders may be broader, but his head is wiser. You would do well not to lock horns with him, for I fear he will outsmart you at every turn."

Antony scowled and turned to the wine-flask. Later that evening, when the others had retired, he dismissed the slaves and broke out into loud complaint.

"I have served the General loyally for almost ten years. I have stood by his side in battle. He has never given me a commission which I have failed to execute. And now, he encourages that brat to make a fool of me. Brat? Did I say, brat? Worse than that."

He pulled himself up from his couch and slumped across the table.

"We all know the General's morals. The brat's his catamite. Well, let a man fuck where he will. It's no reason to let his infat – infat" – he had some difficulty with the word – "infatation," he tried, "make him disregard his loyal friendsh."

He looked up, his eyes bleary, yet his mind – which, despite its well-known deficiencies, never lacked penetration – still working. "Ah, that cut you to the quick, Moush. You didn't know? You can't deshieve me, I've sheen the way you look at the brat. Now the General'sh shlipped in and cut you out. Well, remember thish: that brat has an eye for the main chansh. He'll never givc himshelf to Moush when he can get Sheashar . . ."

I did not believe him. But from that moment I was disturbed by jealousy. I could not forget the suspicions he had aroused, and I found myself watching the way Octavius flattered Caesar, and found myself remarking the coquette in him. And I could not doubt that Caesar was capable of anything.

To this private turmoil were added doubt and perplexity concerning what we would find in Spain. Word came to us that the whole peninsula was in revolt against Rome, and that the dissident generals, Gnaeus Pompey and Labienus (the traitor, as we then thought of him) were encouraging the native rebels, and even colluding with them. This was a sad measure of the debasement that results from civil war. The same thing had happened in Africa, when the Pompeians had surrendered a Roman province to King Juba. Even so, it was hard to credit that the mind of a man like Labienus could be so distorted by personal resentments and ambition that he could place his own interests so absolutely above the interests of Rome and Empire. I was dismayed and angered when I reflected how many Roman legionaries had perished, how a succession of noble generals had striven, in the great endeavour to bring Spain under the benign and fruitful rule of Rome, and now saw this great enterprise undermined by the selfishness of faction.

Reports brought us terrible news. Troops loyal to Caesar were executed by order of the Pompeys or Labienus; this was all the more bitter to hear in the case of Labienus for he had formerly commanded some of the men whom he so callously committed to the sword. Moreover, Gnaeus Pompey was operating what was no less than a reign of terror against those provincials who, acknowledging the benefits they had obtained from Rome, tried to hold fast to Caesar. The family of the great financier Balbus, Caesar's loyal friend, without whose assistance he could never indeed have maintained his army throughout these terrible wars, had to flee from their mansion in Cadiz disguised as peasants. The house itself was sacked, and Balbus later showed his generosity (and his wealth) by accepting his losses philosophically and neglecting to seek the recompense from the public Treasury which Caesar would have felt obliged to make.

*　　*　　*

It was winter, and the landscape of central Spain is terrible in that season. The rivers are foaming torrents through a sea of rock. It is like the desert in its immensity, and yet unlike the desert in its meaning. The desert denies man; Spain breaks him as even the backs of its mountains are broken. I have never been in a country which spoke so clearly of its indifference to man and his meaning. Perhaps it was this indifference which accounted for the atrocity of the Spanish War.

We fought our way to the south, battling against the elements and geography rather than the enemy who fell back before us. So we advanced through the wake of the destruction which they wrought. Food was scarce and supplies difficult to organise. I have often said that the most important officer in the army is the quartermaster; it was never truer than in Spain.

At last we caught up with Labienus and Pompey on the plain of Munda a few miles out of Cordova. They could avoid battle no longer. We knew it was by Labienus' counsel that they had drawn us so far forward, weakening our army. Gnaeus Pompey would have been rash enough to offer battle weeks before. But Labienus said "no". Perhaps he had been hoping that Caesar's well-known impatience would lead him to make a rash move; there was, after all, no officer who knew Caesar's mind better than Labienus, except myself. And indeed Labienus' strategy had almost worked, for Caesar had been tempted by the notion of trying to outflank the enemy, and had been on the point of essaying this audacious enterprise (which would, of course, have exposed his flank to a counterattack while he was still on the march) when I had urged him that, in accepting the apparent invitation offered by the enemy's movements, he would be falling into a trap laid by Labienus. He was displeased at the suggestion, but one aspect of Caesar's genius (which, as you know, Artixes, I have never denied, and which indeed you Gauls have felt so severely) that never deserted him was his ability to let reason in the last resort speak loud. So, although he was piqued by my suggestion that his judgment was in this instance unsound, he yet gave the matter due consideration, and acted as I had advised. And I am bound to say that he showed no resentment of the fact that my judgment had been better than his, though he did not acknowledge it publicly either. Indeed, when Antony urged the outflanking movement, arguing forcefully that it would surprise the enemy and offer us the chance of a quick victory, Caesar employed my arguments against Antony as if they had been his own. But I suppose that is ever the way of genius, which must always be supreme.

Labienus had chosen their position. One could see it was his work at a glance. They were drawn up on the crest of a rise. Behind them the ground rose gently again towards the little town of Munda. It was not a steep hill, but from the plain we would still have to climb perhaps a hundred feet. That may not sound much, but it is a lot to ask of soldiers attacking a well-armed and well-trained enemy, not deficient in number. Labienus and Pompey had, we were assured, some thirteen legions. These were drawn up in the centre. The Moorish and Spanish auxiliaries, half of them cavalry, were on the wings. The ground was steeper there. There was no choice but to make a frontal attack.

The night before the battle was very cold. It was the day after the Ides of March, and a hard frost. Meteors blazed in the sky. The priests reported that the images of war we carried in our baggage had sweated blood. A deserter assured us that the eagles of the Pompeian legions had dropped the golden thunderbolts from their talons, spread their wings and flown to our camp. When none arrived, the man was soundly whipped. I suppose he was either drunk or demented.

The battle began with a brief cavalry skirmish, which was no more conclusive than such things usually are. Then the lines were locked. It was not a day for manoeuvring, and there was indeed no scope for any clever device. This was a battle, I saw at once, that would be gained by whichever side pounded the hardest. In such battles what matters most is morale. As long as men feel they are supported, they will hold their ground. They know besides, if they are experienced troops, that they have only two choices: to break through, or to engage in that most difficult of movements, an orderly retreat. Two fears dominate the mind of the experienced officer to the exclusion of all else. The first is that his own troops will break through on too narrow a front, with the result that they can be cut off and massacred. The second is that panic will set in. The officer's task therefore is to hold the line steady.

I have never known such fighting as at Munda. Our own troops were wonderfully resolute. They had not marched through Spain, enduring terrible hardships, to lose everything now. On the other hand, I was amazed by the enemy's spirit. This was quite different from anything we had previously encountered in the civil wars; it was as if the hatred which Labienus and Pompey's sons felt for Caesar had communicated itself to the whole army. I saw something else in one of those flashes of insight that can come upon one when nerves and body are fully stretched: this resolution was the justification of the policy of atrocities which the enemy commanders had deliberately pursued. In earlier campaigns the enemy's morale had been undermined by Caesar's declared policy of clemency; that, of course, was what he had intended. Now, as a result of their own actions, they knew that they had put themselves beyond his mercy. For them, as for us, it was a matter of conquest or death.

After some two hours of fighting, we had gained little ground. The enemy had yielded perhaps twenty yards, but their position was if anything stronger than before. A ripple of doubt ran along our lines. At that moment Caesar's self-control snapped.

He yelled: "Soldiers, are you going to betray me now to these boys?" and, snatching up a sword and shield from a wounded soldier, dashed against the enemy line. For a moment he disappeared from my view.

"Save the General," I cried. "Will you let him die alone? Will you be thus disgraced?"

I grabbed a centurion by the shoulder and pointed towards the mêlée around Caesar.

"There is where the battle must be won. Save the General or die disgraced."

Waving my sword high, but quickly couching it in the attack position, I led a charge of some two hundred men towards where the troops around Caesar were struggling. It turned the issue. For a moment the battle stood still. Then, very slowly and still in good order, the enemy left began to withdraw.

Our position was now one of the greatest danger. I could imagine Labienus smile as he watched the battle develop from his vantage point at the gates of Munda. Another fifty yards, he must have thought, and I shall be able to loose my cavalry on the enemy's flank. I shouted orders to halt the attack and re-form our ranks, but in the noise and press no one heard me or had sufficient self-control to obey. I looked across and up the hill. I could see cohorts of Labienus' cavalry and infantry moving from his right and centre. Our position was more dangerous than ever, and all, I cursed, as a result of Caesar's moment of uncharacteristic panic. (It is fair to say that this may have been the result of an epileptic attack he had suffered a few days before.)

But . . . Caesar always declared that he was a favourite of the gods, and if ever a day proved this to be the case, it was Munda. Labienus' manoeuvre, admirably intelligent though it was, destroyed him. The rapid and unexpected deployment of the troops was remarked and misinterpreted by the men in his front lines. They did not realise that he was about to unleash the blow that would give them victory. Instead, they thought that it was the beginning of a general flight. Panic set in, rapidly as it always does. Except for one legion, which retreated in good order, and died fighting almost to the last man, the army of our enemy disintegrated.

I have never known a battle change so completely in such a short time.

One wing of the enemy army broke, fleeing to the safety of Cordova. The rest were thrown back into the ditch before the walls of Munda. There was no escape. Few prisoners were taken. Our legionaries were determined to make an end of the wars, then and there, that grey afternoon. They could not have been restrained from slaughter, even if that had been Caesar's wish. And it was not. For the first time in the civil wars no quarter was given.

"I have often fought for victory," Caesar said as night fell on the field, whence the groans of the dying and the wounded still prevented the silence of night from descending, "but this is the first time I ever fought for my life."

It was reported that the enemy dead numbered almost thirty thousand. Among them was Labienus himself. I looked on that strong, proud, aggrieved countenance.

"He chose the path he has followed," Caesar said.

That night Octavius came to my tent. He was pale and trembling.

"Well," I said, "that is war, the great destroyer of illusion."

*   *   *

It was not quite the end. The two sons of Pompey had escaped the field. Sextus, it seemed, had found a refuge, none knew where. Gnaeus reached Gibraltar to find that all the ships were in Caesar's hands. He fled back from the coast, into the mountains. There he was discovered by a troop seeking fugitives from the battle. They found him wounded in a cave, deserted by all but a couple of slaves. He demanded clemency. Even in his extremity, I am told, he could not keep a note of arrogance from his voice. He received none. The soldiers made short work of him. As with his father, his head was cut off, and sent to Caesar.

Meanwhile Cordova had been besieged. The walls were stormed. More than twenty thousand soldiers and citizens were put to the sword. Antony was mighty in the slaughter, drunk on wine and blood-lust. The word "clemency" rang in my ears like a mocking bell. We had journeyed far from that dawn on the banks of the Rubicon.

CHAPTER

What a strange thing is love, a word we commonly employ as a euphemism for sexual desire. My passion for Octavius had died. Its end was abrupt. A few nights after the sack of Cordova, he came to me in tears. He babbled in confusion. It seemed that Antony (who had been roaring drunk for a week) had tried to ravish him. The boy's tongue stumbled over the story; his beauty fled from him. I was seized with an impulse of cruelty, not tenderness. Even now, I cannot account for the violence of the change in my feeling. I looked on him with contempt, even disgust. He needed my help, perhaps. I had none to offer him. Something in me had snapped.

A few weeks later he left for Greece, to resume his studies, by Caesar's command. He went to join Maecenas; another companion was an ill-bred young officer, by name Marcus Agrippa. Well, I was relieved to see him depart. His presence had begun to embarrass me. There is nothing so dead as an infatuation from which you have recovered. As the months passed, something of tenderness returned. But when we corresponded, there was now a distance between us. There was nothing intimate in our letters, and I knew that when we met again, there would be a gulf between us, like a stretch of inhospitable coastland fringing the sea.

My mother always used to say that lust was a game the gods played to make fools of us, and amuse themselves. When she looked back on her own passion for Caesar, she could no longer understand how it had come about.

Is it the result of a trick of light, of the immediate disposition of limbs, lines, and posture?

How strange to perplex myself with this question now.

For me, it has always been inseparable from some idea of

degradation. My revulsion of Octavius puzzles me therefore.

Perhaps I was attracted by his freedom from experience. I do not know.

When I look on Artixes, I think this may be possible.

As it happened, I returned to Rome and surprised my wife Longina in bed with a curly headed boy. Both sat up, Longina displaying her delightful breasts. Surprise, then indignation, then fear, as he recognised me, could be read in the boy's face. I had no idea who he was. He looked even younger than my wife. Her tongue flicked her upper lip. Then she smiled.

"Husband," she said. "What a charming surprise," she added in Greek.

"No wonder your freedwomen were alarmed to see me."

"They should be whipped for letting you break in on me like this."

She nestled back among the cushions and fluttered her eyelashes at me.

"Fair's fair," she said. "I bet you haven't been faithful to me in Spain. He's a friend of Caesar's," she said to the boy, "and you know what that means. Besides, he's been having the most tremendous thing with Octavius. Does that still go on, husband?"

"I could divorce you," I said.

"Why bother?"

"I could have you whipped yourself. In the days of our ancestors I could have had you put to death."

"Of course you could, but those days have gone. Besides, I know you better than you think. I'm not quite the mophead you take me to be. I've taken the trouble to find out a lot about you, husband, and I could give you quite a long list of your lovers, starting with that famous pair, Clodia and her brother. So don't pretend. Actually, I imagine you're enjoying this as much as I am."

The trouble was, she was right. I found the situation exciting.

"Who's your friend?" I said.

She giggled.

"Can't you guess? We're more alike than you think, husband."

I looked at the boy's tumbling curls, his lustrous eyes, his soft and at that moment trembling mouth. He was slim, and there was a hint of mischief even in his fear.

"Yes," I said, "I see a resemblance."

The boy was Appius Claudius Pulcher, whose father had been consul ten years previously. That father, whom I had known to be proud, corrupt and superstitious (like so many of the clan) had fallen at Pharsalus in the ranks of the Pompeians, though he had despised Pompey himself. He had married his daughter to my cousin, Marcus Brutus, who, disgusted by her infidelity, had put her aside, in order to marry Cato's daughter Porcia, certainly a woman better suited to his priggish nature. This boy must be the fruit of his father's last marriage to a woman half his age whose name I couldn't recall. Appius Claudius Pulcher had hated Caesar. Looking at the boy I couldn't imagine he felt any powerful desire to avenge his father. He probably revelled in his freedom from paternal rebuke, which would certainly have been forthcoming.

There was a silence in the room. My wife appeared content, happy to enjoy what she had provoked. She wanted a scene. So I determined to deny her that. As for the boy, he had clearly got more than he bargained for. I was travel-stained, grim, returned from the wars, a general of renown, not – he must have thought – a safe man to be discovered cuckolding. I told him to get out of bed and dress himself. He obeyed; in some confusion, made uncomfortable by the gaze I directed at him. Then I escorted him to the door of the bedchamber.

"We shall say no more of this at present," I said. "You are not to be blamed. On the other hand, you must understand that you have insulted me. Before I determine what must be done, I must talk to my wife. Then you and I will have to talk also. For the moment, think yourself fortunate that I am not a man of the same temper as your late father."

I turned back towards my wife. She had thrown the coverings aside, and lay on her back, her legs spread, her right hand resting between them.

"How masterful you are, husband," she said.

Her voice was low. I unbuckled my tunic and leaned towards her. She put her right arm around my neck and drew me down, and giggled again.

A little later she said:

"We make a better pair than you thought, don't we?"

*　　*　　*

She proved this to me repeatedly in the weeks that followed. I began to think that I had got a better bargain in Longina than I had thought to have. Perhaps the young Appius Claudius had woken her up. (I soon resolved that problem, by the way, arranging to have him attached to the staff of the Procurator of Judaea. Since the appointment seemed to come direct from Caesar, he did not dare demur. It was unfortunate, and in no way my fault, that he got a fever and died before the end of the year. To her credit, Longina did not protest when I told her that her lover was being despatched into what was effectively exile. I have reason to suspect that they continued to correspond, however, but by the time I came to that conclusion I had other more important matters to consider.)

Longina was not well-educated. Indeed she was scarcely educated at all. She wrote in the same tumbling and ungrammatical manner that she talked. But she was no fool; her wits were quick, and she had a liveliness that one would have looked for in Cassius' daughter.

My father-in-law viewed the progress of our marriage with an ironic detachment. That was a mood, or air, which he cultivated. Cassius was in reality a man of the most intense passion, proud, jealous and implacable. He had made the marriage in cynical fashion: Caesar had conquered; I was a favourite of the dictator; therefore the alliance was desirable. He looked on me still in those weeks after my return from Spain with an appraising eye. In my company he usually spoke well of Caesar.

As for my wife, she was eager to make the acquaintance of the dictator. She urged me to invite him to our house: "For dinner, supper, anything."

"Caesar demands intelligent conversation," I said.

"And we can't provide it? Well, ask that old bore Cicero if you like."

"Caesar can scarcely go out to dinner without finding Cicero in the party. People look on the old man as a sort of insurance policy. Actually, though Caesar respects him, he more and more finds his tendency to dominate the conversation irritating. Besides, Cicero suspects I penned the *Anti-Cato*. He has been cool to me recently."

*   *   *

My objections, which I did not in any case understand myself, were overruled. Caesar was invited, and accepted. At the last minute, my wife added my cousin Marcus Brutus to the party — an invitation which did not please me.

"Is it true," my wife asked Caesar, "that you have invited the Queen of Egypt to Rome?"

We all knew he had, and that Calpurnia was furious.

Caesar smiled: "I hope you will make her acquaintance when she arrives."

"Oh I don't expect she'll want to meet ladies," Longina said. "Not if what I've heard is true."

"And what have you heard?"

My wife screwed up her nose so that she looked like a little girl.

"Well, that she put her brother to death and that he was also her husband. Is that true?"

"Absolutely."

"And when he was her husband, did they . . . you know?"

"Did they what?"

"Well, you know, you must know, go to bed together, fuck?"

"That is something only the Queen could tell you."

"I don't suppose she would though."

"I am sure you will not be too shy to ask her."

I had seen it so often before. Perhaps that was why I had attempted to divert Longina from her intended course. Now Caesar exercised his old accustomed charm. His manner was at the same time intimate and perfunctory. He gave the girl the impression that his whole attention was concentrated on her; and yet he remained aware of his performance, aware of his wider audience whom he invited to admire it.

It was like a play unfolding of which one already knows the conclusion; the chief interest for the audience is therefore to judge the skill with which the dramatist has handled his material. Sometimes, now, especially in these summer evenings, when the mist rising from the valley turns my mood to melancholy (as if there were not already sufficient reasons more substantial than my imaginings to induce such a mood, even a darker one, even despair), then it seems to me that the whole gaudy course of a man's life is indeed no more than such a play, a charade which we enact for the amusement of the indifferent gods. And so I watched the to-and-fro of the conversational dance, saw my wife's lips curve in invitation as she leaned towards him displaying, as if by nature, the rich roundness of a breast, heard her laugh gurgle forth like a stream long dammed-up now breaking free; and all the time, Caesar, the Master, drew her towards him as if there was no more question that she would come than there is that the sun will sink into the western sea.

"What sort of man are you, son-in-law?" Cassius said.

The question was rhetorical.

"If Caesar or any man debauched my wife . . ."

"Come, Cassius," I replied, "there is no need for this pretence. You know very well what you would do. The same as me: nothing, in the case of Caesar. That sort of virtue is out-of-date. Besides, I have shared women with Caesar before, and on some of them he had a prior claim."

"You deceive yourself, son-in-law, only when you lay claim to any equality with Caesar."

"Very well, Cassius. I yield to you on that point, and I acknowledge also that you may have a father's interest in not seeing your daughter disgraced. But then I tell you, she is not disgraced. Longina made the running herself. She is no flower that Caesar has picked."

"And does that not anger you?"

"Cassius," I said, "I thought you were a philosopher."

But if I could not tell the truth to Cassius, I could not hide it from my cousin Casca.

That was strange, for Casca was not a man whom I could expect to understand noble indignation. I suppose it was because he knew me better than any other man. He knew, for instance, that at any time up to the hour of my return from Spain (when I had surprised young Appius Claudius, himself incidentally an admiration of Casca's) I would have been happy to trade Longina to Caesar in return for the many favours he had done me. But Casca also saw, even while he mocked me, that something more than my vanity was wounded. He saw that I had really believed that, simply because I had found in myself an unexpected tenderness for my wife, she experienced the same feeling for me.

And now Casca said:

"So the Senate proposes to grant divine honours to Caesar. It would be appropriate if you were to speak in favour of the motion."

"In favour?"

"Naturally, my dear. To lose your wife to a man, however distinguished, may be thought disgraceful; to be cuckolded by a god is no shame."

"I can see only one objection, cousin," I replied. "While we may indeed grant divine honours to Caesar . . ."

"Say 'shall', not 'may'."

"Very well: shall. While we shall do so, nobody will believe that Caesar is in reality a god."

"Oh," Casca said, "when you introduce the word 'reality', you lose me, and I lose interest. Who is to say what constitutes 'reality' in this fool's world? Are my debts reality? On which subject, by the way, I am distressed that Caesar has betrayed those who trusted him, and declined to cancel debts as we were told he would; not, of course, that I believed that assurance. Certainly my creditors think them real; as for me, I dismiss them from my mind. And as for passion, which some call reality, you are aware – how could you fail to be? – of my passion for Diosippus, when the moon is waxing, and Nicander when it is on the wane, but you also know that if it was in my interest I would have either of the brats crucified – which I mention only as the nastiest death I can envisage. So where is the reality of my passion? I would weep for either lad, naturally, and my tears would be copious and impressive, but they would not prevent me from acting in my own interest."

"So your self-interest is reality."

"Is it? Is it? I wish I knew."

He leaned back and stroked his belly. We were in the hot room of the baths, I remember. He brushed the palm of his hand across the folds of flesh and flicked a stream of sweat and vapour on to the tiled floor.

"Is it? There are times, cousin, when it seems to me that there are only two realities I recognise: the first is physical. The body is real, I can't deny that."

"Many have."

"They have less flesh than I. The body is real and so, as a consequence, are its demands."

"And the mind?"

"Belongs to the body . . . part of the body."

"It controls the body."

Casca laughed: "How can you, an old soldier, say so! You have known fear in battle. Which is in the ascendant then? Mind or body? Or does fear force itself on you from without?"

"If so, fear is real."

"We think it is. And as for the mind controlling the body, let us return to where we started. There is a part of the body" – he fondled it – "which sometimes displays an intelligence of its own. I may wish to stimulate it, and it says 'no' and remains limp. At other times it moves on its own without my permission. In short, it does as it pleases whether I am awake or asleep. Sometimes I am awake and it sleeps. Sometimes I sleep and the dear little thing dances and sweats. So where is the reality of the controlling mind?"

"You said you recognised two realities. What is the other?"

"Boredom."

"That is not a philosophical answer."

"Boredom," he repeated, "which forces one to seek reality in action. Which reality will, of course, be an illusion."

He called on the slave to drench him with cold water, and then waved him away.

"Disappointing," he said. "The dear little thing took no interest. It is only your vanity which is wounded by your wife's adultery."

"Men have killed for that reason."

"What? Kill Caesar? My dear Mouse, that is an interesting idea. That might release me from boredom. How shall we set about it? All the same, Mouse, you will never kill Caesar on account of a chit like your wife."

CHAPTER

10

It will seem strange to anyone who reads this apology for my life that when I have such a short time before me (as I fear) I should spend part of it extracting trivialities from my memory. But if this arouses incomprehension, it will be because such a reader is incapable of imagining the complexity of things. The truth is that we do not know the springs of conduct; we do not know which particular circumstance or feeling drives a man to any particular action. When now I think of Casca arguing for the autonomy of sexual desire, I find that his arguments have an application that may be pushed much further. If we do not know why we experience desire, if this is something which escapes our control, then can we pretend to know why we are driven to still more obscure courses?

It seems to me now that I had never questioned my attachment to Caesar. When the civil war broke out, I was on his side, one of his favoured generals. It was natural that I continued so. I never argued the case, and not only because I was inspired by Caesar's own confidence of victory.

My imagination drifts back to that moment when we crossed the little stream called the Rubicon, and to that strange figure which rose out of the mist, playing the pipes, on the further bank. The image is vivid: perhaps my imagination has enriched or perverted it: was there really, for instance, that suggestion of goat's legs? Were the limbs even covered, as memory insists, in goatskin? Some of the soldiers, you will recall, cried out that the god Pan welcomed us to Italy. We all felt that something rarely mysterious presented itself to us; it gave an aura of incomprehensibility to what was in reality a militarily commonplace action. Had the sun been up, the figure would have appeared absurd.

Yet the memory will not leave me; surely, memory insists, there was some significance to that moment which the mind refuses to grasp. Or is perhaps incapable of grasping.

Now, considering it, it seems to me at the very least, part of a vaster mystery: why we subdued our wills to Caesar.

My cousin Marcus Brutus once spoke in terms of fatalism: we were doomed to submit to Caesar. My father-in-law Cassius rebuked him. The fault, he said, lay not in our stars. The fault was in our natures. No impersonal force, only our own weakness, determined that we should be underlings.

Artixes has just left me. We have been drinking wine, thin, sour stuff such as they make in these barbarian parts, but wine nevertheless, and I think I am a little drunk.

No matter. There is truth in wine, or, as the proverb has it, wine releases the voice of truth.

Caesar: did I submit my will to him that morning when he emerged from my mother's bedchamber and I responded to his smile with a smile? And when I found Longina's door barred against me, and knew Caesar was within, and so left the house, and descended to the Suburra to a brothel where I paid for an African girl, was that merely yet another acknowledgment of my inferiority?

That was the trouble, wasn't it? Caesar diminished me. He diminished all of us. And we could never understand how or why.

There were times – I have recounted some – when I myself, by my words or actions, saved Caesar from the disaster for which he appeared to be heading – in Egypt and in Spain, for example. There were times when he set me tasks which I accomplished better than he could have performed them himself.

It made no difference.

As my mother said: "Of course we all adore Caesar but at the same time we know he cares nothing for us."

"That," some might say, "was because he was truly a god."

I have never seen Caesar afraid. I admit that. Gods are never afraid.

That proves nothing. There was a centurion from Aricia, I remember, a sour, bilious man who was never afraid.

But Caesar had the imagination to sense fear.

Did he? There were times when I have thought he lacked

imagination. Certainly his literary style was peculiarly deficient in that quality. He once showed me a poem he had written. It was embarrassing. Catullus said that to me also.

Caesar . . . Suppose I had joined Pompey. I might have been killed at Pharsalus, but I would have died a free man.

Perhaps I should set myself to try to understand Labienus. We never made that attempt. It was simpler to condemn him.

But Labienus was my precursor. I see that now.

So: Labienus . . .

We spoke of him with bitterness, of course. He was a traitor. No man had been more richly rewarded by Caesar. Had things turned out otherwise, he would have shared the consulate with Caesar in 48, both supported by the authority of Pompey. Well, that was not to be, and in the crisis Labienus proved more mindful of old family loyalties to Pompey than of his long associ- - ation with Caesar. When he departed, he did so scrupulously, not attempting to carry other of Caesar's officers with him. Later he regretted this failure, though at the time he considered his behaviour honourable. He wrote to me once on this matter. I still have the letter, which I recovered from the place of conceal-ment I had thought fit for it, shortly before the disaster that landed me where I now find myself. It was in my travelling bureau when I was captured, and since my documents were recently restored to me, I think it proper to publish it now.

It is dated some months after Pharsalus, from Africa whither Labienus had fled, and directed to me at my mother's house in Rome.

Decimus Brutus,

An old colleague fallen into adversity greets you. I beg you not to yield to what I suppose may be your initial impulse which might lead you to destroy this letter without perusing it.

I write not to excuse myself, for in my opinion my conduct does not require exculpation. Nor do I write to seduce you from your loyalties, which would in any case – I have no doubt – be a vain effort.

You know of course that I was torn between two loyalties, and there is no need therefore to expatiate on the conflict of loyalties which engaged me. Suffice to repeat that I had obligations to both Caesar and Pompey, and that I chose to honour the latter.

It would be easy to maintain that that was all there was to my decision: that, since I recognised my loyalty to Pompey as being superior, and also anterior, to my loyalty to Caesar – a deeper thing altogether – this was the sole cause of my decision to adhere to Pompey. And I have sufficient confidence in your virtue to be assured that you would not question such an assertion, but would indeed honour me for my candour and for my recognition that certain loyalties should properly outweigh others, even when the latter appear more likely to bring personal advantage, and even greater glory.

For I must say this: I did not believe I was acting in such a way as would benefit myself. I had no confidence that I was joining the winning side.

I ask you fervently to believe that.

No man, except perhaps Cicero, was better acquainted with both Caesar and Pompey than I. Indeed, I can claim a deeper knowledge of both men than Cicero could possess, for he has met them chiefly at dinner-tables and in the Senate, while I have served under both in the field. Consequently I was aware that Caesar's star was in the ascendant, Pompey's in decline. Fortune, my dear Decimus, reflects character and capacity. I could not fail to compare Caesar's swiftness and certainty of judgment and the lucidity of his intellect, even the imperturbability of his courage, with my poor Pompey's ever-growing tendency to vacillation, and his inability to distinguish between illusion and reality. He still, as the clouds of crisis enfolded the Republic, could not perceive the nature of his own moral, intellectual and physical deterioration. At most, I could hope that, in adhering to him, I could supply the deficiencies I remarked in him.

Vain hope, as events have proved, for my advice was disregarded while it might have been valuable, and my counsels adopted only when matters were beyond remedy.

My judgment has been proved right, my fears justified, and yet I do not regret the course I took.

Now, when defeat, death, and even dishonour (for I can trust Caesar to see that I am dishonoured) stare me in the face, I can still maintain that I have no regrets.

Nevertheless, Decimus, since no man wishes to go down to the Shades without first speaking for himself and finding at least one man of virtue to attend to his words, I take this opportunity to try to explain my reasons for acting as I did. The world may howl against me, and I am indifferent to its execration; but I would not wish you to think badly of me.

Let me say therefore that I admire Caesar. I retain an affection for Caesar. I recognise the grandeur of Caesar's achievements, to which both you and I have made telling contributions. But none of this prevents me from seeing that the course on which Caesar has embarked is pernicious. It can lead to nothing but the destruction of the Republic which has been the means of Rome's greatness, and which can alone, through its time-honoured institutions, guarantee the survival of liberty in Rome.

The government of a single person sounds the death-knell of liberty. It will convert Roman noblemen into courtiers. Little by little, an Oriental despotism will be established in place of our free institutions. Men will no longer dare to speak their minds; they will suit their words to the wishes of the dictator.

I have heard Caesar talk of the corruption of Republican institutions and of the corruption of feeling which this breeds. I do not dispute that this has happened, though I would lay the blame principally on men like Caesar himself. Yes, and on Pompey too; I do not deny that. When these two, and Marcus Crassus came together at Lucca, they engaged themselves in a criminal conspiracy against the Free State.

If I adhered to Pompey rather than Caesar, it was not because I had greater respect for him. It was simply because I considered him less dangerous. He was weak where Caesar was strong. He was indecisive where Caesar was determined. I never thought the Republic safe in Pompey's hands, but I knew that his dominance was less secure than a victorious Caesar's would prove to be.

You may argue that Caesar plans many beneficial reforms. My respect for Caesar is sufficiently strong to deter me from offering contradiction. Instead I offer this warning: the means by which a reform is effected may negate any benefit which in other circumstances that reform would bring.

If you can believe in your heart that Caesar intends to restore the Republic and retire into private life, then my fears may be unfounded, and my course of action may have been misguided.

But can you believe that?

And, even if you could, can you believe that a Republic restored by Caesar's hand and as a result of Caesar's methods, could possess any vitality?

I accept that I am heading for failure. So be it. I shall fight my cause honourably to the death. And I shall die convinced that posterity will judge me more favourably than Caesar's friends may do. I address this letter to you, however, because there is one friend of Caesar's whose good opinion I still value and seek, and because I hope that it may give you occasion to reflect on the dangers for Rome of the path which you have chosen to follow. You will understand, my dear Decimus Brutus, that I do not question your virtue. I do not doubt that you have adhered to Caesar for the best and most selfless of motives. I ask only that you should consider anew where Caesar is heading, that you should consider the implications for Rome, the Empire, the institutions of the Republic, the great noble families that have made that Republic and finally for liberty itself, which no good man surrenders save with his life, of Caesar's dominance.

Caesar, you may still say, can be trusted. Very well; so be it again. But Caesar will have successors. Will it be possible to trust them in like manner?

Caesar may continue to show outward respect for the institutions of the Republic, even while he subverts them. Consuls may still be elected, even though Caesar may fix the elections and though the consuls will be powerless. But in time the office of consul will become a merely decorative honour. Power will rest with the dictator, who should more properly be termed, in the Greek fashion, the tyrant. Free speech will wither, for it cannot flourish when the government is in the hands of a single person. Orientals will hasten to designate the tyrant a god. Even the Senate will cravenly follow suit. Caesar may accept divine honours with the scepticism proper to a Roman nobleman. His successors will come to think of themselves as gods, with the power of gods, the liberty of gods.

That is the future which Caesar is constructing. When the day comes on which a Roman nobleman thinks it proper to prostrate himself before the tyrant, as Orientals do before the despots to whom they are utterly subjugated, that will be the result of Caesar's victory.

I urge you to think on these matters, dear Decimus, and draw back before you become an agent in the destruction of the liberty that depends on the survival of the Republic.

I am as ever your friend and equal, Labienus, now equal in honour, but one who in the future I envisage, which I shall not survive to experience, would find himself your equal only in dishonour and servitude.

This was a dangerous letter to receive. I was incensed that he should have thought to send it to me. Fortunately, minute enquiries revealed that he had taken the precaution of having it secretly delivered. It was probable, therefore, that it had not been intercepted and copied for Caesar's eyes. Nevertheless I took care to observe him closely when we next met and for some months after, to see whether his manner to me had changed or whether he was regarding me with some suspicion.

Naturally, too, I rejected Labienus' arguments. They were an attempt at putting a brave face on his desertion. Few men can resist seeking public reasons to justify their private behaviour. Labienus had realised that he had made the wrong choice. He had been betrayed by his own ambition. Therefore he now pretended to me, even perhaps to himself, that he had joined himself to Pompey not because he thought Pompey would win, but rather because he recognised his cause as being morally and politically to be preferred. That was nonsense, of course.

Of course it was nonsense. I assured myself time and again that it was nonsense. Only I found myself returning to his letter, extracting it from its place of concealment, and brooding on its message.

Why, I was even tempted to show it to young Octavius. That, of course, was in the weeks of my infatuation with the boy. Prudence restrained me. I might dote on the youth, but my judgment was not so far destroyed as to make me suppose that he could be trusted not to reveal the existence of this compromising letter to Caesar.

Often since, I have told myself that if I had not found something in the letter from the first, I would have burned it straightaway.

Now, I recall words attributed to Cicero when he heard of Labienus' defection.

"Labienus is a hero. Never was an act more splendid. If nothing else comes of it, he has at least made Caesar smart. We have a civil war upon us, not because we have quarrelled among ourselves, but on account of one abandoned and ambitious citizen."

Sedition, as I thought at the time.

After Munda, I sought out Labienus' corpse. The expression on the face was calm. Did a tear escape me?

CHAPTER

11

For the moment, however, all was sunshine and general rejoicing. Even those who had supported the defeated party could not disguise from themselves their relief that the terrible civil wars were over. All felt as if a great weight had been lifted. Women, happy to think that their sons, husbands and lovers would no longer be sacrificed to Mars, united in praise of Caesar. An uncommonly large number of children were conceived in noble families that autumn. When Longina confided her own pregnancy to me, I scarcely doubted that I was the father.

In the Senate, men tumbled over each other in their eagerness to lavish honours on Caesar. Cicero, it must be said, while urging such honours, also recommended that they be kept "within the measure of humanity". But power attracts toadies, and they soon overstepped that measure. It was reasonable to order a temple to be built in honour of Clemency, since none could deny that, except in Spain, Caesar's clemency to his defeated opponents had been remarkable, an honour to Caesar himself and to the Roman people in general. When one thought of how barbarian princes and Orientals were accustomed to make a hecatomb of their conquered rivals, the clemency that Caesar displayed renewed one's pride in *Romanitas* (to use a word then coming into fashion). It was perhaps appropriate that my cousin Marcus Brutus, who was such a conspicuous example of the dictator's forbearance, should introduce this proposal in the Senate; and few people were as critical of his leaden delivery and pompous platitudes as I was. Indeed, the general opinion was that Brutus had spoken in a manner worthy of his noble ancestors. I have never understood how Markie so easily attracted golden opinions. I suppose there was something in his manner – his lack of humour, his incapacity for irony – which appealed to the dullards who in any assembly are bound to be in the majority.

Caesar, with a self-consciously noble gesture, ordered that Pompey's statues be restored to the place from which they had been cast down. Cicero now declared that "Caesar, by resurrecting Pompey's statues, has established his own for all time". This rhetorical flourish was greeted with loud applause.

If those of us who had been Caesar's loyal friends and collaborators from the first perilous days of civil war were disgusted by the sycophancy now displayed by those who had previously declared him a wild beast that must be pulled down, well, that is hardly a matter for surprise.

Antony, however, was distrustful as well as disgusted. He could not believe in the sincerity of those who now declared themselves utterly reconciled to Caesar.

"It does not make sense," he said, "and yet Caesar appears to accept it at face value. Damned if I do."

He persuaded me that we should approach Caesar and urge him to form a guard for his protection. We cited the example of those from the elder Gracchus onward who had been murdered while they thought themselves the favourites of the people. I did not scruple to add the names of certain Greek tyrants to the list, for I wanted Caesar to understand the loneliness of his position, and the dangers to which this exposed him.

Caesar listened to our arguments, and then repeated them in a loud voice so that they might be more generally known.

Then he raised his hand, and smiled.

"I respect your motives, my friends, but Caesar will not condescend to live like an Oriental despot. It is better to die once, than to live in fear of death."

We could not move him.

"Did you ever hear such bloody nonsense?" Antony said.

It was not the first time he refused my advice. I argued against the proposal that he should celebrate his victory in Spain by a Triumph.

"Caesar," I said, "what is proposed is both unprecedented and distasteful. Even Sulla never held a Triumph to celebrate victories over Roman citizens. The Triumphs which you held last year were different. I grant you there was some dishonesty in the suggestion that they all celebrated victories over foreigners. Nevertheless, it is true that, for instance, even if Scipio and Cato were your chief enemies in Africa, the Triumph could be justified on account of the part that King Juba played in that campaign. But it was different in Spain. There we encountered and defeated none but Romans, and it is improper to rejoice in the defeat and death of men to whom we were united by ties of blood and ancient friendships. You have displayed your magnanimity by your decision to honour Pompey. You are in danger of destroying the effect this has had, if you now insist on a display of public rejoicing on account of the death of Labienus, and the destruction of Pompey's family."

I knew at once that I had gone too far. A nerve twitched in his cheek, sure sign that he was moved to anger.

"You are talking nonsense, Mouse. Labienus betrayed me, as Pompey never did. He was a man I valued, and I had frequently given public evidence of the high regard in which I held him. For him to desert me was treasonable. Besides, Munda was the hardest battle I ever fought. Don't ask me not to rejoice in that victory and Labienus' death."

"Private rejoicing is one thing. Perfectly natural. You know I share your feelings, even though I cannot stifle regret that our old colleague was not loyal and so condemned himself to ignominy. But a public Triumph is another matter. It is wrong in itself, for the reasons I have given. It is also impolitic. It will reopen the wounds which in all other ways you have set yourself to heal. You cannot suppose that all those who are connected by family and friendship with the men we defeated in Spain will not bitterly resent the holding of such a Triumph. That resentment will fester. Besides, it seems to me that in order to enjoy a day of glory, you will not only alienate hundreds of people now ready to be well-disposed to you, but you will pin on yourself a badge of undying shame."

"You forget yourself, Mouse. You forget you are talking to Caesar."

I was dismayed by his obstinacy. In former days, I told myself, Caesar was open to reason. He knew he was given to rashness, but he could be persuaded from unwise courses by those whom he had good reason to trust and respect. I had done nothing to impair that trust and respect, but he received my warning as if I was an insolent fellow of no account. I was grieved by his behaviour, not only because of the cavalier manner in which he set my advice aside, disregarding all I had done for him, but, more particularly, because I was certain that my advice was good and his conduct foolish.

So he pressed on with the Triumph, and insisted that I should myself take a place of honour in the procession. Unfortunately, I was stricken with an ague the day before, and my Greek doctor readily signed a certificate stating that he could not answer for my health if I took part. Caesar pretended to accept this at face value, but I knew he was displeased.

The reception of the Triumph was as I had predicted. Of course the vulgar throng, ever delighted by spectacle, applauded with their usual enthusiasm, but among men who mattered it made a bad impression. People said it was shameful to rejoice in this manner at the calamities which had overtaken the Republic, and in wars which nothing but dire necessity could excuse, either in the eyes of men or before the gods. So Caesar's reputation suffered, and Cicero asked, "What price clemency now? True clemency should extend to the memory of Roman dead, in whatever cause they perished. How is concord to be restored if we are invited to celebrate, rather than mourn, the slaying of our friends and relations?"

My argument, I might add, went against my own interest. I had recently acquired the principal stake in a school of gladiators, who were naturally in great demand on account of the Games held in conjunction with the Triumph. Prices were high, and I received a considerable pecuniary advantage; but I would willingly have forgone that to spare my country and my general the dishonour of this Triumph.

I was so perturbed by this episode that I took the risk of expressing my feelings in a letter to Octavius.

My dear Octavius (I wrote)
     You will have received news that Caesar has determined to hold a Triumph in honour of our victories in Spain. I am

certain that your feelings on this matter will be the same as mine.

Nothing can tarnish Caesar's glory. Nothing can make me doubt the necessity of these terrible wars. No man, as you can attest, fought harder in Spain than I, and I am sure you will agree that none has been more diligent in your uncle's cause, nor has served him more faithfully.

It is on account of the love I bear him, and the love I bear you whom I presume to be his heir, that I take pen now to urge you to exert your influence with him in the same manner and the same direction that I do myself.

It is a time for moderation and reconciliation. It is necessary to cultivate these qualities if the Republic is to be reconstituted in the manner we should both desire, and of which we have discoursed. We are agreed, are we not, that the central problem is how to combine liberty with order, how to reinvigorate the noble traditions of the Republic without sacrificing what we have fought to gain?

There is no one (except, of course, Caesar) whose wisdom I respect, and whose counsel I value, as I do yours; and I never cease to be amazed by your ability to combine youthful ardour with prudence more to be expected of a man twice your age. And yet I pause on that sentence, for I cannot but observe that advancing years may impair judgment, and success may breed rashness.

I write this also to warn you of the dangers we still run, and of course to assure you of my undying affection.

You will be pleased to learn that I am to become a father.

I trust your studies go well, and that you will soon return to Rome that I may enjoy the charm of your company, and avail myself of the benefit of your opinion which will always, I am certain, be directed towards the restoration of sound principles of public virtue.

I signed myself "Your affectionate friend".

However carefully couched, this was, I knew, a dangerous letter to send. Yet it seemed to me necessary, for I could not but be alarmed by the rashness of Caesar's conduct, and the dangers this might breed for Octavius and myself as well as for Caesar.

I sent the letter by a trusted slave, with instructions that he was to deliver it to Octavius in person and that he was to wait for a reply which he would bring directly to me.

Mouse of mice,

Congratulations on impending fatherhood. I always knew you had it in you.

As for the other matters of which you discourse so sagely, speaking with the wisdom of Cicero, if not of Solon, be assured that I shall ponder them in whatever of my heart I can spare from my current enthusiasms, the nature of which it would be unseemly to commit to writing. Suffice it to say that Greece has delights to offer in matters other than literature and philosophy. Indeed, only the sternest philosopher could profess himself indifferent to the goods available.

Public affairs seem remote from this idyllic Apollonian setting. Yet I am well aware that they will soon press hard upon me, and I am grateful to you, my dear Mouse, for the care with which you attend to my interests. I shall ever be guided by you in all matters, for I know how tenderly you feel. I know and commend your prudence. I am at one with you in all things, and I recognise that this is a time for caution and conciliation.

We are wise, are we not, to walk warily in the sight of the gods who are ever quick to punish the presumptions of us mere mortals.

I wrote by an earlier messenger today to my uncle, so there is no need to burden you with a request to convey my dutiful love and esteem to him.

Maecenas and Agrippa, though frequently at odds, are in their different ways, agreeable and stimulating companions. I trust their good sense, but I trust you more, and my native discretion most of all.

I send you whatever you would have from me, with the assurance that you will not demand what I cannot offer.

Octavius

That letter provoked a renewed spasm of desire, soon quelled. I admired the boy's discretion, was conscious that the same quality was demanded from me in circumstances which appeared ever more perplexing.

* * *

The question "What will Caesar do?" was in everyone's mouth. Nobody could imagine that he would not mark the end of the civil wars by a thorough reconstruction of the State and its Constitution. After all, even many who had followed Pompey agreed that the civil wars had been caused as much by the decay of the Republic as by Caesar's ambition. There were not many to agree with old Cicero that only a change of heart was needed.

Cicero himself had retired, perhaps in disgust, to his estate at Tusculum where he amused himself with philosophy, which he not only wrote but taught to a group of young noblemen who delighted to flatter him. He also talked of writing a history of Rome, but was dissuaded partly by the report that Caesar did not look kindly on the enterprise. This came as a surprise to him because, whenever they met, Caesar was accustomed to flatter him. Nevertheless Caesar's opposition to the project was real.

"It would of course have the merit of keeping the old man occupied and out of mischief," he said to me, "and that is certainly a consideration in its favour. We would all enjoy the rhetorical flourishes too. But all the same I can't approve. When Cicero sits down to write, he gets carried away. Loose talk at the dinner-table doesn't offend me, but I don't choose that Cicero should give the definitive version of my career to posterity. And his literary skill is such that we all know it would be received as definitive. So warn the old thing off, will you, Mouse?"

Which I did, to Cicero's very considerable consternation; he was terrified to think he might have incurred Caesar's displeasure.

"How could he imagine an old man could undertake such an arduous task?" he said. "Do please assure Caesar that I never speak anything but well of him."

This was nonsense, as we all knew, but I let it pass, even though he continued by saying:

"All the same, I do wish you would do something to prompt him to the right sort of action. When I think of how Sulla employed his dictatorship in an attempt to eradicate weaknesses and restore stability to the Republic, I am astonished by Caesar's indolence and complacency. You know how I honour him. You know the depths of my affection for him. It is my consciousness of my own virtue that allows me to urge you to speak to him about these matters. It rests in Caesar's power now – which is greater than that of any man since Sulla, greater perhaps even than Sulla's – to put things on a sound footing. I am told that he plans to appoint the consuls and praetors for the next five years in advance, making the elections a mere formality, and thus also making a mockery of our proud traditions of liberty. I have denied the rumour, of course, and assured people that Caesar would never do anything so flagrant. Do tell him what I say, how I do all I can to quell these insidious rumours, and warn him that the proliferation of such stories must harm his reputation. Constitutional reform – conservative and moderate reform – is the most urgent task before him. I am quite ready to draw up proposals for what needs to be done. You, my dear Decimus Brutus, know better than anyone – I say that for I admire your powers of perception and judgment – that I am the man best fitted to do this, for I am now bereft of ambition. It cannot be supposed that at the age of sixty-two I retain any hopes, even any wish, of playing a conspicuous part in public life. Not at all; I am happy with my books and my garden. It is only my intense desire to serve, to do something more, even above and beyond the great services I performed which earned me the title of 'Father of his Country' – one that I revere above all other honours – which prompts me to suggest that I may perform this last service for Rome and Caesar. Assure him therefore of my willingness, but stress, I beg you, the absence of any personal ambition in my proposals."

And so on, and so on; a man could empty a wine-flask while Cicero talked.

As a matter of fact, Cicero was far too deeply engaged in the problems of his private life to undertake such a task, even if Caesar had wished it, and even if he had still been competent to perform it (which I no longer thought him) or likely to carry it out in a manner agreeable to Caesar. He had recently divorced his wife Terentia, though they had been married for over thirty years. He claimed that she had neglected him during the civil war, and even left him without necessities. Then he said that she had impoverished him by running up huge debts, that his house had become naked and empty as a result of her insensate extravagance, and that when his daughter Tullia had travelled to receive him at Brindisi after Pharsalus, Terentia had sent her south with an insufficient number of attendants and quantity of supplies. This was all nonsense. The truth was that the old philosopher had had his eye on a girl young enough to be his granddaughter whom he was determined to marry. She had the merit also of being rich, and Cicero was indeed laden with debt, though it was his responsibility rather than Terentia's. The truth was that the old goat lusted after his young bride, and that was the picture that filled my mind, as he jabbered on concerning the need for constitutional reform and his own willingness to undertake the task of drawing up proposals.

CHAPTER

12

All the same, Cicero might be an old windbag nowadays, but I couldn't deny that he had spoken sense. We had endured these terrible wars – wars which no one – not even Caesar, as he so often reminded us – had sought, and they had been fought for one simple reason: that the traditional political system of the Republic no longer answered the needs of Empire.

(I explained that to you, Artixes, you will remember, but you will forgive me if I say now that I then did so in excessively simple terms suitable for the understanding of a barbarian youth, however charming.)

But it was this question which perplexed me throughout that autumn. It was a golden autumn, as I recall, one of those years when each day seems imbued with a crisp clarity that calls on man to worship the gods, and yet with a warmth that encourages him to indulge in all physical pleasure. The heat of the day still invited languor, and the little breeze that blew in from the campagna encouraged reflection. We old warriors deserved the languor; we politicians, who had to consider how reform might best be effected, required those moments of reflection.

Casca mocked me for my preoccupation.

"Take what the gods give and be grateful."

Rumours swept the city that Caesar intended to introduce Gauls and other barbarians into the Senate in such numbers that we Roman noblemen would become objects of contempt.

"It cannot be," said even those who most keenly spread the rumour.

"What is the purpose of a Roman nobleman's career in public life?" asked my father-in-law, and now friend, Cassius.

He answered his own question.

"He seeks dignity and power."

But what did Caesar plan?

Oh he made minor reforms, of course: he adjusted the calendar, for instance, and set great store by that.

"I am a practical man, Mouse," he said, "and concerned with practical matters. There is nothing more practical than the measurement of time. In antiquity our Roman months so ill agreed with the revolution of the year that festivals and days of sacrifice gradually fell in seasons quite opposite to those for which they were intended. It might happen therefore that the sacrifice intended to bless the sowing of crops might, in one year, fall at the time when the corn was yellow. Could anything be more absurd, my dear fellow? Well, King Numa, the great law-giver so revered by our ancestors, took thought and devised a remedy. He ordered that the priests, when times seemed too abruptly out of joint, should order the interposition of this month called Mercidonius, which, as you know, is of the type described as intercalary. But even this has proved ineffective. I have, however, taken counsel of the wisest sages, Greeks and Egyptians for the most part, and we have propounded a new scheme of things, a new calendar, which eradicates these ancient defects, and which will set things right for all time."

He could continue in this vein for hours. It was extraordinary: Caesar, so swift in action, so witty in repartee, the man whom the ladies called "Quicksilver", could also be the most frightful bore.

But I suppose that is true of most men when they mount their hobbyhorse.

I could get him to talk of these things. I could get him to expatiate on a plan he had projected to cut a canal through the Isthmus of Corinth, to the great benefit of traders no longer compelled to skirt the dangerous coast of the Peloponnesus. He would talk also, again at length, of how the Tiber might be conveyed directly from Rome by a deep channel cut directly from Rome to Circeii, and so into the sea near Terracina.

"The merchants at Ostia may grumble, but what of that? In any case, I shall clear the shore there of its secret and dangerous obstructions."

Then he proposed draining the marshes by Nomentum and Setia, to employ many idle hands in agriculture.

And so on . . . There was no end to his schemes for social and physical improvement.

This was all very well. It proved that his luminous mind had lost none of its accustomed invention and activity.

But when I ventured to ask him, yet again, how he intended to reform the Constitution, with the implication (I admit) that any effective reform would make a future career like his own impossible, he frowned and declined to answer.

Let me, as has ever been my endeavour throughout this memoir (which is not, I insist, primarily intended as a work of self-justification, but rather as a treatise which may edify such future generations as may chance upon it), let me then try to speak with all the honesty which I can muster.

It may be beyond the wit of any man to restore the State. It may prove impossible, given the universal nature of our Empire, ever again to combine order with liberty.

This is a matter which I had discussed with young Octavius. He responded to the question with all the pessimism character-istic of youth.

"There has to be a supreme ruler of such an empire," he said, "and my uncle has made himself its master, as Pompey failed to do."

"Sulla was such a master," I said. "He drew up a revised Constitution and then retired from public life."

"And how long did his Constitution last?"

We were in an arbour in his stepfather's garden. Ilex trees shaded us from the afternoon sun. A lizard ran along the wall. A slave brought us wine and we dismissed him. Then he was summoned by Octavius' stepfather, Philippus, as he lay at his ease, half-drunk, at the other end of the garden. We talked in low voices though none could hear us. It was about a month before we set out on the Spanish campaign, before Octavius had made clear to me that relations between us must now change.

I said: "What do men want? Dignity, first of all."

"Well, that can be arranged, can't it?"

"Freedom from fear."

"More difficult to ensure?"

"The ability to exercise their powers to the full."

"And if these powers clash, one man's with another's, as my uncle's did with Pompey's? What then?"

He stroked his thighs. For a moment I was distracted, amazed as ever by his ability to be so conscious of his own body, yet capable of allowing his intellect to work independently of such preoccupations.

"Do you know what has changed in Rome?" I said.

When I recall my conversations with Octavius, I am perplexed – I was perplexed then, am even more so now – by what I can only call my consciousness of duality. This came on me in two forms. In the first place, there was that duality that philosophers have expounded. It was like those dialogues of Socrates: where you are aware that abstract philosophical questions are being debated in an atmosphere of highly charged sexuality. Such duality is always disturbing, and always alluring.

But there was another duality that disturbed me more deeply. I could never be certain which of us – the experienced General, the man of action, the almost grizzled man of affairs – or the beardless boy who had his thighs shaved with red-hot almond shells, and who delighted in his beauty as the most mindless of women does – which of us was master and which disciple. Did I play Socrates to his Alcibiades, or was Alcibiades giving lessons to Socrates?

So, now, when I said, "Do you know what has changed in Rome?" I did not, even as I spoke the words, know whether I was about to instruct him, or whether I was seeking information.

Of course I must have been about to instruct him, for what could he tell me on such a matter?

"Yes, of course," he said. "Rome made itself, or was formed by the gods, as an assembly of free men, exercising voting rights in the Forum about matters which concerned them intimately and of which they might be expected to have arrived at an informed opinion; and now the Roman populace, who still exercise, nominally at least, the same voting rights, who still claim to be the fount of political power, is composed of idle, workless layabouts, whose votes are for sale either to the highest bidder, or to the man who shouts the stupidest but most violent cry."

I paused. He smiled.

"Come on, my dear, contradict me if you dare."

"You have told me what I was going to argue myself. And what is the consequence?"

"Well this time, my dear, since we are in such evident agreement, let me urge you to provide the answer."

"The answer is that popular politics, the politics of the elections, the politics that determine the magistracies, the politics that choose the men who must guide the destinies of Rome, have become a sham."

"A lie," he smiled. "A game which the most honest among noblemen finds himself compelled to play most cynically."

He sipped his wine, then, doing something which I had never seen done before, took a deep purple grape from the dish on the stone ledge beside his couch, and peeled it delicately with the nail of his forefinger.

"My dearest Mouse," he said. "There is nothing to be done. Which is why men of intelligence like you and me – yes, and my uncle most of all – are driven to action, in an attempt to persuade ourselves that something worthwhile may yet be done. On the other hand, look across the garden, at my stepfather. He is drunk now, though it is early afternoon. He will stay drunk. Why not? He is rich. He has no part to play, not because he considers any part unworthy of his abilities, which by the way he grossly exaggerates, but because he considers his abilities unworthy of any task that might present itself to him. Somebody said to me the other day that a cynic is a man who knows the price of everything and the value of nothing. Do you know what my friend Maecenas replied? 'Not so,' he said, 'a cynic knows the value of everything and knows it is not worth the price demanded.'"

I was displeased to hear him quote Maecenas, but could not dissent from the judgment.

And yet, Artixes, I find myself here, your father's hostage, your father's prisoner, and let me be honest, your father's destined victim, since none will pay the price he might demand for my release.

Where stands cynicism there?

CHAPTER

13

But there was one other subject about which Caesar would talk as autumn turned to winter. This was his proposed campaign against Parthia. Now, let me admit that in other circumstances these plans would have been justifiable. The Parthians were insolent and aggressive. Their victory over Marcus Crassus at Carrhae had given them a contempt for Rome. They threatened the security of the eastern frontier of our Empire. There was also the question of Armenia, that kingdom which, protruding south, must be dominated either by Rome or by Parthia.

Yet these were not the real reasons why Caesar was determined to embark on this enterprise which exceeded in audacity all that even he had ever attempted. Nor was it the case that he was persuaded by Cleopatra, whom he had now installed in a palace on – if I remember rightly – the Esquiline, and whom he visited nightly for an hour before supper, sometimes indeed remaining there for the meal, and even for hours afterwards. It was true that as an Easterner she was eager to see Parthia humbled, and she admitted to me herself that she had a further reason.

"I have realised, Mouse, my poor Mouse," she said in that tone which would have sounded caressing to any man who did not retain the echoes of Clodia's speech in his memory, "that here in this dull, conventional Rome, which is so boring – why did nobody ever warn me how boring Rome is? – here I can be nothing but Caesar's plaything – his piece of foreign skirt, as some rogue said the other day – a piece of insolence for which I am glad to say he was soundly whipped. But in the East, in Parthia, Caesar and Cleopatra may reign as Sun and Moon –

we shall be beyond compare. Do you wonder that I urge the campaign upon him? Besides, Mouse, he needs little urging. Caesar is one of those men who must ever journey further and into more dangerous territory to fulfil his Destiny. And . . ." she smiled like a kitten just developing into a cat ". . . it has been borne in on me that Cleopatra is part of that Destiny. We are yoked together. How he can tolerate that dreary Calpurnia is a mystery. I suppose it's part of the great boringness of Rome."

No doubt her urging played a part. No doubt she scarcely needed to urge.

For the truth was that Caesar was indeed bored. That marvellous sagacity, that balance, that sense of the possible, seemed to me to be fleeing from him, as the god fled from Hercules. Caesar, who had once said to me, pinching the lobe of my ear, "Always remember there are two rules of politics, Mouse. First, that politics is the art of the possible; second, that what is possible may be enlarged by the manner in which the dice fall," now looked on Rome and its politics with loathing.

"What have I achieved, Mouse? I have gained great glory. We have won glory and successes such as only Alexander may have exceeded. I dominate Rome as no man has since Sulla. Sulla! You know how I have ever loathed and despised him; and yet here I am, after so many battles, so many campaigns, no more, it seems, than another Sulla. Mouse, I am fifty-six. This is no way for Caesar to end, arranging who shall be consul this year and the next, which nonentity shall hold which praetorship, who should be fobbed off with this and who with that. Have I proved myself the favourite of the gods, I who am the descendant of Venus, only to find myself compelled to listen to lectures from Cicero, however carefully couched in respectful, even timid, language? Do I care which noble faction seeks that office, and which the other? Do I even care for the plaudits of the mob which any man of intelligence, sensibility and genius must despise?

"No, Mouse, what shall it profit me to spend my declining years adjusting this, repairing that, meting out laws which Caesar himself despises to a stinking multitude that worship him while he gives them shows and Triumphs, and would as soon revile him if Fortune fled from him?

"Mouse, Caesar, as you whom I have loved almost as my own

son know only too thoroughly, cannot rest content with such dull matters, such petty business. What have we known? Clanging fights, where a man renews himself, burning towns, where a man sees his glory godlike shine, sinking ships, where our enemies are delivered to the gods that rule the sea, praying hands, to whom it is in our power to respond with life or death? And you would have me surrender such knowledge for . . . the administration of a corrupt and stinking polity?

"Mouse, consider Parthia, that all but boundless empire across wastes of sand, those sands where Marcus Crassus – my equal for a few months in power, my superior in wealth, my inferior in all else – those sands where Marcus Crassus so ignobly perished. I have heard that there still remain Roman legionaries from his army, taken in that terrible battle, and ever since held in captivity. Would it not be a glorious action to restore them to their homes and families, to bring them back to the tutelage of their familial gods?

"And Parthia, Mouse, is the heir of Persia which Alexander conquered. When I was in Egypt they asked me if I wished to visit Alexander's tomb, to gaze on the embalmed countenance of the greatest conqueror the world has ever known. But Caesar would not, Caesar refused, and all wondered. Some whispered even, 'Caesar is ashamed that he has not yet matched Alexander.' None dared say this to Caesar, but I could not fail to be aware of how the whispers ran. And in my heart I knew they spoke truth. I felt in my bosom a keen jealousy of Alexander who all his life had been free from the petty constraints of political necessities that have bound me; and I knew in my heart that till I had equalled his achievement, I could not gaze upon him . . ."

"But Caesar," I tried to say, "think of Gaul, consider Pharsalus . . ."

He brushed my intervention aside.

"And so, Parthia, to subdue that empire as Alexander subdued the majesty of Darius. And then . . . to follow my star still . . . wherever it shall lead me . . . to India perhaps where Alexander himself was stopped, or, a still grander scheme presents itself to me, a campaign which would be seen by all as a new wonder of the world . . . to traverse the Hyrcanian wastes, and march on the north side of the Caspian Sea to where the frosty Caucasus proudly challenge the heavens themselves, the Caucasus where Prometheus was held, victim of his unparalleled audacity. Then to carry war into Scythia, that unknown land of terrible barbarians, to march up the Danube into the dark forests of Germany, and so reach the Rhine from this new and strange direction. After which, I would again be received in Gaul as a godlike redeemer. I would have drawn the new boundary of the Roman Empire and extended its limits to the ocean on every side . . .

"Would this not be a fit culmination to Caesar's career? And why not? I cannot rest here in this stew of corruption. Caesar is a man unbound, who will not consent to be confined . . ."

I cannot swear, now and in my present distress, that these were Caesar's precise words. Furthermore I have condensed into one oration the gist of innumerable conversations we had on these matters at that time. But I remember three things which, at different moments, came to my mind, though I did not choose to utter any of them to him.

The first was, with what difficulty he had advanced a few paltry miles into the mist-shrouded island of Britain.

The second was my memory of how Clodia had told me that when Caesar first informed her (in bed) that he was a god, she had imagined he was inviting her to share a joke; and only much later had realised that he spoke in all seriousness.

And the third was that a priest once told me it was written in the Sibylline Books, those repositories of ultimate wisdom, that "The Romans could never conquer the Parthians unless they went to war under the conduct of a king . . ."

Artixes said to me:

"But from what you say, this Caesar of yours was a madman. In Gaul we venerate such beings but we do not entrust them with responsibility."

"Don't you remember, my dear," I replied, "that I told you Cato once said Caesar was the only sober man to set himself to destroy the State?"

"Many madmen are nevertheless sober," Artixes said.

CHAPTER

14

I must hurry. The days shorten. Artixes assures me that no reply has yet arrived by way of the emissaries his father, the Prince, sent. But there is a look in his eye which suggests to me that his father no longer has any great hopes of receiving a substantial ransom.

As the days shortened then too, in that, my last Roman winter, the mood of the city grew ever more tense, and sharp-knifed.

Casca remarked to me one day: "It's odd, isn't it? We fought all these battles and nothing is settled. A few great men have disappeared – none of my creditors, unfortunately. The parties have re-formed. Cicero has less to say for himself. But otherwise nothing seems to have changed, except that, I'm sorry to say, Diosippus has quite lost his looks. Even that diet I put him on hasn't worked. It merely makes him look his years. However, I have had some hopeful reports from my agent in the slave-market. He tells me he expects a charming cargo from Phrygia very soon. Don't see how he can be telling the truth, not with the seas as they are. They'll either be wrecked or arrive utterly wind-blown and ugly, while if they attempt the overland journey it'll take months to get them into any desirable condition."

There were days when Casca was a considerable comfort. On the other hand he went on to say, "Don't you think our Lord and Master is behaving really a bit oddly these days? Too bizarre for words. Only the other afternoon he was seen to be wearing knee-length red boots. Yes, bright red boots. And when someone had the nerve to ask him what this was in aid of, he declared that his ancestors, the Alban kings, had always been accustomed to wearing such boots as a sign of their rank. Well, to me of course, that simply explains why the Alban kings haven't lasted. I can't think of anything to make anyone look sillier than knee-length red boots, like a comedian in a low pantomime. But, well, our Lord and Master – I mean I know he has some pretensions to a certain wit, but I've never thought he had a sense of humour. Indeed I remember once suggesting to you that it would take a surgical operation to get a joke into Caesar's head. You bit my head off, I remember. After all, those were the days when you thought the sun shone out of Caesar's arse, and, to be fair to you, he had something of the same idea about you. Well, as you know, I followed him with the utmost and most admirable loyalty, for quite different reasons: because I saw that the old boy was a winner, and, except at the gaming-tables, your fat old Casca has always preferred to be on the winning side. In any case, when it came to a choice between the noble and fortunate Caesar and that great lump of lard they used to call the Great One, it was as simple for me as choosing between a pretty lad and, let us say, Calpurnia; but – how I do ramble on, I've always noticed that garrulity is the sign that I'm worried. Anyway, to cut a long matter short, as the man said when he made a eunuch of a Nubian, do you suppose our esteemed master is going off his rocker? Because, darling Mouse, if he is, I'm going to find another bed to lie in. What do you say?"

What could I say? I certainly couldn't start talking about the Parthian plans and the Hyrcanian wastes and the frosted Caucasus. So I said:

"You've always underestimated Caesar's sense of humour. Besides, he's a dandy. He's always been famous for being a dandy. And dandies take strange whims at times. Do you remember that chap – who was it? – one of the Dolabellas, I forget which – who had his hair permed with goats' piss because he thought it gave it a most distinguished sheen?"

But others were worried too. One was Calpurnia. She summoned me to her presence, taking care to do so on a night when she knew that Caesar was with Cleopatra.

I obeyed, without enthusiasm. As I've made clear, I always disliked Calpurnia. She has less charm than any woman I have ever known except the Madam who ran a certain brothel in Cadiz.

She looked even more than usually scraggy and nervous that evening, with her hair unsuitably dyed a dull red. She had been drinking too; her breath stank of acidulous white wine. Her hands, the fingers loaded with rings, were never still. They patted her hair, plucked at her neck, twisted around each other. She could not sit still, but, having directed me to a couch, immediately leapt up and flitted about the room, her gait unsteady as she embarked on a monologue.

"He's bewitched, that's what it is, that woman, whether she has actually given him some potion, I can't say, but she's bewitched him. And she's not really beautiful, you told me that yourself, and others have confirmed it, so what does he see in her if she's not bewitched him? I could strangle her with my own hands, yes I could, look, just like this, like wringing a chicken's neck, I'm told he calls her 'Chicken'. And this boy she has with her, this child, she says he's Caesar's son. I don't believe it myself, I've good reason not to, you know, think of all the women Caesar has had, and have any of the others claimed he has fathered a child? No, of course not, well there's that bitch Servilia, she's sometimes hinted, or let others hint, or not denied, that that toad Marcus is Caesar's child. But it's not true, because I don't believe he's . . . well, I've never said this to anyone and you're to keep it to yourself, but though I've never had children myself I had three miscarriages by my first husband, and Caesar has never made me pregnant. So, what conclusion do you draw from that? It's obvious, isn't it, he's sterile. Between you and me, that's why he's so determined to be a Great Man. It's to wipe out the shame of not being, well, normal, of not being able to father a child. That's the truth, and that little bitch has the brass neck to call the child Caesarion. And he purrs and goes along with it . . . but it's not true." (Calpurnia was talking nonsense. Caesar and his first wife had a daughter, Julia, later married to Pompey.) "And now he's set on this Parthian expedition, it's madness, I've told him that, but, well, you know him, you've known him all your life, yes of course I know your mother was one of his lovers, that doesn't worry me, it was before my time, do you think he's going mad?

"There's this prophecy, you must have heard it, that the Romans can only conquer Parthia under a king, and when I mention that to Caesar, he just laughs, and says prophecies are nonsense. And only yesterday he said, quite casually, we hadn't been quarrelling or anything, he just said, quick as boiled asparagus, 'I might divorce you and marry the Queen.' That would make him a sort of king, I suppose he thinks, a King of Egypt, imagine. You know how superstitious he can be when it suits him. It's always when it suits him, him, him, never any consideration for me, or anyone else. 'Look,' I said to him, 'you've a big enough mess to clear up here in Rome, why don't you get on with that and stop this Parthian nonsense?' and he laughed again and said I understood nothing about politics. But I understand a great deal, you know, I'm not a fool. I know you don't like me, Decimus Brutus, and perhaps I am not likeable, I have moments when I see that, but I'm not a fool. Your mother would have told you that. So, let me tell you what I see happening. They're going to kill him. I don't know who, but people are frightened of him now as they never were before, not just because he's so powerful but because he has really and truly started to go off his head. There's this clemency business. 'Look,' I said to him, 'you've got enemies, you know. You think because you've forgiven them for fighting on the other side, they are grateful. You're a fool, Caesar, don't you understand, the one thing people can't tolerate is that you have been in a position to say "I forgive you," and that you've said it as if you were some sort of superior being, a god of some kind. People can't stand that. In politics, if you have enemies and defeat them, you should get rid of them, finish, that's what Sulla did, yes, and your uncle-by-marriage Gaius Marius, they knew how people behave and feel. But you've forgotten. You think because you're a Great Man, everything will be easy for you and the world will arrange itself to suit you. It's not like that, Caesar.' Do you know I taste every dish that is put before him, myself, first, in case of poison, yes, I risk my own life for him at every meal, that's what I do. I put myself at risk, and is he grateful? Oh no, he laughs and tells me not to be foolish. Besides, I can only do that when he dines at home, or when we dine together in company. He was furious when I did it at Cicero's house last week. He said it was an insult to our host. 'Better to insult our host than have you poisoned,' I said. So he laughed again and said, 'Anyway, since everyone knows you have acquired this curious habit, you might reflect that someone might want to kill you, not me.' You see, he makes a joke of everything. That's mad, isn't it? And then he laughed again as if a new thought had struck him. 'What if they used a slow poison?' he said. 'You can't expect me to let my dinner go cold just to see whether you die of a slow poison. Besides it might be so slow it would kill us both . . .'

"Decimus Brutus," she paused, and stood over me, twisting her hands again, "there is only one way of saving Caesar. It is not enough to get the Queen out of Rome, for that will only make his Parthian mania worse. He will follow the bitch to Egypt, and then launch his campaign from there. It's all he thinks about. No, the bitch must die. I want you to fix it . . ."

She went on and on, explaining how I was to arrange to murder the Queen of Egypt (whom, in any case, you will remember, I rather liked). She had several proposals as to the best method. She wondered whether it might be possible to kill her by magic. There was a Bithynian she had heard of who was very skilled at issuing curses (if issuing is what you do with a curse) that were really and truly effective. Apparently the cursed person just turned his or her face to the wall and wasted away.

"In a matter of days, I'm told."

Unfortunately her informant hadn't been able to tell her exactly where this Bithynian wonder-worker was to be found. Somewhere in Trastevere, it seemed. It shouldn't be difficult for someone of my resources to seek him out. She would do it herself, but people might ask questions.

And so she went on and on, madder than those Eastern priests who derive gratification from mutilating themselves, madder even than the maddest Jews, who, as is well-known, sacrifice stolen children at the full moon. Actually, they don't, but for some reason Calpurnia brought up that subject too.

Why would that have been?

Of course, yes, she compared Caesar to them. She said he was madder even than they were.

I longed to ask: "If you really think him so mad, why are you prepared to go to so much trouble to save him?"

But I refrained. I knew she would reply that when Cleopatra was out of the way, Caesar would recover his wits.

Eventually I got away. I left the house with a new feeling in my breast. For the first time in my life I felt sorry for Caesar.

He had inspired many emotions in me, but I would never have thought that I could feel pity for him.

But who wouldn't pity a man married to Calpurnia?

No wonder he was so keen on the Parthian expedition.

It was a relief, for the moment an exquisite relief, to escape from Calpurnia into the turmoil of the night city. I mounted the Capitol and gazed down over the Forum. It was a cold night, the full moon threatening a frost. Stars sparkled, remote, inaccessible; how, I remember wondering, could men really imagine that the distribution of these spots of light at the hour of birth could determine a man's fate? I looked down, at the lines of wavering torches carried by slaves escorting the litters in which my equals were borne to and from dinner-parties. Was Caesar among them, swaying from Cleopatra's warm embraces to Calpurnia's bitter tongue?

The din was incessant, for the decree issued a few months earlier by Caesar, which prohibited all transport wagons save those of construction workers from passing through the city in the hours of daylight, and confined delivery carts and other wagons to the dark, ensured that no hour was free of the clatter of hoofs, the ring of iron wheels, the execrations of drivers jostling against each other and losing their way in the narrow alleys.

It was from this Rome of endless bustle, of uncontrollable animation, that Caesar wished to flee. I gazed across the valley at the dark shapes of pine trees on the Palatine; I turned aside to look across the river where the moon threw her light upon the Janiculum, and I could not understand the revulsion from the city which he experienced. Below me, in the warren of streets that confusedly scrambled towards the river, footpads and murderers might lurk, on the lookout for victims. Yet, Rome by night . . .

Is it because I know I shall never feel its pulse beat again that I think of it with tenderness now?

I descended from the Capitol, I remember, and found my way into a cheap tavern. My appearance silenced the company, till I indicated that I was there on my own business. The proprietor brought me a jug of wine, and after a few moments' consultation, escorted me to a back room lit by a single candle. There was a girl sitting in there, dressed only in a shift. The proprietor gestured towards her and left us. The girl stretched her arms upwards, got to her feet, took hold of the hem of her shift, and in a single languorous gesture drew it over her head and tossed it to the ground. The flickering candle cast strange dark shadows on her body, as she stood waiting my pleasure. She was very young. I laid my left hand on her shoulder, my right between her legs, feeling on my wrist the rough prickle of her bush. I eased her on to the couch and kissed her belly. Then, removing my toga, and folding it carefully at the head of the couch, I enjoyed her. She was silent and skilful and acquiescent. When I was spent, I lay beside her till the candle guttered. I gave her nothing but money. She gave me a glimpse of desolation. I would have slept there if I had not feared to do so.

When I had paid the proprietor, not informing him that I had also given a silver coin to the girl, I sent him to find me a night-watchman to guide me safely home.

I entered our matrimonial chamber. Longina awoke.

"You stink of some slut who has rubbed herself with fish oil, husband."

I kissed her breasts.

"Yes," I said, "that excites you."

She aroused me quickly. Our coupling was intense, energetic, violent. Longina was all eagerness. She took the lead. This time it was I who drifted into indifference first. She leaned over me and bit my neck. She lay on top of me. I put my arms around her, held her close, kissed as if our bones would bruise each other.

She was a wonderful animal. I was still alone, in a valley, as the thin light of the winter dawn crept upon us.

"Where is your father?" I said. "I must speak to him."

"In Campania, on his estate. Why must you speak to him?"

"Because I am lost," I said. "Because we are perhaps all lost."

"Husband," she said, "husband, husband, does any of that matter? Feel my belly. Soon, in a few months, you will feel our child stir there."

* * *

For two days, perhaps three, I lingered. I remained at home, with Longina. She held me with desire and an affection that was almost love. We Romans have never been uxorious. We are brought up to respect our womenfolk but we do not in general permit them any part in public life. Those who push themselves forward, and insist on being regarded as worthy of political consideration – women like Servilia and Calpurnia – are properly resented. They easily become objects of mockery. Longina had no such ambition. But what she wanted from me was what I could not honourably give. She was afraid for me. She would have had me abstain from public life, withdraw into a domesticity which all my peers would have regarded as contemptible.

"You know," she said, between kisses, "that I married you because my father told me to do so. I disliked you at the time. I found you remote and chilly. Besides, I adored Appius Pulcher even before I knew you. Of course he was never my lover before I was a married woman, because everyone knows that a lady has to be a virgin at the time of marriage, and I was very strictly brought up. But I still adored him, and when you went to Spain, I admitted him as my lover. And then you came back, and found us together, you remember."

"Yes, darling, I remember."

"And oh . . ." she put her arms round my neck and pressed herself upon me, "that morning I saw the difference between a boy, a pretty boy who was great fun, and a man who had achieved great things. And you made me feel a woman, not just a girl. And then you encouraged me to flirt with Caesar, yes, you did, don't try to deny it, and of course I was flattered, and, as you wanted me to, I went to bed with Caesar. Well, who wouldn't?"

"Who hasn't?"

"All right, quite so, but for a few days I hated you and despised you because you seemed to me to believe that Caesar's continuing goodwill towards you was more important than anything that there might be between us. But . . . Caesar . . . after the first time . . . do you know, husband, husband, husband . . ." Her tongue sought out mine . . .

(I torture myself with these memories, of her warmth, her presence, of which I dream in my nights which are ever more empty of all but despair . . . not fear, for I shall not admit that . . . but despair, of ever again . . . Artixes, with whom I try to amuse myself; in whose being I seek to recover something of sunshine . . . is nothing of comfort, when I recall, as I nightly do, Longina's embraces . . . lost . . . sacrificed . . . on account of . . . what? Duty? Ambition?)

"Husband" . . . hours later, in bed, warm, together, sticky with passion and happiness. "Husband, Caesar has had too many women, you know, too many, to feel anything for them. They are a convenience. He used me, as you might use, I don't know what, I have no gift for words, but there was a contempt in his treatment of me . . . do you think the Queen of Egypt feels that too . . .?"

"I think the Queen of Egypt is a girl who is in full charge of her own life, whose ambition is boundless, and who can out-Caesar . . ."

"Well, I couldn't. Whenever he left my bed, I felt diminished. Not because he had gone but because of the way he had finished with me. And the day came when he returned and I said 'no'. And do you know how he responded? He laughed . . . He laughed. Why do you think he did so?"

"You tell me."

"Because that is how Caesar has to treat any rebuff. Another man would be angry, but Caesar will not stoop to anger. He has to maintain his superiority. So he laughed. And the glance he gave me . . . horrible. Then he threw a jewel into my lap and left. Husband, Mouse-husband, I love you, do you know that . . . ? There, I've said it. I swore I never would. To tell someone you love them puts you in their power. But, please, please, please . . ."

Please what? What did she mean? I knew even then, and I knew even then that she was asking what was beyond me, and what, if I had acceded, would have caused her in time to despise me.

For this is something I have learned: that we love most what is denied us. That winter I adored Longina, I adore her memory still; and it is because I could not do as she wished. I could not give her what she asked for, my submission to her will; and if I had done so, she would have turned away from me. She loved me, had come to love me, for my virtue. And my virtue would have fled if I had submitted to the indulgence of uxoriousness.

There is only one character who is wholly contemptible in Homer, and that is Paris, who allowed his passion for Helen to unman him. And I think Helen came to despise Paris, as all who read the *Iliad* despise him.

Wasn't the intensity of those days in December all the greater, all the more invigorating, all the more delightful because we both knew that the gods decree that men and women must demand of each other what the other cannot in honour give?

Our idyll was broken. It was broken first by a letter I received from Octavius in Greece.

Mouse:

Rumours reach me which are disturbing. You will understand that I must speak carefully for it is foolish to give credence to rumour. Nevertheless certain rumours, which are persistent, threaten my future career, in which I know you continue to take a lively and affectionate interest. Maecenas, whom you dislike, is a wise counsellor as well as a fruitful source of gossip, and the word that reaches him is that the paternity of a certain child may be acknowledged. Very evidently, if this were done, which naturally appears improbable, my own position would be impaired. My uncle is of course the most honourable of men, and would not, I am certain, contemplate such an acknowledgment which has, I am certain, no basis in truth. Yet these rumours persist. Since your counsel is properly so highly valued by all parties concerned, I cannot believe that any action would be taken without prior seeking of your advice. Therefore, I write to you, not in any trepidation, but rather because rumour is insidious; it can lead to unpredictable consequences, which, however unpredictable, could nevertheless be to some extent anticipated as being to my (and perhaps even your) disadvantage. I can well understand that the lady in the case has powerful reasons for urging the course of action which is rumoured. Can I beg you to make any enquiries that may prudently and sagaciously be undertaken? Would it, I wonder, be wise for me to abandon my studies, delightful and stimulating as they are, and return forthwith to Rome to protect my interests? Naturally of course I shall acquiesce in whatever is determined, and if I have to seek another route to fortune, then I shall do so with all the resolution and intelligence at my command. But I wish to take no action now which you, as my valued friend and adviser, would deem precipitate, unwise or unnecessary.

I send you warm greetings and the assurance of my affection.

Octavius

I wondered, of course, who had been kind enough to pass on the rumour that Caesar contemplated the acknowledgment of Caesarion as his son. Despite the suggestion that it came via Maecenas, I couldn't help but suspect Calpurnia. I could see that she might consider it in her interest to stir up trouble between Caesar and his nephew and presumptive heir. It could only help her campaign to bring the rumours about Caesarion into public notice, for the more discussion there was, the more Caesar would realise how offensive the Roman nobility would find it if he even hinted that he might make a half-foreign bastard his heir.

So, I replied soothingly:

My dear Octavius:
There would seem to be something fretful about the air of Greece. It stimulates the imagination and disturbs the judgment. The rumours you have heard are only rumours. What you fear will not come to pass. You say you trust my judgment: very well, rest assured that the influences you fear are exaggerated.

On the other hand, I hear that your friend Maecenas enjoys three new catamites a day.

Can this rumour be true?

I remain your dear friend than whom you have none warmer.

D. Iunius Brutus

There was nothing, I thought, compromising in my letter, which would certainly be intercepted at some point, and a copy sent to Caesar. If he learned in this way that Maecenas was a disreputable associate for young Octavius, so much the better.

But he must have known that already. That thought made me wonder if there was truth in Mark Antony's claim that Octavius himself had been enjoyed by Caesar.

All the same my gibe was a mistake. I would have been wiser to cultivate Maecenas, however I despised him. I am sure that he poisoned Octavius' ear against me. Certainly that was the last letter I ever had from Octavius which spoke to me in terms of trust and affection. I should have realised that Maecenas had taken my place as the principal influence over the boy – he had the advantage of being with him, and of being addicted to every vice, something always attractive, even glamorous to the young. Had I realised this, I should have set myself to flatter Maecenas (who, like all effeminates, is peculiarly susceptible to flattery). In the manner of his type, he is also jealous, malicious and vengeful. He made it impossible later for me to effect a reconciliation with Octavius. But for his malice, I might not find myself in my present unhappy state.

And another thing: it occurred to me that if Calpurnia was right, and Caesar was indeed now sterile, then Caesarion might be my son, not his, the fruit of my one luscious and lustful encounter with the Queen. The dates would have fitted just as well in either case. The thought amused me, but it was one which I considered wiser not to share with Longina: or indeed with Caesar.

CHAPTER

15

During the Festival of the Saturnalia, in the dark afternoon of the shortest day of the year, Mark Antony arrived at my house, half-cut and still crapulous from the previous night's debauch. He demanded wine and leered at Longina, who properly retired to her own chamber.

Antony stretched himself on a couch, drank the wine the slave had brought in one gulp and held out the goblet to be refilled.

"You're a lucky bugger, Mouse, always were," he said, and leaned over sideways and vomited on the marble.

He watched with a smile curling his lips – a smile that contradicted the bleariness of his gaze – while the slave cleaned up the mess.

"Sorry about that. More wine's the answer. Keep bunging the stuff down till some of it sticks, I always say."

"Well, Antony, you are always welcome to my hospitality, within reason."

"Cagey bugger, aren't you, always were. Tell you what I've been trying to decide. Am I celebrating or am I not?"

He gulped more wine, steadied himself on his elbow.

"That's better. Send this little brat away. We don't want slaves to hear what we have to say. Bloody gossips, every man jack of them. Fuck off, do you hear, and leave the sodding wine. That's better."

He poured himself another measure with a trembling hand that made the jug rattle against the goblet.

"D'you understand what I said? Am I celebrating or am I not?"

"You tell me, Antony. You ought to know after all."

"Ah, crafty . . . crafty . . . but that's the point, I don't know.

So I come to you, little Mouse, to find out. And when I say 'I', I include you. Are we celebrating, or are we not? Here, you're not drinking. Bloody drink, will you. It's uncivilised to leave a man to drink on his own. Uncivilised and ungenerous. But I'm generous, so I'm offering you one."

"Very well. And let me answer your question. You appear to be celebrating, but not perhaps very happily."

"Got it in one. I knew I was right. Said to myself, bloody Mouse'll see the bloody point. I am celebrating, been celebrating for two, three days, maybe four, but not happy. Good. So next question, next question . . . Very diffy one. Why? Got everything to be happy about, don't I. Antony starts his consulship in ten days, maybe a fortnight, lost count 's a matter of fact. But not happy. Why?"

"I can't answer that. You ought to be happy. You'll make a fine consul."

(As long as you can contrive to be at least half-sober at the necessary official ceremonies, I thought.)

"Mouse, you've let me down. Little Mouse, let old Antony down. Never would have thought it . . . Tell you why, give you the answer myself. We won the bloody civil war, didn't we? Yes, can't deny that. But we're losing the peace, that's why. All those buggers on the other side, like your esteemed father-in-law, like that prig of a cousin of yours, Marcus Brutus, are slipping back into power. By Hercules, there was a fucking Augean stable to be cleansed, and nothing has been done. There are plots against Caesar, Antony, loyal old Antony, goes and tells the General, and he laughs, says, go and sleep it off, there's a good chap. So: answer. I'm not celebrating . . ."

And then he fell asleep.

I am aware that throughout this memoir I have presented Antony in an unfavourable light: as uncouth, boorish, impetuous, wrong-headed. He was all these things. But he was also more, and different, something which many who had not served alongside him failed to realise. His charm was formidable. When he chose to exert it, the radiance of his smile, the eagerness with which he charged at life, lit up the existence of those around him. And he was no fool. He said many foolish things, but he was also capable of flashes of unexpected intelligence. And strangest of all, this man who appeared so heedless of the impression he made, who even at times seemed to delight in presenting himself as disreputably as possible, was also possessed of a rare sensitivity: a sensitivity that quivered, sunbeam-like, in response to the moods of others. This was one reason why his soldiers adored him. There is no general men will follow so eagerly as one who has an intuitive understanding of how they feel at any moment. And Antony had that quality. Even in drunkenness, he was never cut off – as I have seen other drunkards separated – from the way others felt. He was an utterly social being, one who could not be imagined in isolation. And because he was this, he understood far more than those who are wrapped up in their own concerns ever do.

Now he opened one eye.

"Fuck the Queen of Egypt, I say. But when I tried, she said, fuck yourself, old boy."

He closed the eye again and began to snore.

If Antony believed that men like my father-in-law and Marcus Brutus were plotting against Caesar, he was almost certainly correct.

This left me in an alarming position. As Caesar's closest adherent, known to be the favourite among his surviving generals, was I the object of such a plot also? Was it possible to plot against Caesar alone, and leave the Caesarian party unmolested?

The next afternoon I encountered Antony in the Forum. He had just emerged from a barber's shop, spruced, shaved, pomaded and sober.

"Afraid I was a bit of a bore yesterday, old boy. Sorry and all that. Hope I didn't say anything I shouldn't, specially to your lovely wife."

"Not at all. You indicated you hadn't got far with the Queen of Egypt, that's all."

"Did I now? Between you and me and the gatepost, old boy, she's a bit more than I'd care to tackle. She may be only a child, but she's a man-eating one, don't you know."

"Antony," I said, taking his arm, "this Parthian campaign. Will he go ahead with it?"

"Oh, I should think so, wouldn't you? The old boy's bored, you know."

"And after it?"

"After it? Well, I should think it might be the end. First rule of war: don't invade Parthia. I've tried telling him that. Imagine you've done the same in different words. Doesn't do a bit of bloody good, does it. So, it's us for the desert song, and us for . . . who knows what?"

"That's my opinion. So how do we set about stopping it?"

He lifted his head, like a lion sniffing the breeze.

"Wind's blowing cold from the East. Think you can stop that, old boy?"

I had to admit Antony was right. My fears were intensified when I learned that various members of the old Pompeian party, including some who had affected to be most closely reconciled to Caesar's rule – for that of course is what it was, despite the punctiliousness with which the traditional posts in the Republic were filled – that some of these, as I say, were urging the Parthian campaign on him. The ignominy of Crassus' defeat was a stain on Rome's reputation, they said, that must be wiped out; and Caesar was the only man capable of doing so. This of course was music to his ears, and he did not reflect that these men urged him to the enterprise in the hope that he would fail.

I confess that the same thought had also occurred to me: that Caesar's death on the Parthian campaign might be the most honourable way out of the difficulties that his continuing and ever-growing ascendancy was now so evidently presenting. But it was not a way of escape that I could honourably dwell on.

Instead, I went to see him at his own house, choosing an hour in the morning when he would not be over-tired as a result of the business he had been transacting, for I had noticed that in recent months, he was more amenable to reason in the first part of the day; and that when he was tired his mind delighted in ever more extravagant flights.

He received me kindly, as was his wont, and dismissed his secretaries when I said I had important matters which I wished to raise.

For a moment we sat in silence. All at once he looked an old man. It was the first time that thought had ever struck me, and I experienced a wave of tenderness and affection.

"Well, Mouse," he said, "it must be a grave matter that brings you here at this time of the day when you know I am accustomed to be at work."

"It is precisely of work that I wish to speak."

I then explained to him the causes of my anxiety: that it was now nine months since the Battle of Munda; that there could be no question but that the civil wars were at last concluded; but that it seemed to me that we were no nearer a resolution of the problems that had caused the wars.

He frowned when I said that, as if to remind me that in his opinion, and as he had so often asserted, the cause of the wars had been the determination of his enemies to destroy him.

So, to prevent him from raising the point and thus provoking an argument that might divert me from the course on which I had determined, I interpolated an acknowledgment that this had been the immediate cause of the wars. That of course, I admitted, had properly been removed. But I hastened to add that we both realised, as historians and politicians well versed in these matters, that the underlying causes of the wars went beyond personalities and turned on the question of the Constitution. Now Caesar had been granted the title of Perpetual Dictator, which ensured that authority could be maintained in Rome and throughout the Empire. Yet I could not see, I said, with all the respect that I could muster, how a perpetual dictatorship could answer.

"I must warn you," I said, "that there are even some who put it about that you wish to be crowned king. It is naturally a rumour which I deny whenever I hear it."

Again he frowned, then waved a hand to indicate that I was to continue.

Very well, I said; he had made minor reforms. He had enlarged the Senate, and although many of our fellow members of the old nobility complained that those he had admitted were scarcely gentlemen, I was in full agreement with him as to the value of the enlargement. Likewise, I was in favour of his decision to increase the number of praetors and quaestors, not only because it gave more men the rewards of office, but because there was more public business of a greater variety of sorts to be transacted. And yet such reforms could hardly be thought sufficient to tackle fundamental problems.

I hurried on here, for I could see that he was becoming bored, and I did not wish to exhaust his patience.

And now, I said, he was engaged in preparing for war against Parthia. There were good reasons for such an undertaking. Nevertheless it must distract us from other business for two or three years, and in this interval, with Caesar absent from Rome, it could not be imagined that any of the causes of our discontents would be removed. The Parthian expedition, dangerous in itself, was therefore in a sense an act of evasion. I spoke respectfully, of course, but it seemed to me that the most urgent task before him was the repair of our fractured State . . .

I paused, dismayed. He had ceased to listen. His gaze had drifted away. He had withdrawn himself, perhaps into boredom, perhaps into dreams. Then, made aware of my silence, he gave me a smile that had all its old accustomed charm.

"The Queen of Egypt tells me that the title of King would be of great service in the East. I care nothing for the nonsense of titles, but she may be right. Naturally, many in Rome would object, for men grow fond of their old ways and hate innovation. Perhaps anyway, in time, the name Caesar will come to mean more than 'King'. Who can tell? But I have been wondering whether I might not permit myself to be entitled 'King' beyond the boundaries of Italy, while retaining here in Rome simply the style of 'Perpetual Dictator'. It might be a way out of the dilemma. What do you think, Mouse?"

What I thought was that he had been paying no attention to my argument at all. Nevertheless, I replied:

"I do not see how that would solve anything, though of course I understand the Queen's argument comes naturally to her. But the point, Caesar, turns not on titles – and you are quite right in believing that everyone in Rome would resent the assumption of the name of 'King'; it turns on the relationship between you, and the immeasurable power you now wield, on the one hand, and the best means of reviving the traditional institutions of the Republic on the other."

"You don't understand, Mouse. Perhaps you have been listening to Cicero. I revere Cicero myself, and am delighted to converse with him, so long as we confine the topics of conversation to literature and philosophy. Incidentally, he is doing useful work there, finding Latin equivalents for Greek terms which are necessary to the development of the subject. But when he talks of the Constitution, he is talking of something as mythical as the Minotaur. For all his brilliance, he doesn't understand that history is a living thing. When he speaks of the Constitution in terms of reverence, I admire his sentiments, but I know that he is talking of something which ceased to exist before he was born. What does he really believe in? He seems to think that our armies should be commanded by a noble officer – once it was Pompey, now perforce it is Caesar – while Rome, Italy and the pacified provinces are governed or administered by the Senate under the guidance of honourable, public-spirited conservatives prepared themselves to be guided by his golden oratory. He should know that such an assembly doesn't exist, even if it once did, and he should be modest enough to acknowledge that his own record is littered with gross blunders and misapprehensions."

He rose, and took a turn around the room. He still moved, even in his middle fifties, with that athleticism which his soldiers had so admired.

"You should realise, Mouse, for you have followed Caesar, that for the last two, even three generations, our Republic – that wonderful, resounding, moribund name – has proved itself incapable of performing the simplest and most necessary part of government: the maintenance of law and order here in Rome. During this period more Romans – including members of the nobility – have fallen in civil wars, been killed in street battles, or just assassinated – than in any foreign wars. That is not on account of my ambition, or Pompey's ambition, or my uncle Gaius Marius' ambition, or even the ambition of the loathsome Sulla; it has been because the old institutions are no longer answerable to circumstances . . .

"You call for reforms, Mouse. I have no reform to offer. Once, perhaps, I too thought things might be restored simply by the eradication of abuses. No longer. Such hopes are but an idle dream. You imply that there is resentment because I have appointed consuls, praetors and other magistrates, and made the elections into a merely formal ceremony of confirmation.

But you know, in your heart, that for longer than our lifetime, these elections have been either fraudulent or farcical. They have also been dangerous, for they have provoked the violence which government should restrain, and which the Republic has failed to restrain.

"And so, I say . . . the Republic is dead. You cannot breathe life into a corpse. What is left is a sham, and a dangerous sham.

"Things must change. But they will change gradually, as men grow accustomed to new realities. The first reality is that power now rests with the army and whoever controls it. Well, fortunately for Rome, Caesar controls it. As long as Caesar controls the army, Caesar controls Rome. That is the reality against which Cicero's dreams shatter themselves like a piece of pottery thrown against a wall. Time, that is the watchword. Time and I against any two; that is my faith.

"Yes, I shall go to Parthia, because it is necessary. What I choose to call myself is immaterial. In Rome, I am Caesar, and Caesar rules. In the provinces Caesar may be king, even a god, it is not important. What Rome needs is a period of calm, free from civil strife. Only Caesar can provide it, and Caesar can do so only while he controls and commands the army. That is reality, Mouse, I insist on it.

"So, don't listen to Cicero, there's a good chap. He represents the past. The future is quite different, because it will be based on an understanding of the ultimate reality of power: the sword. Naturally the Senate will survive; has Caesar not refreshed it, even as you admit yourself? So will the magistracies for there is necessary work for them to do. But remember: the strong govern the world, and Caesar is the strongest, while he commands the strength of the legions.

"Nobody will ever hold power in Rome again unless he commands that support. If he relinquishes command to others, he will perish. Rome is an Empire, not a city-state. Tell me, in your heart, don't you find it absurd that a mob of greasy unwashed plebeians should be entrusted with the choice of their government, when that government has the responsibility for the whole Mediterranean world . . . and after my next campaign for the government of Parthia also . . ."

*   *   *

I left in despair, for he had sketched a future in which liberty was dead, and in which honour was at the disposal of whoever had seized power . . . It was not for that reason, not to achieve this, that I had fought from the Rubicon to Greece and saved the day at Munda.

CHAPTER

16

Although the year began traditionally on the Kalends of March (a date altered by Caesar's reform of the calendar) my father-in-law, Caius Cassius, was accustomed to throw a party at the January Kalends, for, as he rightly said, "Janus, the guardian spirit of entrances and the god presiding over the beginning of all things and all deeds, deserves our respect." The fact that the party, coming so soon after the debauchery of the Saturnalia, had been known to revive the spirit of that festival and thus degenerate into something which might fairly be described as an orgy, didn't alter my father-in-law's determination to honour the god.

His party in this momentous year took on an unusual significance, for Cassius had pruned his guest-list of all those who were known to be the most devoted to Caesar, even though, as a precaution, he felt it necessary to invite the dictator himself.

Perhaps my presence reassured Caesar that he was not among enemies for he was in genial form throughout his fairly brief stay at Cassius' house. Some say it was the presence of my cousin Marcus Brutus which calmed the agitation he revealed when he first looked round the room, but this is not so: he was on bad terms with Markie on account of rumours that my cousin was ambitious to replace him in the dictatorship.

"Surely Brutus can wait till the breath is out of this frail body," he said.

Besides, any of those present – and alas, some are no longer among us – could confirm that it was to me that the dictator directed most of his conversation that evening. Cassius had asked me to make sure that Caesar was happily engaged, and of course I was delighted to oblige. My father-in-law knew very well that the dictator neither liked nor trusted him; and so, after a brief and ceremonious greeting, he was pleased to see me take him off his hands, as it were.

Caesar departed early, saying that, however festive the occasion, he had work to do.

"Work with the Queen of Egypt," young Cinna sniggered, as soon as the dictator was out of earshot.

After we had eaten and drunk – the sucking-pig was especially delicious, I recall, because, Cassius assured me, the sows on his farms near Tivoli were fed a milk diet which ensured that their own supply of milk was both plentiful and rich – Cassius dismissed the slaves, having first ascertained that they had left an ample supply of wine, both white and red. It was one of his maxims that, in honour of Janus, it was proper to drink alternate glasses.

There were some twenty of us left, reclining on couches and all at our apparent ease. Yet, when the slaves departed, a tremor ran round the room, as if we all sensed the imminency of something of great moment. I may say that my father-in-law had given me no warning of his intentions, which is proof of the confidence in my virtue which he had learned to feel.

We were a varied party. Let me stress that from the start. Cassius himself and Markie had been Pompeians; they had fought (or, in the case of Markie, found safer occupation) at Pharsalus. Quintus Ligarius was a Pompeian, pardoned (as I have related) as a result of Cicero's eloquence. Decimus Turullius and Quintus Cassius (from Parma), more obscure figures, had also fought in Pompey's army. There was the young Cato, less gloomy and uncouth than his father, more intelligent too, as devoted to the Republic, but with a truer appreciation of what was possible; a young man indeed of some charm with his chestnut hair and melancholy expression. He was of course now Markie's brother-in-law, though I had observed with some amusement earlier that he had removed himself from my cousin's conversation, and not only, I was certain, because of Markie's unfortunate habit of occasionally spitting in his interlocutor's face; this was due to a childhood infirmity which he had never overcome, rather than to bad manners. Probably Cato knew this; so he had, I imagined, removed himself simply because he was bored. I couldn't blame him for that. Another

Pompeian was Lucius Cornelius Cinna, married to the Great One's daughter.

But I had old colleagues of my own there: Casca, of course, Lucius Tillius Cimber and Caius Trebonius, men with whom I had fought side by side. There were others whose position was more dubious, and whom I would be disinclined to trust: Ser Sulpicius Galba, well-born, skilled in the military art, but of a sour and truculent disposition. I knew he hated Caesar because Caesar had refused his request to be nominated as consul for any of the immediately succeeding years. More disreputable was Lucius Minucius Basilus, whom Caesar had denied the governorship of a province on the grounds that he was unfit for the responsibility; instead the dictator had offered him money. Basilus claimed to have been insulted, but he took the money all the same.

I knew from my father-in-law's manner that this was not a purely social gathering. Though he had been polite and courteous throughout the reception and the meal, I was aware that his nerves were drawn taut as a bowstring.

"Balbus told me an odd thing the other day," my neighbour, the younger Cinna, said. "You know, Balbus the banker."

"Of course I know Balbus. What was this story?"

"Well, it seems that some of the veterans who had been discharged and granted farms in the region of Capua were breaking up some ancient tombs to obtain stone with which to build their new farmhouses. Now it seems that one of these tombs belonged to Capys, founder of the city, and on it they discovered an inscription which read: 'Disturb the bones of Capys and a man of Trojan stock will be murdered by his friends and kinsfolk and later avenged at great cost to Italy.' What do you make of that, eh?"

"Not a lot," I replied. "After all, I suppose all we Romans may lay claim to being of Trojan stock, in some remote manner, and there are Romans murdered by their friends and kinsmen any day of the week."

"No, but," he said, "naturally I'm not superstitious, but it makes you think, doesn't it?"

"Does it?" said Casca. "Well, that's quite an achievement, my dear. On the other hand, once you start heeding old wives' tales of that sort, you'll never come to the end of it. Why, only yesterday my fat old mother told me a story which she'd had on the best authority – her manicurist's, I suppose – that a herd of horses which our Lord and Master dedicated to the River Rubicon, on account, you know, of its significance in his career, crossed the stream – a miserable ditch as you would know if you had been with us – and began to eat the grass on the other side. As soon as they did so, my ma was told, they evinced a great repugnance, and some of them actually started to be sick."

"Good heavens, that's extraordinary."

"Isn't it? It would be more extraordinary still, my dear, if Caesar had ever dedicated a herd of horses to that beastly little stream. But can you imagine him taking the trouble to do so?"

"It would be still more extraordinary," I said, "if any such horses, even if they existed, had been sick. But horses can't, you know. That's why colic can kill them so easily. If you get a disturbed stomach you vomit. So does a dog. But a horse can't. End of story."

"Well," young Cinna said, "I admit I don't know anything about horses, can't stand the brutes, bite at one end and kick at the other as they say. It's not that I'm frightened of them, it's just that they have an unfortunate effect on me. So I didn't know that. But, don't you see, that makes the story more extraordinary still. It's against nature, and when something happens that's against nature, that's really significant."

"Oh dear," I said.

That was the sort of story, and that the sort of conversation, common in Rome that winter. Credulity ran riot.

Our talk was interrupted by Cassius banging the handle of a knife on the table to attract our attention.

Then he said:

"I don't intend to make a speech, my friends. As some of you know, I detest after-dinner speeches. That's why Cicero isn't here." (An obedient titter ran round the table.) "But I have a few things I want to say to you. They are not entirely safe things to say. If you listen to me, we could change our lives, and restore liberty to Rome. So I'm asking two things of you, before we start. First, I would ask anyone who isn't prepared to take the responsibility of action to leave us now . . ."

Nobody moved.

"Good, I've judged you well. Second, I would ask you all to swear, on the honour and reputation of your ancestors, and in the name of whichever gods you reverence, that everything said here tonight from this moment will remain confidential, that you will speak of it to nobody who is not now with us, unless you have my permission, and that you will not discuss it beyond this circle or in other company. Will you swear? Will you swear such an oath?"

Again nobody moved, nobody spoke.

I was the first to rise to my feet and swear a formal oath in the terms requested. One after another, some slowly as if with fear, each man rose and followed suit, most of them employing the very words which first Cassius, and then I myself, had uttered. At last only my cousin Markie was left seated.

"Marcus Junius Brutus, heir to one of the noblest names in Roman history, will you swear . . ."

Markie crumbled bread.

"This disturbs me," he said. "I have indeed been much disturbed of late. I am vexed with perplexities, ideas which I feel it proper to keep to myself. Many of you will know that I love honour more than I fear death. But now, I suspect that you are about to urge a course upon us to which I cannot honourably reconcile myself."

"Come, Brutus," Cassius said, "there is no man in Rome held in higher respect than yourself. I have heard people say that they wished the noble Brutus had eyes to see what is plain to others. I'm afraid you are too bound up in your own perplexities. I can't force you to swear, but I can urge you, even beg you. We would not wish to be deprived of your counsel."

"Well, naturally" – the bread was now in crumbs – "I'm honoured that you should think so well of me. But suppose I hear something said in this room tonight which honour would urge me to reveal, and suppose I have bound myself by an oath to remain silent, then that will make my perplexities worse. Cassius, you know I love and respect you, but I cannot deviate from my sense of what is right . . ."

("Little prig," whispered Casca, "fucking little cowardly prig.")

"So, with respect, Cassius, I cannot bring myself to offer the promise you demand. Therefore, I think I should take my leave.

Which I do, wishing you all well, and sound judgment in whatever you choose to deliberate."

He folded his napkin and got to his feet. He went round the table and embraced Cassius, and so departed from us. It has always been said that he left with dignity. My memory is that he scuttled from the room like a frightened rabbit.

The young Cato looked for a moment as if he would follow his brother-in-law, glanced across the table, caught my eye, and remained where he stood. Only one young man, whose name I did not know (it was Favonius, I later discovered) chose to follow Markie.

When they had gone, Cassius resumed his couch and motioned to us to do likewise. Then he began to speak.

"I am sorry that Marcus Brutus, whom I admire as I am sure you all do, has felt unable to remain with us. He is a man I honour and respect. Perhaps, you will say, he is over-scrupulous.

"There was another man with us earlier today of whom that cannot be said. You all know that I speak of Caesar. Men have said many things against Caesar but I doubt if anyone has ever accused him of being over-scrupulous . . .

"I would ask you to think of Caesar and of the relationship in which we now stand to him, in which Rome now stands to him.

"I can't tell what you and others think of the life we lead, but speaking for myself, I would as willingly cease to breathe as continue to live in . . . awe . . . of a man no different from myself.

"I was born in liberty, as was Caesar. I was born his equal. We are men like each other, heated by the same sun in summer, shivering in the same cold winter blast.

"Equals, did I say? I remember once when we were young Caesar challenged me to swim across the Tiber. The river ran high, but I plunged in regardless. Then I heard a cry behind me, and looking over my shoulder, saw that Caesar was in difficulties. And so, just as Aeneas, our noble ancestor, carried Anchises from the flames of burning Troy, so I bore Caesar from the turbulent water, brought him to the bank, and safety. You may imagine I have often dwelled on that moment since.

"And others have performed similar feats. My son-in-law, Decimus Junius Brutus Albinus, here today, why . . ." he turned his gaze directly on me, ". . . why, did you not rescue Caesar from the storm of battle at Munda?"

"Yes, I can make that claim."

"And now," Cassius said, dropping his voice to a whisper, as actors do when they wish to silence the murmurings in the theatre, "and now, this Caesar is a god, and Cassius or Decimus Brutus, or Metellus Cimber who has done great things in battle, or Casca, or young Cato sprung from the noblest stock of Rome, or any of you here – any, in the Senate, camp or temple, must bow and bend and scrape, and flush with pleasure, if Caesar should condescend to nod his head at us.

"Is that a way to live, an honourable way?

"I remember too that Labienus, the noble, honourable Labienus, told me once of an occasion when Caesar fell sick in Gaul, and lay on his pallet bed and called for water. It was pathetic, like a little girl.

"Some of us have seen him suffer fits, have seen him shake, have seen this god tremble, all control departed from his limbs.

"This god . . . this man like us . . .

"And now he is the eighth wonder of the world. Why, he bestrides the world as the great Colossus you have seen at Rhodes, and we others, little men, men become petty inconsiderable things, must walk about peering between his legs, as if we searched for a dishonourable grave.

"Caesar talks of Destiny. There is no word more often on his lips. The stars, the stars, as if it was decreed by Fate that we should be subordinate, subservient, subdued.

"But I say . . ." and again he broke off, again he rapped the table with the hilt of his knife, again he paused, holding us, while each man both longed and feared to hurry on the conclusion to which he was inexorably driving. "I say, the fault does not lie in the stars. It lies rather in ourselves.

"What meat has Caesar fed on that he has grown so great?

"If our ancestors, the men who broke Hannibal, laid Carthage waste, pursued the great King Mithridates to his doom, conquered Spain and Africa and Asia, if these men whom we revere, could see us now? If they could observe our fallen State? If they could see how abject we now seem? If they could see how Caesar, a man of our own stock, a gambler, debtor, lecher, one who has broken the historic links that held the State together, if they could see how he lords us, dominates us, holds us as his . . . subjects? If they saw all this, would they laugh or weep, or weeping laugh and laughing weep?

"This is the question that I put to you tonight: are you not ashamed, as I feel shame, that we have come to this abject condition? Or are you ready to bow down and worship Caesar, call him God, even King, regard him as a creature of a wholly different order from ourselves, his fellow nobility of Rome?"

Then he was silent, very pale, sipped wine, looked hard at each of us in turn. One by one eyes fell away, unable to hold his gaze, and there was silence. It was broken by the one man who had not met his gaze, had not done so for the excellent reason that his eyes were closed as he lay on his couch, in apparent indifference: Casca, of course.

"Words, words, words, Cassius, Cassius, Cassius, you have out-Ciceroed Cicero. There was no need indeed to ask the old man here tonight, for he couldn't have given a better exhibition of rhetoric than you have treated us to . . ."

"Do you think I mean nothing but words?"

"Can't say for sure, old thing, can't say." Casca hauled himself half upright, slapped his belly. "I am fat, fat, fat. That was a good dinner you have given us, Cassius. Caesar thinks only lean men are dangerous, and I am fat."

Metellus Cimber interrupted:

"Enough of this comedy. You have given us much to think of, Cassius. If it is any satisfaction to you, you have brought the blush of shame to my cheek."

"And to mine."

"And mine."

"And mine . . . alas."

"Well, Casca?" Cassius said.

"Put away shame a long time ago, old dear. Give me comfort, wine and a bit of slap and tickle – kill my creditors or let them live as long as you keep them off – and what more could Casca seek from life? I am fat, you see. Words, words, words. Well, I'll reply in words – the proof of the pudding's in the eating – how's that for a proverb? Your cook has a light hand with the pastry, Cassius. Congratulate him from me on those lobster patties . . ."

Again Metellus Cimber broke the silence:

"What you have said, Cassius, can only be a beginning. I would wish Marcus Brutus had stayed. That's a man whose opinion I value. But you have given us all much to think of. Therefore I invite all here tonight to dine with me in seven days' time. Meanwhile we shall ponder these matters, consult our hearts, consciences, interests, whatever; and observe the oath of silence which we swore. Casca, you will find my cook, an Armenian, has a light hand with pastry too, and a deft imagination when it comes to the filling. So, shall we conclude here, and resume our discussion as I have invited?"

We all assented, but, as we made to leave, Cassius beckoned to me, and laid a restraining hand on young Cato's shoulder. When the three of us were alone, he said:

"An interesting response, better than I had dared hope for. But if we could have another word before you follow our friends, I should be grateful."

So we resumed our couches. Cassius poured more wine.

"Mouse," he said, "you know Caesar better than any of us."

"I owe him much."

"He is as greatly in debt to you."

"Well, I won't deny that."

"You knew what I was driving at . . . and yet you stayed."

I spat out an olive stone.

"There are loyalties and there is loyalty."

"What do you mean?" Cato said.

"One owes something to one's friends and benefactors, one owes more to oneself, one owes most to Rome."

"Precisely my thought," Cassius said.

"Oh, you made that clear. I do no more than echo what you said. For months I have been seeking an alternative. I see none."

"If Caesar takes the name of King," Cato said, "the people themselves will quit us of responsibility. They will tear him apart."

"They might," I said. "In any case, he will not assume the title, not yet, not here, not in Rome. If he sets off for Parthia, then, yes, somewhere in the East he will permit himself, with a deprecating smile, to be called King. Perhaps there he will share a throne with the Queen of Egypt. It would be a long campaign, two or three years. In that time the people may grow accustomed to the title. Who knows? But he may never use the name in

Rome. Caesar is indifferent to mere words. He suggested to me recently that the name 'Caesar' might itself come to have a grander sound than the name of 'King'. He may well be right. When I said I saw no alternative to what you, Cassius, did not quite bring yourself to propose this evening, that is because I have already explored the possibility of abdication, that he might follow the example of Sulla, and retire into private life. I did not mention Sulla to him, of course, since we all know that he detests the very name, but even the hint displeased him. He is determined to keep hold of power. He is determined to conquer Parthia."

"He might not return from Parthia," Cato said.

"He might not," Cassius said, "but it is a risk we cannot take, for if he did return, in triumph, then . . ."

He swept his hand, palm uppermost, before him, then turned his thumb down.

"Rome, all of us, in his grip for ever, liberty dead for ever. Cato, you and I stand in the same relation to Marcus Brutus . . ." This was true, for as Cato's sister was married to Brutus, so also Cassius himself had taken Brutus' half-sister as his own third wife the previous summer. "If you are committed to the enterprise I have suggested, Cato, I wish you would urge it on Brutus. I shall myself in private conversation. His nature is slow, reluctant, I was not surprised when he left us tonight. But we must have Brutus. Will you speak to him?"

"Certainly. I shall speak to my sister Porcia also. As you know, she was devoted to our father, has indeed made almost a cult of his memory. Consequently she loathes Caesar more than anyone I know. And she has great influence on her husband."

"Excellent," Cassius said. "I would trust few women with our intentions, but I am ready to make an exception of Cato's daughter."

When young Cato had left us, my father-in-law looked on me with something approaching affection.

"You are ready to bear the accusations of treachery that will be levelled at you?"

"Yes," I said.

"I know you don't share my regard for your cousin Marcus, nor the general high opinion in which he is held. I believe you underestimate him. Sometimes indeed I wonder if you are jealous of the golden opinions he wins."

"Jealous of Markie? No. But I question his capacity, and I don't see why you think him so essential."

"You have chosen the right word. I do think him essential. So much so that I believe we have no chance of success if he refuses to join us. Oh, we might succeed in our immediate aim. We don't need him for that. But it is precisely because he is held in such high esteem by the people."

"Oh yes, as the model of 'antique Roman virtue' – Markie. Yes, it baffles me."

"And by the senators . . . so I truly believe that his adherence is necessary if we are to succeed in what must be our wider aim – the restoration of the Free State. If he joins us, our act will be considered disinterested. If he refuses, our own regard for the Republic will not be credited. So I must ask you to lay aside your prejudice, and woo him also."

"It goes against the grain."

"Nevertheless . . ."

"And he will blunder, I warn you."

"Nevertheless . . ."

"Very well, I submit, reluctantly, to your judgment."

"Thank you. How is Longina?"

"Blooming, and a joy. Indeed, we are now so happy that I could easily be tempted to subside into contented domesticity."

"No, son-in-law, you are too much the Roman. And it is the noblest and most Roman of enterprises to which we have now committed ourselves."

We both rose. He embraced me, and I departed into the cloudy night.

CHAPTER

17

"Let the dice fly high." Caesar's words came back to me many times in the days that followed. "Let the dice fly high" – no matter how they land. It perplexed me – I had never been a gambler. Mark Antony used to mock me for my reluctance to take chances. I replied that that was all right for a genius like Caesar, but even a genius required sober men like Labienus and myself to keep him straight.

"And what about me?" Antony said.

It was a question I could never answer. I never knew Antony's capacity. He fascinated me, I suppose, because he seemed so careless in all he did, careless of everything he did, careless of reputation, careless of consequences. Now I argued with myself, argued with Cassius, whether we should invite Antony to join us. He was consul that year. That was a point in favour, for it would mean that we had the legally constituted authority to back us. On the other hand, I could not be sure of his answer. He was incalculable. Besides there was the danger that he would reveal things in his cups. Cassius made two points: first, that Antony's adherence would repel Markie whose participation he was still eagerly seeking; second, that we would find it easy to approach Antony after the deed.

"He will be alarmed for his own safety. He will have no choice but to assent."

I wished I could be as certain.

Longina kissed me soft on the lips. My fingers danced on her belly, scarcely swollen yet.

"My father . . ." she said, ". . . it worries me that you and he

. . . I don't know how best to put this. My father pretends to detachment. What does his philosophy say? Moderation in all things, isn't that it? He assents to that only in his mind, you know. He's impetuous, impulsive, dangerous. He always finds a respectable reason for anything he wants to do, but the real reason is different. Don't forget I've studied him all my life. I'll tell you something else, something I never . . . he's always frightened me. It's because he's bitter, disappointed."

"Don't worry," I said, and tried to kiss her fears away.

"It's because I don't want to lose you," she said, "and that's what's dangerous about my father. He costs other people things they prize."

For a little her tenderness unmanned me. Then I thought of the son we would have. I thought of the two avenues before him: the free life of a Roman noble: the subservient existence of a subject.

"Citizens!" Thus had Caesar addressed the mutinous soldiers of the Tenth.

But it was an honourable title too. How long could it survive in Caesar's Rome?

The *tramontana* continued to blow harsh from the north. Caesar occupied himself with the planning of his campaign. He was as ever meticulous in his arrangements for the legions' supplies – or he saw to it that others were meticulous.

He said to me: "I know you are due to take up the governorship of Cisalpine Gaul, and of course I have marked you down for the consulship in forty-two. But, we may have to find a substitute for you as governor. I think I shall need you in the East. Now that we no longer have Labienus, you are the only General I can trust with an independent operation."

"There's Antony," I said.

"Yes, there's always Antony. But I never know when I can trust Antony and when I can't. I have always been able to trust you, Mouse. That's why I've named you in my will as guardian to my nephew and heir, Octavius."

"There are rumours that you intend to acknowledge the Queen of Egypt's son as your child."

He frowned.

"Silence these rumours, please. They would only upset Calpurnia."

"I have always been able to trust you, Mouse." The words returned to me at night. I stretched my hand out to my sleeping wife, and woke her, to drive the memory away.

Calpurnia still insisted that I find her Bithynian magician.
"I know he's not left the city."
"Perhaps he's in hiding on account of his crimes."
"I don't believe you have really tried to find him. It makes me wonder if you are not on Cleopatra's side."
Her distress had made her scrawnier, more yellow in complexion than ever. I could not pity her, looked on her only with dislike, wondered yet again why Caesar tolerated this unequal marriage. Her nagging caused him irritation. Almost alone in Rome, she would not even pretend to see him as a godlike figure. She insisted on his frailty. Perhaps he kept her by him as a salutary reminder that the image he presented to the public was false. That thought made me pity him. Then it offered itself as a spur. Perhaps Caesar could still be redeemed. If, in his innermost being, he retained such doubts, then indeed he might be diverted from the course that promised disaster to him, unimaginable consequences for Rome.

"Caesar," I said, and hesitated, like a fisherman gazing on a turbulent sea, and uncertain whether to launch his boat or stay safe on shore. I swallowed twice and cast myself upon the waves.
"Caesar, I have come to urge you to a course from which I fear you will immediately recoil."
"This is portentous stuff, Mouse."
"I have fought long and hard at your side, upholding your cause. You have been kind enough to praise my efforts. No battle required of me the courage I need now: to tell you what you do not wish to hear."
"I've never doubted your courage. Carry on. They say it's good for all men to hear unwelcome opinions . . . from time to time. So carry on. How have I offended you, Mouse?"
"You have offended Rome, Caesar."
"Be careful what you say."

"You have offended Rome, Caesar. Every conversation I have, with men of our own rank, yes, and with inferiors also, leads me to that conclusion. Your monopoly of power is increasingly resented. It is resented even by your dearest friends. And that's not all. The other day, I was writing a letter. It doesn't matter to whom. And I found myself writing this sentence: 'It is a rare felicity to be allowed to think what you like and say what you think: how long will this still be permitted us?' I crossed it out, did not despatch the letter. Caesar, I know you as well as any man can claim to know you, and I know that you are not a tyrant. Many men who know you less well than I, think you are. That may not matter, though I cannot be certain, all the less because of your refusal to surround yourself with a personal bodyguard. But you are erecting a system which will breed tyranny. You control the army. You have in effect abolished the elections. All public appointments are in your gift. You will have a successor who will cement your system. He will have successors who will not consider that there could be another way of governing the Republic and the Empire. They will not have your virtues. Liberty will be no more, and we shall no longer enjoy the rare felicity of being permitted to feel as we please, and speak our minds."

I kept my eyes fixed on him as I spoke, watching for the signs of anger I knew so well: a straightening of the upper lip, a harshness in the eye, a red spot on his left cheek and drumming of the fingers of one hand against the back of the other. But I saw none of this. Instead a friendly smile lit up his face.

"And what would you have me do, Mouse?"

"I would have you withdraw, abandon, or at least postpone the Parthian campaign, give our institutions the chance to work freely under your benevolent eye. Caesar, as long as you live, you will surpass all in authority. But there is a distinction to be made between authority and power. You cannot share your authority, for that has been acquired by your deeds and virtue; but you can relinquish power. You have stabilised the State; now you can restore it."

"Well, Mouse, I can see that it took courage to nerve yourself to speak to Caesar in this fashion. But what you recommend is absurd, impractical. I have already explained this to you. The

Republic is moribund. Its institutions are no longer equal to the task of government. If I withdrew, as you advise, the order I have restored would again disintegrate. Rome would once again be a prize to be fought over by warring factions. Liberty is a fine word, but liberty can only be enjoyed when men also enjoy security. That Caesar has provided. There is now in Rome, and throughout the Empire, an ordered liberty. It is all men are fit for. It is only on that basis that the Empire can be governed. Do not suppose that Caesar has not thought long on these matters. They disturb my nights. You offer me a great temptation. Do you suppose I don't have moments when I yearn for the tranquillity of my villa overlooking Lake Albano, when I do not imagine how I might fruitfully employ my last years in the pleasures of literature, philosophy, and country life? We were all educated to revere the memory of Cincinnatus, called from the plough to save Rome, and then, having performed the necessary task, returning home to guide his team of oxen; or of Scipio Africanus, my greatest predecessor in the annals of Roman war, whose exploits were all but equal to Caesar's; who, having conquered Hannibal and Antiochus, retired, disdaining the squabbles and petty jealousies of the Senate, to his country seat at Liternum in Campania. Yes, Scipio's example is a temptation, for his virtue has ensured him enduring fame. But Scipio is also a warning. Like Caesar he was offered the dictatorship for life; unlike Caesar, he declined it. Was Rome better for his act of self-abnegation? Or was it not the case that his disinclination to accept the power he was offered opened the way to a sea of troubles? Caesar will resist temptation. Caesar will do his duty, whatever the dangers – and do not suppose I am unaware of them. I repeat what I have said to you before. You cannot breathe life into a corpse; and the Republic is all but a corpse. No, it is already a corpse. Rome and the Empire require the government of a single person; by which I mean, the concentration of authority and power in a single pre-eminent being. It does not matter what he is called: Dictator, King, Imperator, Caesar, God. Names are devices to satisfy the vulgar. Reality is different. Those who pretend that the Republic can be restored, that Rome can flourish again by means of institutions suitable only for a city-state, delude themselves with charming dreams . . ."

He rose, walked behind me, stroked my neck (on which I felt the hairs rise), pinched my ear.

"Reality . . ." he nipped harder. "Read Thucydides, Mouse, not Plato, history not philosophy. It is courage in the face of reality that distinguishes Thucydides from Plato. The great philosopher is a coward before the harsh imperatives of reality; so he flees into the Ideal, where, by the way, Cicero follows him. But Thucydides confronts the facts, exercises self-control. Therefore he also maintains control of things. So also with Caesar. Idealists are all cowards, for they would have things as they are not. Caesar's goddess is Necessity; who is therefore also Caesar's guide."

I left him in sadness. He was a great man, and I owed him much, but the more stridently he talked of reality, the less his ear seemed to be attuned to any murmurings which might disturb his devoted contemplation of his own glory. What is this world, O soldiers: it is Caesar. What is this waste of sand but Caesar? What is Rome but Caesar? What is Parthia but the means of fulfilling Caesar's Destiny?

"It is a strange thing to remark," Cicero said, "but Caesar has no hinterland."

"What do you mean? I don't follow you." My cousin Marcus Brutus frowned. "No hinterland? I don't understand you." He was like a soldier advancing beyond the frontier, lost as soon as he had left the road with its regular milestones.

I had arranged a small dinner-party. My original intention had been to ask only Markie and his wife Porcia. Then I added Cicero. He would be indiscreet, and therefore stimulating, I thought; besides, with him there, Markie would be less suspicious of my motives. I had also invited Cicero's young wife, to satisfy my own curiosity; but he did not bring her. They had fallen out, decisively perhaps.

"Ah, you are puzzled, Brutus." Cicero was delighted by the admission. "Well, it is natural. Caesar's genius is so dazzling. But of course I have the advantage over you; I knew Caesar well before he was Caesar, with all the connotations that illustrious name now bears. Of course he has always been brilliant; yet his brilliance sheds no light around him. It is, you might say, a concentrated brilliance. And when I say he has no hinterland," he continued, with no pause for breath between sentences, lest someone should interrupt him, "I mean simply this: Caesar has no real sense of the past, no sympathy with the way others may think, no sensitivity to immemorial affections. Perhaps this is one reason for his success: his very limitation. That's an interesting thought, which it might be fruitful to explore. Is it even, one wonders, a criterion for a certain type of worldly success that a man should never pause to consider the other side, the other side of the question, to gaze, if you like, across the valley that divides the present from the past?"

"But I don't understand," Markie said. "Caesar is always talking about his ancestors."

"Remote ancestors," Cicero said. "So remote as to be unreal. But the tradition of the Republic – ah, that is a reality from which he prefers to avert his eyes."

Longina sighed and caught my eye. I imagined that she was thinking how very much more entertaining Caesar was as a dinner-companion.

Porcia said: "My father always used to say that Caesar was a careerist, nothing else, that he cared for nothing but his own position, and would be absolutely unscrupulous in advancing it."

"But that precisely confirms what I have been telling you," Cicero said. "I would expect, of course, nothing but good sense and accurate observation from Marcus Cato. Caesar is essentially limited. He feels none of the affections which bind men to each other and to their ancestors. I do not think it has ever occurred to Caesar that society is a partnership between the living, the dead and those yet to be born."

"I have heard Caesar deny the very existence of society," I said. "In his opinion, society is an invented concept which enables men to acquit themselves of full responsibility for their actions."

"Precisely," Cicero said again. "I have talked to you, before now, Decimus Brutus, of the threat which I choose to call individualism – which, by the way, is my own poor attempt at providing a Latin equivalent for a Greek philosophical term – the threat which this presents to the community of Rome, and by community I would wish you to understand that I mean all that we have inherited from our ancestors who forged the

Republic and the means of Rome's greatness, and also what we are in duty bound to transmit to our children and grandchildren. I am an old man, near the end of life, near at least the natural term of days, and I see very clearly that, however conscious each of us may be of his own self, and of the demands it makes, the desires it engenders, yet we are all caught in a web of circumstance and connection, which in our case is Rome — its history, its political structure, the duties it imposes. Therefore, in the last resort, I say that whoever injures Rome, injures me, injures my friends, injures all I hold dear and reverent."

Cicero left early, explaining that, at his age (which in conversation he sometimes liked to exaggerate, perhaps to make himself seem more remarkable, or in an effort to attract sympathy) he required longer hours of sleep — "not that I sleep sound, you understand, but I must at least rest in bed" — than vigorous youth or beauties like Longina and Porcia.

It was, incidentally, absurd to describe Porcia as a beauty. She was very thin, and her lower jaw was of the type described, I believe, as "lantern" — long and lean. Moreover, her eyes were dull, without sparkle. You had only to look at her to sense that she was devoid of imagination.

"What an old bore he is," Longina said. "I had to keep pinching myself to keep awake and not yawn in his face." She giggled. "He would have liked that, I don't think."

Markie frowned again.

"He is a man of the very greatest distinction. I confess I find it difficult sometimes to follow his conversation, partly because it's so copious, but I never leave Cicero's company without feeling enriched."

"Yes," Porcia said. "A very great man, but a thinker, not a man of action, and as my father, the great Cato, used to say, 'Action is the test of a man.' I think that's so true. After all, anyone is capable of speaking virtuously, even the greatest hypocrites, even Caesar when he pleases, but to act virtuously, in accordance with the example of our ancestors, and the duties enjoined on us by the gods, that's a different matter."

"There's something strange, and disturbing, about which I wish to consult with you, cousin," Markie said. "I don't know quite what it means or how I should respond."

"Well?"

"It's been reported to me, reliably reported, that a paper has been found under the statue of our great ancestor who destroyed the Tarquins, with the legend: 'O, that we had a Brutus now! O, that Brutus were living at this hour!' Then, when I took my seat as praetor at the tribunal today, I discovered a message laid before me there, which read: 'Brutus, thou sleepest. Thou art not a true Brutus if you will not wake from your shameful slumber.' I am puzzled to know the import of these things."

"Husband," Porcia said, while I still deliberated how I should best answer my wooden-headed cousin, "husband, you are too modest, and it makes you slow. These messages which puzzle you so strangely ought not to do so. They are arrows directed at your conscience. They call upon you to imitate the action of your great ancestor, and rid Rome of a tyrant."

"A tyrant? Caesar?"

Longina shifted on her couch. Like me, I think, she suspected her father's hand in these messages.

"Yes," Porcia said, "a tyrant. One who is smothering liberty in Rome as surely as he destroyed my noble father. And so the people turn to you, Brutus, as one whose virtue they recognise."

It was as if she had forgotten our presence. She was concentrated utterly on her husband.

"But Caesar has been kind to me," Brutus said. "I bear him no grudge, have nothing with which to reproach him. And, compared to those who have gone before, like Marius and Sulla, he has displayed a notable clemency to those who fought against him. I can't forget that, or ignore it. What do you say, Mouse?"

"What do I say? I say that I owe as much to Caesar as you do, but I owe more to Rome. Whatever Caesar's virtues, and nobody is more conscious of them than I am, his position in the State has become vicious. We may have nothing with which to reproach Caesar himself, personally, but Caesar will have an heir . . ."

And so, with infinite patience, I spelled out again, in still greater detail, on account of my cousin's slow understanding, the arguments I had employed to Caesar himself.

And I concluded: "Think of Caesar as a serpent's egg. An egg does no harm, but when hatched, it will breed vipers who will poison Rome with their sting. So, what do you do if you find a serpent's egg? You crush it."

"Husband, darling," Longina murmured in my ear, when our guests had departed, and we lay in bed, having made tender love, "Mouse-husband, I am afraid."

I stroked her breasts, ran my hand over her belly, and between her legs. I brushed her lips with mine.

"It is not a fear that you can banish with kisses."

But she clung to me and kissed me hard; yet I felt a trembling run through her body.

"I'm not going to question you, but again I'm afraid of my father's influence on you. At the moment all is imaginary, in your head. Let it remain there, please, not translated into action . . . it's not Caesar I'm thinking of, though when I think of him, and of how he is so full of life, I'm horrified to think of the plans you are brooding on. But it's not Caesar, it's you. My father is rash. His enterprises go astray. I'm afraid that everything will go wrong."

"There's another fear you might consider," I said. "Suppose I stand out. Suppose I even tell Caesar what is planned. It won't be the last attempt. There will be others, and one will succeed, since Caesar refuses to take precautions. What then? What will be the fate of someone known to be Caesar's ally? How long would I last in such circumstances?"

CHAPTER
18

My nights are disturbed. I woke this morning in cold terror. Caesar had visited me in a dream. At least I am sure it was a dream, and not his ghost – small consolation. I was in bed with Longina, who lay damply weeping in my arms, overcome with the sadness that succeeds desire and its performance. Her grief was the greater because she had revealed to me that our little son was dead: "crushed in the egg", she said, over and over again. I do not know whether this is true, for I have had no word from Longina. Her silence distresses me, even though I tell myself that she may have no means of knowing where I am, may not have received my letters, and may ache because of my absence, as I do on account of hers. The pains of love, once satisfied, now denied, are sharper even than the pang of unattainable desire. To lose what you know and trust is more cruel than never to have what you hoped for.

But Caesar stood at the end of the bed, displaying his wounds. He did not speak, but his gestures, as he touched first this gash, then another, finally that which was my own work, were pitiful.

I wanted to cry out that I could acquit myself of envy, that that had not been my motive as it was (I now realise) Cassius', but there was an obstruction in my throat, and though I could form words, I was unable to utter them.

Then Caesar beckoned to Longina, and she withdrew herself from me, and slipped, silver as Diana in the shaft of moonlight, from our bed, and threw her arms around Caesar, and kissed him full on the lips. I was compelled to watch as they withdrew, with many lascivious gestures, both all at once oblivious of my presence, my rights, my very existence. The moonlight slid away with them, and I was left in the dark, and a long silence, which was broken first by a cackle of laughter, and then by a sound which I knew to be my own sobbing, though my body did not move and my eyes were dry.

A dream? Of course. I don't believe in spectres. But it left me like the last, solitary ant of a broken ant hill.

As for Longina, there, undoubtedly, my dream told the truth. She had turned away from me towards the memory of Caesar. She would, I am now certain, deny me if we should ever meet again. And what difference would that make? Would it stimulate my jealousy? I don't think so, I have never been a jealous man. Rather, the thought provokes a serene and sombre resignation, a type of detachment.

It has come to me that if we were to meet again, she might yield to my desires, something might revive in her of her former feeling, but even if this was not the case, even if my love was not returned, it would no longer matter. If we were together again, we might resume our former habits, or we might not. In any case I wouldn't stop loving her.

When I think how I took her for convenience, as an act of policy, and how I despised her, now there I find cause for shame.

My preference for Octavius over her! How callow it seems, how stupid! What nonsense the Greeks talked about the superiority of the love between a man and a youth! Perhaps it merely reflected the inferiority of Greek women? But I don't think so. There is nothing after all like the love for a woman who has given herself to you.

And if both Octavius and Longina now think of me with contempt, well, it is only her contempt that can distress me.

And yet, having written that, with the utmost sincerity, I have to confess that three weeks ago, I wrote to Octavius, pleading with him to intercede on my behalf, and so save my life. I am ashamed of that letter now, and of the terms in which it was couched. Yet if a man was cast into the sea and drowning, would he care on what terms he was rescued? There are two voices at war in my head. Thus:

Reproach: Such a plea is a denial of virtue. It is less than should become a man.

Response: We have made too much of virtue. We have made

fools of ourselves over our concept of virtue. It was virtue brought me to my present state.

Reproach: Ah, then, do you deny the virtue of that act? Would you have it undone?

And then there is silence.

Octavius has not replied. Perhaps there has not yet been time. Perhaps when he received my letter, he tore it into angry pieces. Perhaps – a worse thought – he read it aloud at the supper-table to amuse his companions, to make Maecenas snigger.

On the other hand, starved as I am of news, my letter may have been pointless, too late. Octavius himself may no longer be in a position to do anything for anyone.

That thought doesn't distress me.

Artixes has grown more distant. He no longer asks me to read my memoirs to him. Either his father has grown suspicious of our friendship, or he has conceived an abhorrence for either my person or my history. So I am truly alone now.

History . . . there is a chance, I suppose, that this manuscript will survive me. I write it partly to fill the time, to revive memory and banish thought of the future (which nevertheless keeps breaking in); partly as an act of self-justification. This is my testimony.

Will those who read it understand me, or will they continue to reproach me with that single word Octavius directed at me: traitor?

Very well, I accept the word, adding only this: I had a deeper and more true affection for Caesar than Octavius had. My life had been bound up in his. I served him with the utmost loyalty. Does the boy suppose that it cost me nothing to put a higher duty above my debt to Caesar? Besides, I had been subject to his charm . . . that famous charm.

Another dream: desert sands extend in all directions, grey-purple in the lingering light of the sun that has slid behind the distant hills. I am alone. Around me lie evidences of disaster: dead horses, scraps of armour, abandoned swords, spears, great lumbering baggage carts. But there are no corpses of dead legionaries. It is as if I gaze on the debris of an army without soldiers.

I stumble on, weary, thirsty and afraid. The moon has risen as the chants begin. From a sandbank on a ridge, I look down on a hollow place, where naked figures dance around a stone altar, in barbaric but compulsive rhythm. There is a figure bound to the altar. It keeps changing in the shifting light. Now it seems young, now old, now a woman, now a youth. A squat shape disengages itself from the dancers, and hops in a crouched position towards the altar. Only the head of the bound figure is free and it turns from side to side. The mouth is open as if it is screaming, but no sound comes from those lips which are the colour of dead ashes. Then the crouching thing rises. It turns towards me and I see that it is masked. The company is silent. In the distance a wolf howls. A cloud of birds – kites or vultures – descend on the altar with the slow beating of heavy wings. They cover the figure, so that the last I see is that grey-lipped mouth, stretched wide, emitting screams that never sound. And at that moment, hands pluck at my garments, sharp nails tear at my flesh, and I wake screaming the screams that the figure was unable to release.

In the words of my poor Catullus:
    "*Miser a miser, querendum est etiam atque etiam, anime.*" –
    "Twice-wretched soul, again and again must I sound my sadness."

CHAPTER

19

Enough of these black dreams that come on stealthy feet to make me fear sleep itself.

Let me resume my narrative.

Of all our traditional Roman ceremonies the strangest, and to me perhaps for that reason the most compelling, is the Lupercalia. Its origins, even its purpose, are unknown, lost in the mists of time. It takes place two days after the Ides of February, in the middle of the ten days of ceremonies in honour of our departed ancestors; but whether it is connected with these, no one even among the priests can confidently say.

It centres on the cave of the Lupercal, on the south-west side of the steep and leafy Palatine. It was at that spot that the she-wolf succoured Romulus, our founder, and his brother Remus, and this connection and the name of the festival would seem to insist that in some mysterious fashion it celebrates that deed. If so, many changes must have taken place since it was first inaugurated, for there is no evident resemblance between its rites and the suckling of Romulus and Remus.

The festival commences with the sacrifice of goats and the offering of sacred cakes baked by the Vestal Virgins from ears of corn of the last harvest. Two nobly-born youths have their heads smeared with blood from the knife employed in the sacrifice, and this is then wiped off with wool dipped in milk. Then they are required to laugh. Wrapped in the skins of the goats, they eat a lavish meal, after which they lead two companies of noble youths at the run around the base of the Palatine. All carry *februa*, strips of purified goatskin, with which they lash any women they encounter. Needless to say, the more enterprising among them seek out the prettiest girls, who, regarding it as both an honour and a good omen to receive the lash, make little effort to escape. I have been fascinated by the Lupercalia, since I was myself one of the two chosen youths, and I know how it generates an uncanny excitement. It invites the participants to shed for the moment the trappings of the civilisation which at other times we so highly value.

I attended it this year with Casca.

"I like its savagery," he said. "As you know, old dear, I generally give well-born boys a wide berth. They are rarely sufficiently pliable for my taste. All the same there are always one or two beauties disporting themselves who take my fancy and give me a bit of the old excitement. So, yes, I'm on."

It was a cold bright day, with snow on the hills. There was the usual confusion, yelps of excitement, laughter and taunting. Caesar sat on a golden chair among the dancing priests of the Luperci. He wore a purple toga and a golden wreath on his head. Because of the cold he had a shawl round his neck. He seemed to be paying no attention to what was happening. I let my gaze wander.

Then Casca nudged me in the ribs.

"Look at this."

A large figure, dressed in skins, pranced towards Caesar, bearing a crown. For a moment I didn't recognise him as Antony. He knelt before Caesar, extending the crown to him. Caesar made no response.

Crown of Romulus? I thought.

The crowd fell silent, all eyes now fixed on Caesar.

He stretched out his hand, touched the crown, let his fingers lie on it, while his gaze travelled the thronging mass. Then, without looking at Antony, he pushed the crown away, and let his hand drop. The crowd roared applause.

But Antony did not desist. He remained on his knees, still holding out the crown to Caesar, as if he was a suppliant, begging a favour. This time, Caesar's fingers closed on the crown, while once again his gaze shifted from it, sweeping the assembly. But again he let his hand fall, and again there was a roar of approval.

Antony did not move. He held the crown steady, level with his eyes. He pushed it a little towards Caesar. Caesar stretched out his hand again. He took the crown. Antony loosened his hold. For a moment the crown was all Caesar's. The silence held, to be broken by yells of disapproval. Caesar smiled, still looking at the crown and not at the people. The crown trembled in his hands. Then he thrust it at Antony, almost knocking him over backwards, such was the vigour of the thrust. The boos and hisses which had begun (as if the mob were in the theatre and Caesar a player who had displeased them) were translated into cheers.

Caesar rose, a little unsteadily, so that he laid his hand on Antony's head. He pulled the shawl away, and let it fall. He pointed his index finger at his naked throat. His mouth moved, but what he said couldn't be heard in the tumultuous din. From his action I deduced that he was inviting any whom his response displeased to cut his throat. The invitation was not accepted. The cheers resounded louder. Caesar swayed, and fell to the ground.

Casca whispered: "I expect he's been choked by their stinking breath, they crowd around him so close."

"No," I said. "It's his old complaint, the falling sickness."

A voice close to my other ear said:

"It's not Caesar who suffers from the falling sickness, but us. Yes, and Casca too, we all have the falling sickness."

I didn't have to turn to identify my father-in-law.

"An interesting charade," he said. "We need to talk about it. Come home with me after this is all over."

Caesar had recovered, was on his feet again, very pale, and still trembling. He held up his hand for silence.

He obtained it, which says much for his authority and presence.

"Good people," his voice was faint.

"The poor soul," a sluttish girl near us muttered.

"Good people," Caesar said again, "I apologise for disturbing you with this strange infirmity of mine, which, as veterans of my campaigns will tell you, has often preceded my greatest triumphs. If I have offended any of you in any way this day, think kindly of me, and attribute the offence to the onset of my malady."

Then, leaning ostentatiously on Antony's shoulder, he made his slow, almost regal, way through the crowd in the direction of the Forum.

"The poor soul," the girl said again, "you can see how he suffers."

"He should never have been out today, I could see that as soon as I clapped eyes on the poor man," one of her companions said, "but there it is, he's a martyr to duty."

"Yes," said another, "and he knew how it would disappoint us if he wasn't with us."

"Poor soul," the first girl said again. "You can see how hard it is for him."

"I'm glad he put the crown aside."

"Oh it was a crown, was it? I couldn't see."

"Aye, I'm that glad, though, mind you, if anyone deserves a crown, it's Caesar."

"Did 'ee hear what he said, though, when someone called him 'King' one day? 'My name's not King, but Caesar.'"

"Oh he's quick. You won't outsmart our Caesar."

"No, he's our boy, we're safe with Caesar."

"I don't know what that Antony was thinking of."

"Drunk, I daresay. He nearly fell on his arse when Caesar gave him that little shove."

"What was it all about then?"

"Well, he was just proving, like, if you ask me, that he doesn't want a crown. It's enough for him to be Caesar."

"Too much for most."

"He don't look well. I worry about him, nights, you know."

"Poor soul . . ."

Bombarded by such comments, with praise of Caesar ringing in our ears, we made our way to Cassius' house.

"There's a depth of affection for him, you know, love almost, one mustn't forget that," I said.

"I don't," Cassius said. "It preys on my mind."

"Pish and tush," Casca said. "The rabble is fickle. Believe me, I know. With good reason. Today, yes, that was their mood. If Caesar had told them to go home and stab their mothers, they'd have obeyed him. But that's today. Tomorrow they'll scream equally loud for a new hero. That's the rabble. Trash. You don't want to take any heed of them."

"I hope you may be right," I said.

*   *   *

Cassius called on a slave to bring us wine mulled with spices.

"Drink it up. It was cold out there," he said, handing us goblets, and downing his own.

"That's better. Well?"

"That's better, as you say; and again, as you say, well?"

"I had hoped," Cassius said, "that Caesar's popularity would decline. But it still increases."

"Would they have cheered as loud," I asked, "if he had accepted Antony's gift?"

"Every bit," Casca said.

"If his popularity," Cassius said, "is still waxing, then the day threatens when there will be nothing he cannot do, for there will be nothing, not even public opinion, to restrain him . . ."

"So?"

"So, we must do as we have determined. So also, Mouse, it becomes ever more necessary to recruit your cousin Marcus. He must be persuaded. I have sent for young Cato to consult how we may bring matters to the point. Mouse, it's no use turning down the corners of your mouth. Consider the three of us here. I have no illusions about my own standing: I am detested by the common people as the very expression of aristocratic pride. They loathe what they understand – and misunderstand – about the philosophy that informs my actions. You, Casca, are you respected? I think not. And, Mouse, are you popular? If you make a speech in the Forum, will the people cheer? Who will die for you or your cause?"

"The Ninth Legion is devoted to me. I have led them to fame and victory. They stand to in my allotted province of Cisalpine Gaul, and, believe me, Cassius, you couldn't wish for a finer body of men."

"Mouse, Mouse, soldiers, soldiers . . . they will follow whoever pays them."

"No, they have deeper loyalties. Caesar's strength derives from the army. Never forget that."

"Caesar's strength derives from his being Caesar, and from our weakness. No, however much you dislike it, we need Marcus Brutus. He is the only man we can hope to recruit who is held in high esteem by mob and senators alike. He is the only man who can make our cause . . ." he paused, and smiled; there was a sneer in his smile, ". . . respectable," he finished with a bark of laughter.

"We would do better with Antony," I said.

"Antony?" Cassius said. "After that comedy today?"

I argued the case for Antony at length. I dismissed what we had just seen. We couldn't know Antony's motives, not till we had discussed the matter with him, as I was quite willing to do. Antony was consul, I said, and that alone gave our cause authority. It meant we could take whatever measures were necessary to secure order, and do so legally. I emphasised the importance of legality. It was true, I admitted, that Antony had been a devoted partisan of Caesar's – but no more than I myself; he had rarely questioned Caesar's actions. Well, how many of us had? But he was not infatuated with Caesar; he had resented Caesar's refusal to support him in his quarrel with Dolabella the previous year. Antony was popular with the crowd and, as consul, could legally take command of the legions. I admitted his frailties, but insisted that they were outweighed by his ability. We ought at least to sound him out. If he adhered to us, our cause would be immeasurably strengthened.

"Antony is not respectable," Cassius said.

"The same charge could be levelled at me, old fruit," Casca said.

"Your case is different, and not only because you can keep a secret in your cups, which Antony can't. Mouse, even if I agreed with everything that you have said – and you have argued the case for Antony with an eloquence of which Cicero might be proud – there remains one insuperable objection: we will never secure Marcus Brutus if he thinks Antony is engaged in the enterprise, for Antony is everything Brutus despises and detests."

"Bugger Markie," I said.

"Not me, old boy," Casca said. "You'll have to find another candidate for that job."

My doubts grew when young Cato arrived, fresh-faced, handsome, incurious. He brought good news, he said. His sister Porcia was exercising all her charms ("Bloody few, I'd have thought," muttered Casca) to persuade her husband. Brutus was half-convinced. He had written some pages of an essay on the virtues of the Republic. It was provisionally entitled *Against the Government of a Single Person.*

I remarked that this did not really take us any further.

"Besides, the Republic is easier to applaud than to achieve."

"But I must tell you something else," Cato said. "Supporters of Caesar have crowned his statues with royal diadems. And the mob cheered them as they did so."

"Well," Cassius said, "that warns us that delay is dangerous. Cato, will you accompany me to Brutus? It is time to twist his arm in order to release the obstruction that holds his noble spirit from action."

Even now, I do not know how Cassius truly regarded Brutus. The note of irony was rarely absent from his voice when he spoke of him; and yet no one could have set higher store by his adherence to our party. Perhaps the truth is that Cassius both admired and despised him, valued and resented him, distrusted his capacity and yet felt the need of his reputation for virtue. Perhaps even Cassius shared the doubts that disturbed me as to the morality of our plan, and, feeling such uncertainty, thought it could be banished only if Brutus, whose virtue none could reproach, collaborated with us. I do not know. I know only that his insistence that we must recruit Brutus was the chief cause of our failure, as I shall prove, given time to do so.

Casca and I left Cassius' house together. Our spirits were low. Heavy clouds, threatening snow, had blown up from the northeast. We both felt we had committed ourselves to an uncertain enterprise. Our trust in Cassius had diminished. And yet . . .

"Have you considered, Mouse, that we could still blow the whole bloody thing? Tell Caesar what is planned, and so . . . Yes, of course you have, and we won't, will we?"

"No, we won't. Whatever the risk, we've both been brought to this point. That charade this morning . . . did you see how at the third offering his hands clung to the crown?"

"I saw."

"There's a Greek word."

"There would be."

"Megalomania."

"Well, bugger that."

"If you say so."

"No, I've just spotted something I fancy. See you later, old bean. Be good."

And Casca left me in pursuit of a curly headed epicene with a dancer's gait. I saw him take the boy by the elbow, and the pair disappeared up a narrow alley.

The snow came, lay in the city for two days, silencing the noise of wagons. Then the weather turned wet and windy, staying like that for the rest of February. Cassius reported that Markie was still wrestling with his conscience, but that both he and young Cato were confident that Porcia, reason, and the public interest would prevail. He told me that Brutus was like a general compelled to yield one position after another: "Finally, he will be trapped in the citadel from which he will find only one escape."

Without seeking authority from Cassius, I sounded out Mark Antony. He admitted that he was perturbed by Caesar's state of mind.

"That bitch the Queen has him in a vice. He's no longer capable of thinking straight."

I was convinced that he understood my purpose; yet he affected not to. Nevertheless, he laid his finger along his nose; and it seemed to me that this gesture indicated that though he would have no hand in the business, he would not seek to obstruct it.

"Caesar's not immortal," he said as he left. "And he's a lot older than we are. This Parthian campaign will probably finish him off – his health's not what it was, you know. And then things will revert to normal – whatever that can be said to be."

Trebonius pressed Cassius to include Cicero in our plans. He received some support from Metellus Cimber, but the rest of us were opposed.

"We shall need Cicero," I said, "after the deed. Can anyone doubt that he will approve it? But till that moment is reached he is more likely to be a hindrance than a help in our enterprise."

My opinion carried weight, and Trebonius desisted from his attempt to persuade us.

Diadems appeared again on Caesar's statues. This time two

noble tribunes, men of exemplary Republican virtue, Flavius and Marullus, tore them off with their own hands and cast them on the ground. This action received the approbation of the mob, though some said later that the tribunes themselves had seen to it that their defiance would be witnessed only by those whom they knew to be favourable, and whom indeed they had with them by design. Caesar was incensed by what he termed their insolence. Exercising the authority which he possessed as Perpetual Dictator, he deposed the tribunes, and then, when they were private citizens and no longer protected by their office, had them cast into prison. Of all his tyrannical acts, this made the greatest impression on those who were wavering, eager for the restoration of the Republic, yet held back by fear of Caesar. For they saw that if he could treat the most honourable office of the tribunate with such cavalier authority, he had become capable of anything.

Casca laughed: "It's rich to remember, ain't it, that the ostensible cause of the civil war was the treatment meted out by the Senate to the tribunes who supported Caesar."

"Yes," I said, "and the theme of his memoirs of the war was to insist on 'with what great zeal I sought peace'. What does he seek now?"

That question hung over all our deliberations, and the answers we suspected fortified many minds.

"Your cousin inches towards a resolution," young Cato said. "This business of the tribunes has made a deep impression on him."

The Kalends of March ushered in spring. There was a lightness in the air calling one to action. The sky was soft and blue and the air fragrant. My soul was filled with eagerness. I rose early in the morning, leaving Longina beautiful in happy sleep, and sought out Cassius.

I apologised for the early hour.

"Not at all. I always rise at first light. I study philosophy for an hour, then practise fencing or do gymnastics. When you reach my age, it is necessary to keep both mind and body in training. Otherwise deterioration is rapid. Well, things go merrily, don't they?"

His insouciance annoyed me. It belied his reputation. Cassius was seen, by most, as saturnine, sour, pessimistic.

"We are almost there," he said. "I dined with Marcus Brutus last night. He is on the point of committing himself. Then we must move quickly."

"Before he changes his mind, you mean, or loses his nerve?"

"If you choose to put it like that. But, as I've said before, you underestimate him. He is scrupulous, and that is to his credit. The Senate is scheduled to meet on the Ides of March, ironically in Pompey's theatre."

(This was on account of a fire in the Senate House, necessitating repairs.)

"I have marked that as an appropriate day."

"Very well," I said. "I'm agreed. I shall send Longina to the country."

"Is that necessary? Might it give rise to suspicion?"

"Her pregnancy will serve as excuse."

"You look troubled."

"Then my looks betray my state of mind."

What disturbed me, as I explained to him at length, was that no preparations had been made for anything beyond the deed itself. We seemed to be working on an assumption that everything would fall comfortably into place. I didn't believe that. There would be danger. We might have need of troops to maintain order. It couldn't be assumed that all Caesar's partisans would submit to our will. Antony's position had to be considered. I suggested that the Ninth Legion, which was devoted to me, should be put on the alert; I was ready to give orders that it should leave its winter quarters at Bologna, and march towards Rome.

"Can such an order be given without awakening Caesar's suspicions? Can such a move take place without confirming them? Besides, afterwards, the consuls, Antony and Dolabella, will be legally in command of the armies."

"Legality will have to be set aside. Perhaps Antony should be set aside also. Dolabella is of no account. He'll run around like a headless chicken."

"Well," Cassius said, "your proposal is risky. It will need to be pondered on, and more widely discussed. I have convened a meeting this day week. By then, I am certain Marcus will be ready to commit himself."

Longina protested when I told her she must leave Rome. Her lips formed in a delicious pout. Her eyes brimmed with tears. She met my guarded explanation of necessity with a tilt of the head and further questions. Then defiance. She would not be persuaded, would not obey. If I loved her, I would not ask this of her. Her lovely breasts heaved. I took her in my arms and tried to kiss her mood away. But she disengaged herself, and said:

"I've warned you against my father. I haven't asked what you are plotting together, because I haven't needed to. Are you afraid that I will betray you?"

"No," I said.

"Then I still don't understand."

"I am afraid," I said, "yes . . . Since you know what we are best not to talk about, let me confess my fear. I'm afraid, horribly afraid, that everything will go wrong. I'm afraid of failure, but, where you are concerned, for our failure would not place you in danger, I am still more afraid of success. My friends are blind to the devotion That Man inspires in the people. They therefore take no thought of the possible consequences of our success. Violence, rioting, revenge – that's what I fear. And I want you safe from that. I need you safe from that, if I am to play my part as a man of virtue."

"Very well," she said, "but do you need to play this part? I've been thinking about that."

She took a green apple from a dish and bit into it. The juice ran like a tiny rivulet from the corner of her mouth.

"Lord, I have such a lust for apples. Old wives say that means our child will be a daughter."

"It will be a boy, and in any case, only the first."

"If you were to stand aside, then when it was over, you would be in a strong position, wouldn't you? Especially if my father and the rest are as ill-prepared as you suggest."

The idea had occurred to me. Of course it had. Temptation never fails to offer itself: Caesar dead, and myself innocent of his blood, and in a position to mediate between the two parties. Visions of authority beckoned as insistently as an eager whore.

"I am in too deep for that," I said.

It was true. If I stepped back now, I would earn only contempt from those who held to their word. In extremities there is no place for the man who seeks the palm without the dust. It was months too late for the course Longina suggested.

"You could be sick."

"They would only believe my resolution had failed. Do you suppose a man of your father's penetration would be deceived by a pretence of sickness?"

"Don't you understand," she cried, "I am afraid for you, you fool, because I love you. I am afraid for myself and for my son."

She broke down in tears. I knelt to comfort her. Her arm stole round my neck. I scarcely felt the knife enter my back just below the left shoulder.

As it happened I had turned myself in order to kiss her mouth which was itself averted from me, so that the dagger did not penetrate, and I received only a glancing wound. But the knife came away red, and I felt the warm rush of blood, and Longina held the knife aloft and gazed on it as the drops fell to the marble. We drew apart. She held the dagger, point downwards, between us.

"What have I done?"

"What have you tried to do?" I think I smiled; I hope I did. "I have never been stabbed for love before. You goose."

I took the dagger from her trembling hand. She made no resistance. I ran my finger along the blade, and touched her lips with my blood.

"You goose," I said again.

"I might have killed you."

"With this toy? Unlikely. Anyway, it's no more than a scratch, I think. Deep wounds bleed slower."

"Come, let me bathe it and clean it. What was I doing?"

"There's no need for tears."

Her shame and horror – also unnecessary, in my opinion, for her motive only made me love her more – served my purpose. She abandoned her opposition to my plans for her safety. She was humble and submissive. When I saw her like that, I reproached myself, and came closer than at any other moment to yielding to what she wanted. Our plan seemed feeble, irrelevant to the things that really matter in life. What did I care for public virtue or the seedy old, worm-eaten Republic in comparison with the revelation just vouchsafed me?

"After all," I said to myself, "there is nothing, not even the thrill of battle, to compare with the satisfaction to be had from a woman who truly loves you."

But love dies when respect dies, and that depends on the loved one's self-respect. Otherwise it becomes that debilitating emotion: pity.

A paradox: Longina's love made her fear the course on which I had embarked. I feared her love would die, with my self-respect, if I abandoned it.

I accompanied her two mornings later out of the city by the Appian Way. The sun shone, the light sparkled and the dark pines were touched with gold. Then at the fourth milestone we stopped, embraced, tongue searching tongue, as if by that we expressed not only desire, but unity of word, deed, spirit.

I laid my hand on her belly.

"I felt her move last night," Longina said.

"Him."

"You will have it your way, but you may be disappointed."

"Nothing you do, nothing you produce, can disappoint me."

"I'm not so sure about that."

"Remember," I said, "what I do is for our children, that they may grow up free, and not slaves. It's not for myself. How could it be, when I blossom in Caesar's sunlight? But the course he is embarked on promises only darkness for Rome and her children, for our children and theirs. I wish you could believe that."

"I believe you believe it. That's enough, even though it remains rhetoric for me. So Mouse-husband, the gods go with you."

"And with you."

She laughed as she had not laughed for a long time, a deep full-throated laugh that was one of her glories.

"As if we either of us believed in these gods, to whom we commend each other."

"Oh Longina . . ."

I had mounted my horse. I leaned across the side of the carriage to kiss her a last time. I lingered on her lips, drawing honey and comfort from them. Then the horse shied and we were separated.

I linger on that moment of memory now.

I watched the carriage move away from me, slowly. Once she turned and waved to me, and then looked away and bowed her head, and I knew that tears blinded her eyes. I brushed my sleeve across my own. The carriage passed between tombs that flanked the road. It grew smaller till it was only a speck on the horizon, and then it was no more, and I turned my horse's head, and rode back to the city and Destiny.

So, laughing at the gods, weeping on account of necessity, Longina departed from me. I have never seen her since, except in dreams, waking or sleeping. As I write this, she returns to me; and yet I am mocked by the distance between us.

CHAPTER

20

We convened, as arranged, in Cassius' house, midway between the Kalends and the Ides.

I cannot now recall the precise date, but I recall, as if they were ranged before me now, the faces of my friends and colleagues. There were some I had reason to distrust: Quintus Ligarius and Galba were driven by personal resentment. They believed Caesar had insulted them. Cinna was a mean man, not to be trusted in a crisis. Trebonius, though a friend, I knew to be both rash and irresolute, a dangerous combination of qualities . . .

Many who were not present were cognisant of our intention, had been sounded out, had offered verbal support, would be with us if we succeeded. The dozen who were gathered that evening were the chiefs of what I suppose historians will call the conspiracy. I would reject the term: it has criminal connotations to my way of thinking. We were not criminals: we were executioners of just necessity.

Of all those present young Cato appeared the most nervous. Eager only a few days previously, urging on the deed with an enthusiasm his father could never have equalled, he now seemed pale, weary, filled with apprehension. He confided in me that he had been unable to sleep for several nights. He was oppressed by fear of failure – and of the revenge Caesar would certainly take.

"If we are brave and resolute, we shall not fail."

I spoke with more confidence than I felt myself. That too was necessary. Doubt is infectious, soon transformed into panic. I remembered how Catiline and his friends had lost their nerve, when confronted by Cicero. (My father, as consul-designate, had been the first to demand the death penalty: to their consternation.) Well, we were no Catilines, no discredited and indebted riff-raff. We were among the chief men of Rome, most of us with great achievements, feats of arms, a record of good judgment, to our names. But then, Caesar was more than Cicero, or my poor father.

Casca gave me courage, supported my equanimity. His good sense had fortified me often; Casca was always sanguine. When, on our way to the meeting, I mentioned the possibility of failure to him — in terms quite different from those I would employ to Cato, he scoffed at my fears.

"Caesar is but a man, mere mortal man. He bleeds as readily as you or I."

It was, however, the aftermath I feared most.

Markie had nerved himself to be with us. His long parade of doubt was at an end. For myself, I believe that his decision to join us was determined as much by fear of the contempt with which Porcia would regard his failure to do so, as from the sense of duty about which he endlessly prated. If so, that might be something to put to the credit of Cato's family, if it were not for the malign influence Markie had on our enterprise.

Cassius called us to order. He spoke briefly. His bearing was martial, his tone firm. He outlined the cogent reasons which had brought us together. He deplored the decadence of public spirit which had reduced the Republic to its sad condition.

"If Caesar's system of government were to be confirmed, then all that we know and love in Rome would wither, all that our fathers fought and died for would be no more, as, little by little, step by remorseless step, Rome will sink from view under the weight of an Oriental despotism. Our ancestors — the immediate ancestors of some here present — won the right to call no man 'King', no man 'Lord and Master'. We are called to act if we are not to be despised and hated by our descendants as the generation which, through apathy or cowardice, lost that right, and so condemned the Roman nobility to perpetual ignominy and subservience . . .

"If any man would dispute what I say, I shall not argue with him, but ask him to leave us now."

No one moved, though young Cato trembled and looked as if he might be sick at any moment.

Metellus Cimber got to his feet.

"You have spoken for all of us, Cassius, and we are all of your mind."

There was a murmur of assent.

"Nevertheless," Cimber said – and my father-in-law frowned at the word – "nevertheless, I would like to urge yet again what I have urged before: that we invite Cicero to be one of us. I have two reasons which I would ask you all to consider carefully."

He coughed. Markie, I remember, was looking at him, with his mouth hanging open, a sign, known to me from childhood, that he was concentrating hard.

"In the first place," Cimber said, "Cicero's grey hairs will serve to make our cause appear absolutely respectable. It will help to convince the waverers, for they will say that if a man of Cicero's experience, virtue and reputation has associated himself with us, then our deed must be justified. If we neglect to secure his support, then people will wonder why he is not with us, and probably condemn us as rash young men whom the good sense of Cicero has spurned."

"Scarcely young, Cimber," I said. "Few of us can be called young, and most of us, you yourself of course too, have a great deal of military experience, and great exploits to our names. I doubt whether anyone could dismiss us in the way you suggest."

"Well," Cimber said. "That is only my first point, and with respect to Decimus Brutus, I stick to it. My second is even more compelling, in my opinion. When the deed is done, we are going to have to justify it in the Senate and from the rostra. Can any doubt that Cicero is of all men the most fitted to argue our case?"

This was a valid point, and I said so.

"All the same," I added, "I think your anxiety exaggerated. I have no doubt that we shall be able to win Cicero's support, even his wholehearted support, when the moment of danger is past, and when words rather than deeds are required. So, I propose that we acknowledge the justice of much that Metellus Cimber has said, and then agree to approach Cicero when the time is ripe. I suspect this is what he himself would prefer. He is after all an old man, and has never been conspicuous for courage."

Markie coughed.

"There's no point inviting Cicero to join us," he said. "He would certainly refuse. He will never follow any course which others have set. You know his conceit and vanity."

I knew Markie's jealousy and I guessed that he was afraid that Cicero would outshine him, taking the primacy in our affair, by reason of his talents and reputation; and of course Cassius had promised that primacy to Markie himself in order to lure him on.

Cassius nodded to me, inviting me to speak, as we had arranged he should.

"I have a question to put to you. It is a grave question which needs careful consideration. Shall no man be touched except Caesar?"

Casca said: "Antony and Lepidus. You're referring to our virtuous consul and the Master of the Horse?"

"Chiefly, yes . . . we must secure our position."

"We would be mad not to," Casca said.

"It is indeed a point." Cassius spoke in a considering manner, as if his mind was not already determined. "Antony is loyal to Caesar. Various of us have sounded him out, carefully, and met with no satisfactory response. If he outlives Caesar, are we not likely to find our position endangered? As for Lepidus, he may not amount to much, but he has command of the only troops stationed near the city."

The meeting fell silent. People turned and whispered to their neighbours. Some were clearly agitated, not having anticipated such a proposal. Others nodded their heads in agreement, but none dared to be the first to speak out in approval.

"No, no, no." It was Markie, of course. "No, we are not butchers, Cassius. Think of the horror with which we regard Marius and Sulla and the proscriptions they so shamefully carried out. We are not butchers, I say that again. We are, as it were, priests of the Republic. Caesar's death will be a sort of sacrifice. A necessary sacrifice. I wish it was not necessary. I have, as you know, brooded long on the matter. I am not one to rush to judgment. But I am now convinced. However, if, my friends, you intend to extend the list of victims beyond that single name of Caesar, then I can have no part in your enterprise. I shall withdraw. Kill Caesar alone, and our motive will be recognised for what it is: an act of necessary virtue. Kill Caesar's friends, and it will seem as if we are no more than common cut-throats, bandits, murderers. That will be to invite a renewal of civil war. After the deed, let us practise clemency, and seek reconciliation with Caesar's friends. I repeat: either Caesar alone, or Marcus Brutus can have no hand in the business."

Casca groaned, but Markie carried the meeting. My second proposal, that I should alert the Ninth Legion, and summon them to Rome, ready to subdue any subsequent disorder, was alike defeated by Markie's argument.

"That," he said, "would give the wrong message. This is not a military coup, but, as I have said, an act of sacrifice. I cannot therefore consent, and unless I can freely and of my best judgment consent to any proposal then I cannot in honour be party to the deed. Besides, I am certain that you are too pessimistic, Decimus. There will be no subsequent trouble, for all good men will regard us with favour, and applaud our deed. We shall not be seen as villains, but as heroes who have restored liberty to Rome."

So, it was, ill-advisedly, decided. Only Caesar should die. Then all would be sweetness and light.

The Ides of March, the Theatre of Pompey, then a general acclamation of the Liberators.

Having at last allowed himself to be convinced, it seemed that Markie had cast aside all doubt.

Cassius saw the reason of my arguments, but he supported Markie's rejection of them, because he valued his participation more highly than he valued reason.

CHAPTER

21

On the eve of the Ides of March, Lepidus invited me to dine. I hesitated to accept. This was natural. I had after all recommended that he should suffer with Caesar. At the very least, I had argued, subsequent to our formal conclave, that he and Antony should be arrested. This modest proposal Cassius had also declined to entertain (even though his own judgment approved it) because he feared it would give Markie reason to withdraw from our enterprise. I recognised Cassius' weakness in this decision. For all his merits, and great strength of will, without which nothing would have been done, for he was truly the fount and origin of the business, he suffered from a defect which was the obverse of his singular qualities. He readily fell victim to what I can only call monomania; once he had an idea fixed in his mind, nothing could persuade him to alter it. That fixed idea was the necessity of Markie's participation. There was nothing I could do to shift it. Accordingly, of necessity, I acquiesced.

Nevertheless I was conscious that there was a certain delicacy involved in accepting Lepidus' invitation. Moreover, I would have liked to compose myself for our great action in silence and privacy. Yet there were cogent reasons to accept. For one thing I couldn't tell what doubts and fears my absence might not give rise to.

I was dismayed all the same to discover that Caesar was of the party. So was Trebonius. His presence alarmed me for I knew him to be nervous, and therefore feared that his manner might arouse suspicion. Metellus Cimber was there also, and this displeased Caesar, for he knew that Cimber was anxious that the decree of banishment which his brother had suffered, should be rescinded. He frowned on greeting Cimber, warning him by his manner that the moment was not propitious to raise his brother's case. Seeing this, I took Cimber by the sleeve, and warned him to keep silent. I reminded him also in an urgent whisper that he and his brother had a vital role to play the next morning.

"Very well," he said, "but it offends me to see the dictator so debonair and think of the injustice done to my poor brother, and to recall the indignity he has suffered and the hardships he now endures."

"Let all go well," I said, "and he will soon be restored to you."

Lepidus called us to supper. If I had not known him well, I would have read anxiety in his manner. But Lepidus was always fussy as an old hen. It was strange. Many women were said to judge him the handsomest man in Rome, and certainly in repose he would have made an admirable model for a statue representing heroic virtue; but then he rarely was in repose. Now his fussing irritated Caesar, accustomed though he was to Lepidus' manner.

At last, he broke out:

"Let us be, Lepidus. Your dinner will not be spoiled if we delay a moment before attending it. In any case," he said to me, speaking more quietly, so as not to give offence to our host, "a dinner's but a dinner. I can't be troubled with these fellows who treat it as some sort of sacred rite."

This was true. Caesar was indifferent to what he ate and drank. I had often heard him mock his two former colleagues, Crassus and Pompey, for the care they took for their stomachs.

"I am in this respect a Greek," Caesar would say. "I come to table for conversation rather than food. As far as eating goes I am as happy with a hunk of bread and cheese, as with the elaborate fare these fellows insist on."

By unspoken agreement we avoided politics and war that evening, though Lepidus tactlessly tried to introduce the question of the Parthian campaign. Caesar himself swept that aside.

"If you seek enlightenment on that matter, Lepidus, call on me in office hours . . ."

He turned to me and enquired as to Longina's state of health.

"I am told you have sent her to the country. I trust that doesn't indicate that there is some trouble."

"No," I said, "the air in Rome, you know. And then I think it is easier to get good milk in the country, and that is something for which she has developed a taste in her condition."

He snapped his fingers, to summon a secretary whom he kept always near him, and who, on this occasion, was perched on a stool in a little passage leading to an antechamber.

"Make a note, will you," Caesar said, "that I wish to have a report compiled concerning the quality of the milk sold in the city. It should also tell me the conditions in which cows are kept, the time that elapses before milk is offered for sale to the public, and whether new regulations are needed to control the trade. For instance, whether we should impose a limit on the number of cows kept within a space of a certain size. Oh, and anything else that is thought appropriate. I should like a preliminary report seven days from now, and the project to be completed by the end of the month. I have no doubt that we shall find several reforms called for."

He turned back to me.

"Thank you for bringing this matter to my attention, Mouse. I grow ever more convinced that the secret of successful administration lies in the realisation that ordinary people suffer most from what might seem tiny unimportant matters to such as us, but which in their condition prove irksome. The quality of milk will matter more to a young woman of the poorer classes than the question of whether your father-in-law should be consul in forty-two, as he wishes, or will have to wait till the next year."

Talk at the table had moved on to questions of philosophy while Caesar concerned himself with the city's milk supplies. Someone – I forget who now – was discoursing on Platonism and the Theory of Ideas. He was speaking approvingly. Metellus Cimber repudiated the notion.

"I'm a plain man and a soldier, and I have no time for this farrago. I assure you, it's no good arguing in the middle of a battle that the spear which is being thrust at your belly is only a shadowy representation of the idea of the true spear. No use at all. It's all mystical Greek nonsense and any Roman should be ashamed of spouting it."

"That's rather too strong, Cimber," I said. "I'm at one with you about the spear, of course. Nevertheless, there's a certain charm in Plato's thought, and when you consider abstract nouns – justice, of course, even love – you have to admit that there is some force in the suggestion that our experience of these is always imperfect."

Lepidus nodded his head several times, ducking towards me, to Cimber, and then to the man who had introduced the subject. It always pleased him to hear intellectual matters discussed at his table, even though he was quite incompetent to contribute to the debate himself.

Caesar, usually alert to this sort of conversation, seemed abstracted, and I felt ashamed of what I was saying. After all, I thought, men like Caesar and myself knew the urgency of a reality to which I supposed that Plato had been a stranger. So I said:

"And yet, in the end, this is all frippery when set beside the knowledge of reality which the experience of battle gives you. That is why we Romans are superior to the Greeks of today. We act; they talk."

Now, I wonder: will men still read and debate Plato when Caesar and Decimus Brutus are no more than tinkling names, or perhaps even forgotten?

The conversation turned towards the subject of death.

Someone asked Caesar what manner of death he would choose for himself.

"A sudden one."

Then he signed a number of official letters which a slave brought to the table.

I walked home with Trebonius and Metellus Cimber. They were excited by Caesar's reply to that last question.

"It is as if he had some foreboding."

"Well," Cimber said, "there have been a number of strange happenings. Did you hear that some have seen men of fire struggling against each other in the heavens? I'm also told that a soothsayer – some say Spurinna, others Artemidorus – has warned Caesar to beware the Ides of March."

"Yes," I said, "and the same man – it was Spurinna by the way – warned him with equal zeal to beware the last Kalends of December."

A flash of lightning dazzled us. The ensuing thunder seemed to shake the roof of the Capitol. We took refuge from the sudden teeming rain in a doorway. The storm was brief. Later, of course, many reported that they had seen strange and wonderful things that night: a lioness was said to have whelped in the streets, ghosts to have walked, the rain turned to blood. It was all nonsense, provoked by excitement and the brief experience of an intense but ordinary thunderstorm. Nothing perverts reason like superstition and the credulity it engenders.

The storm abated, as abruptly as it had broken forth. We resumed our journey, till our ways diverged, when we embraced, bidding each other good sleep and a brave heart for the morn.

But I was reluctant to retire. I feared that sleep would elude me. I ached for Longina. I recalled as I splashed over the cobbles that night before we crossed the Rubicon. There had been exhilaration then.

I found myself in the vicinity of Markie's house. A servant answered my knock, led me to Porcia.

"Is all well?"

"Save the night."

"Marcus is studying and has asked not to be disturbed. He is working on his translation of the *Phaedo*. It composes his mind. He is resolute."

"Good. Tell him I called. Tell him all is well, all prepared. Caesar is free of suspicion."

Later in my wanderings I encountered Casca. He had been dining with Antony, and had left him drunk.

"Don't feel like sleep, old boy. Let's go to a tavern."

I let him lead the way to a mean hovel under the rock of the Quirinal. There were some old soldiers there, on leave, playing dice. They laughed about the chances of the Parthian campaign.

"All I want," one said, "is a farm of my own, with a young wife and bairns. It's been promised me often enough. Now, they say, after Parthia. My father went against Parthia with fat old Crassus. He never came back."

"They say there are still Romans held in captivity there."

"Well, they're as far from a retirement farm as if they were fucking dead."

Then they recognised us and the veteran apologised for his words.

"We all get a bit down sometimes," he said, "thinking of the future. I've been in thirty-seven battles. It seems enough, that's all."

"But you don't need to apologise," Casca said. "Every man's entitled to his say. That's one of the glories of living in a Free State."

They joined in his laughter, and he ordered more wine for them.

The boy serving it caught his attention. Casca clasped the back of the boy's thigh, running his hand up below the tunic.

"Well, you're a pretty piece," he said.

The boy dipped his curly head and giggled. Casca made a sign to the landlord, and retired with the boy behind a curtain.

"Well, the General's in good form," the veteran said, leaning across to me.

"Casca is always Casca," I said.

"Aye, that's a comfort."

I went out into the streets. A whore accosted me. I had her up against a wall, paid her more than she demanded, and felt no relief.

I was still awake when the dawn brought light to my chamber.

I rose, bathed, had myself shaved, and dressed in a new toga. My dagger was concealed within its folds, in a sheath attached to a belt.

It was a grey morning. A wind shook the branches of the trees and unleashed bursts of rain as I made my way, with firm step, to the Theatre of Pompey where the Senate was to meet. There were more rumours, I heard, that Caesar would be offered, or would claim, the crown. So much the better; they lent authority to our enterprise. Business was already under way; those of my colleagues who held the office of praetor hearing cases and giving judgment. I admired the resolution of their manner. Even my cousin Markie proved himself worthy. When a certain person appealed from his judgment to that of Caesar, Markie said: "Caesar neither does, nor shall, hinder me from acting and judging in accordance with the law." His voice sounded a little petulant, but his sentiments won a cheer, and he smiled. (There were those, by the way, who habitually described his smile as "sweet", one of his admirers even going so far as to compare it to sunshine after rain. I always thought it smug myself. Nevertheless I was glad to see Markie smile that morning, because I had feared that his nerve might fail, as I had so often known it do.)

Cassius embraced me. His elder son had that morning put on the *toga virilis* for the first time.

"It could not have happened on a more propitious day," Cassius said. "It is, after all, for our children and their children that we act this morning."

He moved around our band of friends, smiling and offering encouragement. Casca clapped me on the back.

"And what happened to you last night, old boy?"

"Much the same as happened to you, but with a being of

a different gender, and more briefly, and probably with less pleasure."

"You couldn't have had more. I must say, I feel unaccountably well. Perhaps I am still a little drunk. Look at Antony – he is still reeling. He can't take wine as he used to, you know, for I matched him cup for cup."

Antony certainly seemed crapulous. Indeed he retired behind a pillar and vomited, then summoned one slave to clean up the mess, and another to fetch him a jug of wine. He caught my eye and winked.

Cassius said to me: "I have told Trebonius to attach himself to Antony when Caesar arrives, and to hold him in conversation."

"Trebonius?"

"Yes, he has sufficient resolution for that part, if no other."

"I've just had a nasty moment," Casca said. "Do you see that old fool over there, can't remember his name, he's a connection of the Dolabellas. Well, he came up to me and said, 'Allow me to congratulate you. You've kept your secret well, but Marcus Brutus has let it slip.' Well, I was just wondering, old fruit, whether it mightn't be prudent to let the blabbermouth – both of them perhaps – have one in the guts, when he went on, 'All the same I'd like to know how you became so rich all of a sudden as to be able to stand for election as aedile. It'll involve you in enormous expense, you know.'"

"What did you reply?"

"Oh, I said, 'Ask my creditors, old boy.'"

That was not the only alarm, for Popilius Laena, a notorious gossip, accosted Cassius and myself and wished us luck.

"I am with you in heart and spirit," he said, "only be quick, for I fear your secret is out."

Cassius turned away, uncertain what to reply. So it fell upon me to soothe the old man, and to assure him that all was in train and that we were grateful for his expression of sympathy.

And still there was no sign of Caesar.

One of Marcus Brutus' servants approached, looking agitated.

"Where is my master?"

"There: dispensing justice."

"There has been a calamity."

"Tell me."

"No, I must tell my master first," and he ran over to Markie, plucked at his sleeve and whispered in his ear. Markie concluded the business he was engaged in as rapidly as possible, and announced that the sitting was suspended.

"I must leave," he said. "This man has brought me terrible news. Porcia has collapsed. She may be dead."

"I fear she is," the servant, a freedman, said.

"If she is dead," I said, "your presence will be to no purpose. Your place is here."

"No, no, I must go."

I wondered (of course) whether this might not be some ruse prearranged by Markie to provide him with an excuse to quit the field. It would have been in character. On the other hand, Porcia would have flayed him with her tongue if he abandoned the enterprise, and I doubt if she would have thought it proper for him to do so even for her sake: so deeply did that woman hate Caesar, her hatred could overcome even her egotism. I was, of course, the last man to be able to persuade Markie; so I turned the matter over to Cassius. I did so even though I had thought we would manage the affair better without my cousin. I had good reason. We had neglected, as a result of his insistence, to take the precautions which I thought necessary. I was not confident of success, but I was determined that, if we should fail, Markie should not escape the consequences of the decisions he had urged on us.

Cassius began to argue with him, but made little headway. If only Caesar would arrive . . . but he didn't. Someone whispered that he was not coming to the Senate that day.

"But that's nonsense," I said. "I happen to know that his old uncle, Julius Cotta, is going to make public his discovery of the prophecy in the Sibylline Books that the Romans will only conquer Parthia under the leadership of a king. You can't tell me that Caesar will miss seeing his enemies' faces when that particular piece of news is imparted."

"Calpurnia, it seems, has had a dream; and therefore Caesar will not come."

"Pish and tush," I said. "I never knew the day when Caesar's actions were controlled by a woman's fears."

Nevertheless I was doubtful, for I knew only too well these moods of lassitude which could suddenly overtake him.

Markie pulled away from Cassius.

"I must go," he cried. "Nothing is more important to me than my wife."

Fortunately, the action provoked by this sentiment – so unworthy of a Roman nobleman – was abruptly checked, for, as he broke away, he bumped into a second freedman sent, puffing and panting, from his house in search of him.

This man babbled that Porcia had recovered. She had only fainted. She insisted that her husband should not turn away from the work in hand.

Was it dismay that made Markie look so sullen?

It was confirmed: Caesar would not come.

"So the matter must be put off to another day," Markie said.

"We cannot afford delay," I said.

"Not for an hour." Cassius was brisk. "Mouse, you must at once to Caesar, persuade him to come. You alone can do it. If Caesar does not attend today, then I'm afraid we are all lost. A secret which is known to Popilius Laena is no secret. It's a miracle that Caesar himself has not yet learned of it."

"Perhaps he has," I said. "Perhaps that is why he isn't here. Well, I'll make the attempt. If Caesar knows our plans, I have nothing more to lose."

There was relief in action. I was glad to be free of the highly charged atmosphere of the Senate. Nothing in the streets suggested anything of that febrile excitement which can run through a crowd when it feels that events of great moment are about to unfold. The stallholders yelled their wares as usual. The taverns were filling up as usual. The people went about their business as usual. I passed a gang of gladiators being escorted to the practice arena; they looked surly, as usual. I hurried round the base of the Capitol and entered the Forum. Perhaps there was less activity than was normal, but then that was often so on days when the Senate met. I passed along the Via Sacra towards the Regia, the house opposite the temple of the Vestal Virgins where Caesar had recently taken up his residence, as he was entitled to do in his office as Pontifex Maximus.

"Here's Decimus Brutus," Calpurnia's voice was harsh and almost hysterical. There were tear-marks on her cheeks.

"Caesar, Calpurnia," I said. "I am giving myself the honour of escorting Caesar to the Senate."

"Thank you, Mouse, but I'm afraid it's an honour which you must do without today. I cannot come. No, that is untrue, and it would be still less true to say 'I dare not come.' So simply take the message that I shall not."

"Say he is sick," Calpurnia said.

"No, I am not sick, and I would not burden you with a lie, Mouse. Say only: I shall not come."

"Can you give me some reason? The Senate will be offended if I return with such a blunt message. They will say that Caesar . . . well, never mind what they will say. You know it as well as I do."

"I do not choose to come. That is sufficient reason for the Senate, who have no right to question my actions. Still, Mouse, I owe it to you to be more explicit. Calpurnia has had a dream which disturbs her; therefore, for her sake, I choose to stay at home."

"You never knew such a dream," Calpurnia said, her voice rising to a shout. "I saw his statue," she hurried on, "and it was running with blood. And then the people, stinking plebs, came and bathed their hands in it, and some of them smeared their faces with his blood; and so I am afraid, and have begged Caesar to remain at home. For that's not all. There were ghosts seen in the streets last night, shrieking and lamenting, and others saw bloodstained men fight in the skies. And then there was that business of the sacrifice. You heard about that, Mouse. When they killed the ox it was found to have no heart. These are all dreadful portents, which it would be impious to ignore."

I sat down, and acted the part of a man thinking deeply.

"I was in the streets last night and saw no ghosts. I have just come from the Senate. The mood there is certainly excited. Your old uncle, Julius Cotta, is going about saying that he is about to reveal something of great moment which he has discovered in his researches in the Sibylline Books, and when anyone asks him what it is, he lays his finger along his nose and says, 'Wait till Caesar comes and all shall be revealed.' More important still, there is a proposal to be put to vote you a crown and the title of King, to be worn beyond Italy, in all parts of the Empire save at home. Even the staunchest Republicans are not averse to this, or so it seems, and there is a rumour that Cicero intends to come to the Senate, entering as you might imagine with the utmost drama when he has been assured that you are there, in order to support the motion. Now you know Cicero better than any of us, and you know what a blow it would be to his vanity if I brought the message that Caesar does not choose to attend the Senate today. I'm afraid that the proposal would be shelved and would probably not be resuscitated. As you have often said yourself, the great art of war and politics is to seize the moment. The moment has arrived, but if Caesar does not choose to come, why, then the moment will pass.

"And then," I said, seeing that my words were having some effect, "Calpurnia's dream . . . perhaps I, not having dreamed it and not having experienced the fear it caused her, can offer a better interpretation. This business of the statue spouting blood and the Romans smearing their faces with it. It seems to me probable that they were indeed drinking Caesar's blood, but that this signifies that Rome has sucked, as we know it has, reviving blood from you. It is a dream signifying regeneration, nothing dreadful.

"Finally," I said, "you know you can trust me to be silent as to the reason why you do not choose to come. But you know also how men speculate and you know how fleet of foot is rumour. So I've no doubt the reason will emerge or will be guessed, or even that some cynic will happen on it by chance, and cry out, 'Well, let's adjourn this meeting till, by chance, we hit on a day when Caesar's wife is not troubled by bad dreams, or has had a good night's sleep.' And then a fellow of similar fancy will cry out that Caesar has little chance of beating the Parthians if he is kept at home by his wife's terrors.

"I'm sorry," I said, "if my frank language gives offence, but you know, Caesar, that I have always spoken my mind in council, and you know that I am a simple plain blunt soldier, and you will forgive me my lack of tact and of nice rhetorical skills, because you know my anxiety proceeds from the . . . love . . . I bear you."

And so I convinced him, and, leaving Calpurnia to her terrors (more justified than she could have guessed, poor bitch), we proceeded from his house.

As we came into the Forum, a lean, mad-looking Greek with long dirty grey hair approached him yelling something which I did not understand. It was Greek certainly, but in his excitement, the words escaped me.

Caesar smiled to see him:

"So, Spurinna, you see the Ides of March have come, and I am well."

"Aye, Caesar, but the day has far to go."

This time I could understand him; he spoke in Latin, made curious by a lisp.

He thrust a rolled-up parchment at Caesar.

"Read this, I beg you."

I said: "I have something for you to cast your eye over also: a suit from Trebonius."

"Read mine first," the old man said, "it concerns you closely."

"Then I fear it must take second place," Caesar said, and handed it to me.

"You did right to persuade me," Caesar said as we approached the Theatre of Pompey. "But Calpurnia was pressing. She has been in a strange mood, almost unbalanced in its intensity. Now that Caesar is away from her, Caesar is himself again."

I slipped from his side as we entered the theatre. Cassius smiled at me. Now that the moment had arrived he was calm as the sky on a windless night. He held Markie to his side. One glance at Markie's face told me this precaution was unnecessary. He had screwed up his courage to a point where he could find release only in action. Then his hand tightened on Cassius' arm. I followed his gaze, and saw that Popilius Laena had approached Caesar and was deep in conversation with him. Impatient murmurs ran round the Senate. Caesar's uncle, Julius Cotta, fussed with the rim of his toga. They had been kept waiting a long time, many of them. I looked about me. Cicero was not present.

Trebonius had seized Antony's attention. After a few minutes' talk, they left the theatre.

Caesar smiled. Popilius Laena gave a little titter and backed away.

Metellus Cimber approached Caesar and knelt before him. He spoke at some length, quietly, so that his words did not carry to me.

Caesar frowned, made a dismissive gesture. Cimber seized the hem of his robe and Caesar twitched it free.

Cassius and Markie now closed on him. Cassius knelt, supporting Cimber's plea, as we had arranged. Markie stood a little apart. He had refused to kneel.

Again Caesar swept his arm across his face in a gesture of refusal. It wouldn't have mattered if he had assented, but that refusal of so reasonable a request was as the ultimate justification of our intent. I drew near enough to hear Caesar say:

"No, and forever no. The decree of banishment stands. If you all kneel before me and fawn on me, I reject your demands as I would dismiss a mongrel cur. When will you learn that Caesar is constant as the northern star, fixed like none other in the firmament?"

"When will you learn that men are still men?" said Casca, and stabbed him in the neck.

Cassius was next to strike, then Markie aimed a blow. It ran through Caesar's toga and the dagger stuck there.

Caesar struggled to his feet, but we were all upon him.

"This for Pompey . . ."

"Dictator for life . . ."

"Tyrant . . ."

"For my brother . . ."

He caught my eye. For a moment horror and reproach filled the theatre.

"Not you, my son."

I thrust my dagger under the breast-bone.

Amazement crept over his countenance. He pulled the toga over his head, and slumped to the marble. His hands clutched at the pedestal of Pompey's statue. Even as he lay there, others of our friends drew near and stabbed him. The body kicked and was still, as the blood ran across the floor towards the rostrum.

We stood in a ring around the body. I think we were all astonished, that it had been so easy.

One moment, Caesar; and the next, a piece of bleeding flesh, authority and majesty departed, like a door slammed by the wind. The tune of the piper who had lured us into Italy sounded a moment in my imagination, and was still.

A senator who had not been of our party picked up a fallen

dagger and knelt over the thing that had been Caesar to add his wound to the many it had received.

Cassius detained him.

"We are not butchers," he said, "and you had no part in the danger. Therefore, no part either in the honour."

My left arm was bleeding, gashed by a blow aimed at Caesar. I bound it up with a rag.

Markie advanced into the open space where the actors played, and raised his voice:

"Do not be alarmed, Conscript Fathers. We intend no harm to any other man. I pray you, keep your seats."

He might as well have bid the wind be still. They scrambled for the door, jostling each other in their fright and anxiety to be clear of the place.

In a moment we were left alone with Caesar's body.

Trebonius entered.

"Where is Antony?"

"Fled in terror, though I assured him he was in no danger. But there is general consternation, panic even, in the streets. I could not restrain Antony."

Markie said, "Very well. We have done what we set out to do. Let us now go, bearing our bleeding swords, to the Capitol, and proclaim to Rome that liberty has been restored."

He spoke like an actor. I did not protest. It was for this moment that Cassius had been so determined that Markie should be one of us: we would see if he was right.

I was the last to leave the scene. I looked back at the body: so small and insignificant; so many battles won, so much distance travelled, so much glory, so great renown: all silenced, expunged, concluded in a flurry of knives.

I almost longed for tears that I might let one fall on Caesar.

I stood over what had been the Perpetual Dictator.

"Cruel necessity," I said, and followed the others into the grey of the March morning.

CHAPTER

23

Markie led us from the theatre to the Capitol to give thanks to Jupiter for the deliverance of the city from tyranny. He behaved as if he was enacting a ceremony. In its way it was impressive. I should have preferred that he realised we had in reality effected a *coup d'état*, which we still required to secure. Our advantage would be brief if we did not seize it immediately. Some of my friends and colleagues brandished their bloody daggers and cried out, "Liberty! Liberty!"

For my part I chose to remain silent and watchful. The crowd fell away on either side as we passed, silent, shaken, perhaps reproachful. That did not disturb me. I had never supposed the rabble would applaud us.

We rendered thanks to Jupiter and the other gods of the Republic. No doubt that was suitable. And then we waited, uncertain how to act. It was still only the fifth hour of the day.

"Is there any news of Antony?"

Cicero appeared, wafted there by rumour.

He congratulated us on having set Rome free.

"But I wish you had consulted me," he said. "You should have realised my advice would have been invaluable."

He did not remain long, being uncertain, I suppose, how things would turn out, and reluctant to be too closely associated with the consequences of an act in which he had had no share.

Other sympathisers made equally brief appearances, nervous, divided between elation and terror.

Casca yawned, and sent a slave in search of wine.

"What do we do now, eh?" he said. "Buggered if I know," he added.

I was dizzy from my wound, unable to think clearly. Two ravens rose from the roof of the Temple of Jupiter and flapped their slow way towards the Tiber.

Dolabella appeared arrayed in the insignia of the consulship which in other circumstances he would only have assumed when Caesar departed for the Balkans. He, too, neither knew what to say nor whether he should be with us.

"Have you seen Antony? Where is he? Does anyone know what has become of him?"

Below us in the Forum the crowd was thickening. A confused babble rose to our ears. I searched for a note of rejoicing.

I said to Cassius:

"We are in danger of losing our advantage. This is our hour and we must act on it. We can't sit here and admire our handiwork."

It was agreed that Markie should address them. The proposal disconcerted him.

"Why me? It was not my idea. Perhaps Cassius . . . ?"

"Listen," I said. "You are the man they want to hear. It was you who received all those pleas urging you to be worthy of our ancestor. Well, show us that you are. Cassius may have been our leader. Without him we wouldn't have got where we are. But you, cousin, are the man with the spotless reputation. So, get on with it, or I swear I'll mingle your blood with Caesar's on my dagger."

Vanity and fear are the two great motivating forces. They snapped at Markie's heels as he descended to the Forum.

A cheer broke out. He approached the rostrum amidst cries of "Noble Brutus" and suchlike nonsense; encouraging in the circumstances, of course.

He raised his hand for silence. The murmuring died away. Someone shouted, "Let's hear Brutus . . . let's hear what the noble Brutus has to say."

He began to speak. He spoke well, I have to admit that. It is a strange gift, oratory, and one you wouldn't have expected Markie to possess. Of course he wasn't in Cicero's class – there was no music in his voice – and he didn't have even Antony's wild eloquence, but he was effective. If you didn't know him – and of course the mob knew his reputation, not the man himself – you would have said: "This is an honest man. I can rely on him to speak the truth." So close is oratory to acting.

"Friends," he said, "fellow citizens. This is a day of sun and rain, a day to weep, and a day to rejoice. Hear me out, I urge you, before you pass judgment on what we have done this morning. There are many here who loved Caesar. I count myself among them . . ."

He was well-launched. I turned my attention to the crowd. There was a fellow just below me, a big, black-stubbled, sweaty fellow with the look of a butcher, his wrists bloodstained, whose chest heaved with sobs. He tore a dirty rag from around his neck and mopped his eyes. When Markie paused, he raised his head and emitted a bellow of pain, rage, grief, I know not what. A companion passed him a flask. He took a swig and a rivulet of yellow wine ran from the corner of his mouth to his chin. He pursued it with his tongue and then wiped his chin with the rag, and drank again.

Markie drew his dagger, and waved it above his head.

"This knife which slew Caesar is ready to be employed against my own person, should the good of Rome require me to die."

Perhaps my threat had inspired this dramatic stroke? The crowd roared, madly, contemptibly. Markie was the hero of the moment, stern, just, noble, selfless, everything he would wish to be taken for. I could not but reflect that the same mob would have cheered as loudly to see us strung up, naked, by the heels.

Cinna, never bright, responded to what he thought to be the mood of the crowd.

"Caesar was a bloody tyrant," he yelled, "and don't any of you forget it."

A clod of dung struck him in the face. Other missiles followed, and we withdrew in disorder back to the Capitol.

Antony had not been idle. When he recovered from his initial moment of terror — quite understandable in my opinion and justified, of course, if I had had my way — and realised that his life was not in immediate danger, he had hastened to Caesar's house. He found Calpurnia in paroxysms of grief, or perhaps fury. He wasted little time in comforting her, the task being as vain as it was unnecessary. Calpurnia was of no importance now. He had never liked her and knew her to be a bitch who would soon find some other man to torment. That poor wretch's state would be worse than Caesar's for he would have to endure comparisons with the dead hero. So Antony brushed her aside and took possession of all Caesar's papers, acting in his capacity as consul. Even Calpurnia couldn't argue with that, though I imagine she tried to do so.

He summoned a conference of Balbus the banker, Hirtius who was not only Caesar's secretary but consul-designate for the next year, and Lepidus, the Master of the Horse. So he secured to himself money, respectability – nobody being more respectable than Hirtius, who was never shocked, Caesar used to aver, by a dirty joke, because he was too virtuous to see it – and, of the greatest immediate importance, soldiers, since Lepidus commanded the only troops in the immediate vicinity of Rome. Then he sent a message to us, proposing an "armistice" and a peace conference. To show his confidence in our virtue, he entrusted the message to his eighteen-year-old son.

You had to grant Antony nerve. I compared his energy and confidence with the pusillanimity of my confederates.

I spent that evening writing letters: to Longina, Octavius and Cicero. You can imagine with what eloquence I argued our case. But I was well aware that I might be dead before darkness fell again.

I was awakened with the news that Lepidus had stationed three cohorts in the Forum and had reinforced the guards at the city gate. Rome, which we had liberated, was now our prison, if we failed to reach an agreement with Caesar's heirs. Lepidus had the good manners or political sense to send me a note explaining that his only desire was to secure order and prevent riots. He sent a similar note to Markie who found no difficulty in believing him.

Then, before I was dressed, another note arrived, this time from Antony himself. Its tone was friendly, but I discounted that, for obvious reasons. He had summoned the Senate to meet the following day at the Temple of Tellus: "It is necessary that things be arranged in an orderly and legal manner." The word "legal" was underlined, twice, with bold strokes. He invited Cassius and me to dine with him that evening, adding that Lepidus was issuing a similar invitation to Markie and Metellus Cimber. There was a footnote: "Don't be alarmed by the measures Lepidus has taken. I would have prevented them if I had known his intentions, but the poor fool must play the Great Man. You know what he is like, Mouse."

I armed the slaves escorting me to Antony's house with truncheons. There had been disturbances in the city. A poet, unhappily named Cinna, had been mistaken for our confederate and bludgeoned to death in an alley. He was, I was later told, a very indifferent poet, but his lame verses scarcely excused his murder.

Antony was sober, but called for wine as soon as I was announced, and drank a beaker before he entered on conversation.

"I hadn't taken you for such a fool, Mouse."

"I understood from the tone of your letter that there were to be no recriminations, this evening at least."

"Granted."

"Besides, I gave you sufficient indication. I all but openly invited you to join us."

"Granted again."

"Have you heard what Cicero is saying?"

"Could I be interested?"

"You might. He asks whether there was anyone but Antony who did not desire Caesar's death, and is there anyone but Antony who is not happy on account of what has happened? I'm not so certain he is right to make the exception."

"That's as may be. I'm still amazed you let yourself be led by the nose. By your father-in-law of all men! I would have credited you with too much sense to get involved in such a ham-fisted, botched affair."

"Thank you, Antony. Certain things would have been better managed if my advice had been taken."

"Meaning I'd have shared Caesar's fate?"

"Meaning you'd have been removed from circulation, shall we say."

"Thanks. But since I'm still in circulation, in my way of looking at it, I'm the man who's got to tidy things up and restore some degree of rational control."

We might fence like old comrades but the dinner was awkward. It could not fail to be; it was as if Caesar's body lay naked and bleeding on the table while we carved up his inheritance. Hirtius was near weeping.

"I would never have thought it of you," he said to me, time and again.

Antony smiled, extended his hand, closed his fingers tight.

"I could have you all hurled from the Tarpeian Rock, and the mob would yell in glee. Don't think it's beyond me. As consul, I command the armies of Rome."

"With your colleague Dolabella," Cassius remarked.

"Don't give me that. Ask Mouse here which of us the soldiers will obey."

"There's no question."

"There's Lepidus," Cassius said.

"If you think I can't control that fool, you're a fool yourself. There never was such a botched business."

"Hardly that," Cassius said. "Caesar is dead."

"And your lives are mine. I'm tempted, I admit it. But relax. For now. For one thing your benighted crew includes friends of mine, Mouse here chief of all. Thank the stars you don't believe in, Cassius, that you've got Mouse on your side. Otherwise . . ."

He cracked a walnut. The shell shattered.

"And you all have families, connections. I've no wish to copy Sulla. I agree with Caesar in loathing that example. And I grant that you may too. Otherwise you wouldn't have stopped at Caesar. So: no proscriptions. Rome's had its bellyful of citizens' blood. Besides — this'll shock Hirtius — I wasn't nuts about Caesar myself."

He beamed on us, and tossed back another mug of wine.

"Oh, he was a genius, granted. He dazzled me, like he dazzled everyone. But I wasn't crazy about him. Not sure I even liked him."

"Liking's a pointless word applied to Caesar," I said.

"Fair enough. Oh I felt his charm. Who again didn't? But — Mouse knows — I agreed with him that the old boy was going off his rocker. This Parthian campaign. Well, thank you for saving us from that. So why did I stick to him? Why did I pretend I didn't understand the hints Mouse dropped? Simple: he may have been heading to be a tyrant, but he wasn't one yet. And he maintained order, which, in spite of my private life, I value as the first public good. Tyranny's more tolerable than civil war. We've all seen too much of that. So that's why you're here. So we can work out how to avoid civil war, how to divvy up the State. All right?"

Cassius sniffed, as if Antony had emitted a bad smell.

"You're plausible," he said. "That's why I find it hard to trust you. But I'll try if you can answer me this: that . . . that charade at the Lupercal. Can you explain that?"

Antony laughed. I remember wondering if there was any other laughter in Rome that night.

"Easy. I was playing silly buggers. Besides, it was Himself's idea. He was trying out the people. If it had gone right – for him – what difference, eh? What's in a name – King, Caesar, Perpetual Dictator – it all comes to the same bloody thing. Besides, I was pissed. You can't hold that against me . . ."

At such moments I loved Antony: for his vitality, his refusal to take himself absolutely seriously, for being the opposite of Markie, and – yes, I still say it – a better, more honourable man. For his laughter. Markie couldn't laugh. I am melancholic myself; Antony supplied a lack in me. Then he outlined his proposals. They surprised Cassius, who despised, and therefore failed to understand, him.

"They'll do," I said, "if you're sincere."

"Sincere?" Antony laughed. "Do you doubt me? Your old mucker?"

As we left, Hirtius plucked me by the sleeve.

"Why? Why? Why, Decimus Brutus? If Caesar loved any man" (it was a big "if" of course) "he loved you. I wish we may be able to rely on Antony, but his judgment, his character . . . oh dear. But who else is there?"

"You can rely on me, Hirtius. We have always been friends."

"Yes," he said. "But you would have spoken the same words to Caesar."

"I never dared call Caesar friend."

Resentment, suspicion, fear and rancour poisoned the Senate.

Tiberius Claudius Nero, partisan in succession of Pompey and Caesar, unstable as water, rose to propose: "Public and exemplary honours for the noble tyrannicides." Some cheered, others shifted in their seats, others howled him down. I was ready to deprecate the motion, to appease Caesar's friends. But

Antony got in first, silencing Nero with a gesture that dismissed the motion without debate: "Neither honours nor punishment." The thing was done, the deed committed; no good would come from dwelling on it. We must look ahead, to ensure the stability of the Republic. Therefore – he brushed a lock of hair aside – the office of dictator should be abolished, that we might never find ourselves in such straits again; all should be confirmed in their offices and appointments, both actual and designate; finally, though it was accepted that Caesar had been killed by honourable and patriotic citizens, nevertheless all his acts – even projects as yet unpublished – should have the force of law.

He smiled on us.

"I warn you, friends, that if you don't accept this last measure, we shall be in the deuce of a legal pickle."

I could see Markie itching to speak. Silence was painful to him. He bobbed up as Antony sat down, but found himself unable to do more than reiterate the sentiments he had expressed in the Forum (though the time for that was past and anyway they sounded even emptier when deployed before a more intelligent audience), and then support everything Antony had proposed.

Cicero couldn't be kept down either. He called for a general amnesty, to include even Sextus Pompey and his gang. He too supported Antony's measures, though, such was his antipathy to him, he contrived to do so without mentioning him by name or title, and even managed to convey the impression that the proposals were all his own. One could not fail to admire his old rhetorical skill, and even Antony was more amused than resentful of this insolence.

Calpurnia's father, Lucius Calpurnius Piso, then urged that Caesar's will should be published and that he be granted a public funeral.

Such was the mood of relief that even this dangerous proposal was carried, and indeed Cicero rose again to support it.

"We must create a new concord in the Republic, commencing here in the Senate, Conscript Fathers," he said.

It was an old tune, reassuring in its familiarity; unfortunately he failed, as he had failed for forty years, to explain how this desirable consummation was to be achieved.

*　　*　　*

It had gone too easily, as if Caesar could sink without trace. Markie swelled in fatuous complacency. He held court in front of the Temple of Tellus; senators, knights, ordinary citizens crowded round him, taking up the refrain of "Noble Brutus".

"Bloody fool," Casca said. "He believes them, you know. We've buggered it, haven't we, old dear?"

"Yes."

"Well, I never thought we wouldn't. But it had to be done."

"Yes," I said, "but we've buggered it."

We had lost our chance of gaining an ascendancy in the Senate, though we had had, I think, a majority. The fate of the wretched Cinna showed the mood of the people. We had no troops at our command, and so depended on the continuing goodwill of Antony, even Lepidus. We were to be punished for our lack of foresight, for our scruples too. We had even failed to suborn Dolabella. Cassius would have none of that. Dolabella, he had said, was a mischief-maker, like all his family, not to be trusted.

"That went off very well," Markie said as the crowd thinned and made for home or tavern.

Such was his judgment on the sitting of the Senate at which Antony had secured his primacy in the Republic.

I did not attend the funeral. It would have been in poor taste. As things turned out, my life would have been in danger also. Trebonius who did attend, protesting that he had not actually struck Caesar, was recognised and pelted with mud. A costermonger hurled a cabbage into his face, another landed him a blow with a stick, a third seized his toga and tore it, so that Trebonius fled, terrified and half-naked, to the nearest friendly house. The mob pursuing him was ready to set fire to the building if Lepidus had not despatched troops to prevent them.

Antony delivered the funeral oration. Cassius and Markie had agreed to that; they could have done nothing to prevent him. According to reports, he began by saying he had nothing against Caesar's murderers. They had acted, in their own opinion, for the good of the Republic. They were honourable men who feared Caesar's ambition. He made great play on the word "honour", and perjured himself when he denied Caesar's ambition. The sarcasm delighted the mob; they roared, demanding more of it.

Then – his masterstroke – he showed them Caesar's bloody toga. He pointed to every rent. He identified each dagger-thrust, pausing for emphasis. It was all acting, of course; we couldn't ourselves have claimed responsibility for particular gashes. But the crowd howled.

I heard the noise and ordered my slaves to set up barricades around my house and bolt the doors.

Then Antony read the will. He told them of Caesar's benefactions to the people, and none remembered that Caesar had lived for thirty years on borrowed money and soaring debts, until he became rich by the plunder of Rome's enemies. They didn't even recall that he had had charge of the State Treasury for five years now, a circumstance which had elicited some of Cicero's most acid jests.

The crowd surged forward, seized the body and burned it in the Forum. They cried out that Caesar was a god. Urged on by an agitator called Herophilus, who claimed to be a bastard grandson of old Gaius Marius, they set up an altar and a pillar in the Forum, offering prayers and sacrifices to Caesar's spirit.

"His bloody murderers would be the best sacrifice," Herophilus cried, and they shouted approval, then set off to fire the houses of those of us whom they could identify. The smoke filled my nostrils all night, but the precautions I had taken kept me safe, in spite of my slaves' terror.

Next morning reports came which convinced me that we had lost Rome and were in mortal danger.

Antony, maintaining the pretence of civility, even friendship, sent me a note to inform me that I was named in the will as guardian to Octavius.

> Since you have been on such intimate terms with the boy, I trust you will use your influence to remind him he is still only a boy, unfit for public life. Do so, and I shall be in your debt; Rome also, more than ever.

Antony's unease, his evident fear that Octavius might challenge his leadership of the Caesarean party, did something to restore my hopes that all was not lost. I therefore wrote to Octavius in appropriate terms.

The flimsy unity of the Ides of March disintegrated. Markie's nerve broke with it. He fled the city, to seek support, Cassius said, in the municipalities of Latium. My father-in-law soon followed. We parted without regret, each reproaching the other for our mistakes and misfortunes. My accusations were justified. He had been the originator of our enterprise, and bore chief responsibility for its failure. "If you had listened to me . . ." I said. It was too much for him. Conscious that he was in the wrong, he left me without even seeking news of his daughter.

Two days later I set out for my province of Cisalpine Gaul. Civil war could not be long delayed. Word came that Octavius had landed at Brindisi and won the support of the legions there. Caesar's heir was on the march.

I would have gone to Aricia to see Longina. But I dared not delay. Wretched news from all quarters spurred me on. Poor Longina.

Careless of danger, Casca, alone among us, refused to alter his way of life. He was surprised in a brothel by a handful of Caesar's veterans. They broke into the chamber, thrusting the terrified master of the place aside. Casca was naked and defence-less, but for his fists. They stabbed him twenty-three times, the same number of wounds as Caesar had received. I believe that most of Casca's were inflicted after death. Then they mutilated the Syrian boy with whom he had been taking his pleasure, and dragged Casca's corpse into the alley where it was discovered by the watchmen towards dawn.

CHAPTER

24

I wept for Casca. I feared for myself. Therefore I made all haste to my province. There I discovered puzzled and near-mutinous legions, discontented municipalities, few subordinates worthy of trust, fear and uncertainty everywhere.

I did not repine. Despondent letters came from Cassius and Markie, both of whom had now fled to the East, ostensibly to their respective provinces of Cyrene and Crete. Cassius declared civil war certain, no longer hoped for victory. Markie admitted that I had been correct in my assessment, and he mistaken: "I have trusted too much in virtue and benevolence; you, cousin, were wiser in your cynicism." I would have respected him if he had not contrived to combine his confession of error with a renewed claim to superior virtue. But I was too busy to brood on such matters.

My first business was to raise an army. The bulk of experienced legions adhered to Antony, though some might join Octavius. The boy had arrived at Brindisi and announced that, as Caesar's heir, he would now be known as Caesar Octavianus.

Cisalpine Gaul was good recruiting ground, and I soon commanded a sizeable force. Yet I could not delude myself, for I knew only too well the difference between raw recruits and the veterans of many wars. I was also compelled to dilute the quality of my best legion (the Ninth) by seconding centurions and veterans to new formations, both for training purposes and to stiffen morale.

Time was what I needed; time was denied me. First, Antony had himself appointed to Cisalpine Gaul in my place at the end of his consular year. Then, with unparalleled insolence, he held a plebiscite on the Kalends of June, to secure himself the authority to assume immediate command of my province. The proposal, unsanctioned by precedent, tore the mask of friendship from Antony's face. His ambition was now naked: to secure an absolute ascendancy in the Republic.

This alarmed Octavius, who wrote to me at last in friendly terms, offering a meeting. His letter reached me while I was making war on the Alpine tribes. The war, necessary in itself, was more valuable on account of the experience of combat it gave my troops. They performed better than I had dared to hope. It was therefore with a new optimism that I set out to meet Octavius at Orvieto, ignoring a peremptory demand from Antony that I should surrender my province to him within the month.

We met at a villa, belonging to his stepfather Philippus, in the hills outside the city.

"What a lot of soldiers you have brought, Mouse. I hope you have supplies for them. We certainly can't feed them."

He hesitated before accepting my kiss. Maecenas sniggered in the background. Young Marcus Agrippa, who had served under me in Greece and whom I respected as an efficient officer, glowered. I had hoped Octavius and I would be alone together.

"Oh no," he said, "I'm far too susceptible to your dangerous charm, my dear. Maecenas and Agrippa stay."

This time Maecenas smirked. He was dressed in the Greek fashion, his eyebrows were plucked, and he was drenched with a sweet, spicy scent.

Wine was offered, and produced with little almond cakes. We sat on a terrace overlooking a golden valley. The olive trees glimmered in the noon heat.

"Well?"

"Well," I said, "these are strange circumstances in which we meet."

"Very strange."

"You've done well," I said. "Antony is furious with you. And you've got Cicero to approve you. I admire you for that."

"Cicero is respectable," he said.

"And you're an adventurer."

"I am Caesar's heir."

"Antony disputes that."

"Naturally."

He was altogether at his ease. It was difficult to believe he was only nineteen. He still looked like the boy whom my caresses had delighted; his lips curved in the same enticing way. His skin glowed. He stretched out a bare leg and scratched his thigh.

"You've done extraordinarily well," I said.

"I know nothing, of course, about war," Maecenas, to my irritation, intervened. "It's not my thing at all. But politically we're ahead of the game."

He giggled.

"It'll come to war, though," I said, "and then where are you? Even politically, things are not quite as you think they are. You're proud of winning Cicero's support, and, as I said, that was a good move. But you can't trust him. Nobody has ever succeeded by trusting Cicero. Besides, have you heard what he's been saying? 'The boy must be flattered, decorated, and disposed of.' That's what he really thinks of you."

"Perhaps."

He bit into a peach. Juice trickled from the corner of his lips. He dabbed at it with a napkin.

"Cicero thinks he's using me," he said. "I think I'm using him. One of us will prove mistaken. Probably him. I've got an army, you see."

"Yes," I said, "and no experience of war, no experienced general."

"Are you proposing yourself, Mouse?"

"Our interests are the same."

"Well, really, ducky, that's a bit of a whopper," Maecenas said. "You did kill Caesar, you know. Or have you forgotten? And we're out to avenge him. Least, that's what our men believe."

"There is a certain difficulty there, Mouse. You must see there is." Octavius smiled. "In the long run certainly."

"The immediate concern is Antony," I said. "He's your enemy and mine. He's ordered me to surrender my province, and you to surrender your legions."

"Oh, you know that, do you? All the same, I can work with Antony, once I've taught him to fear me."

"And how will you do that?"

"Any way that's necessary. That's something I learned from my father."

"Caesar, you mean?"

"Yes, Caesar, of course. I call him my father now, you know. It goes down well with the men . . ."

The shadow of dead Caesar fell on the table between us. Octavius turned away. His profile, chiselled against the distant hills, held my gaze. I remarked what I had never seen before: the set of his jaw.

"He's a god now, you know. I had that officially decreed. His altars rise all over the Empire, even in your province, I'm told."

"Yes," I said. "Foolery. Caesar would have laughed himself."

"I don't think so. He was prepared for deification. You call it 'foolery', Mouse, but I have legions to support it. And the Senate approves me; I was elected consul two weeks ago. Has that news reached you?"

"Quite an occasion," Maecenas said. "My dear, you should have seen it. Twelve vultures flew overhead as the dear boy took the auspices. Well, you can imagine how that delighted the crowd, especially since there were those quick to remind them that Romulus himself had been greeted in the same way."

"Foolery," I said again. "Who released the birds?"

"Does that matter?" Octavius said. "They flew."

"Something else you should know," Agrippa spoke for the first time. "We're going to rescind the amnesty offered Caesar's murderers. You've had it. Your number's up."

"More wine?" Octavius pushed the jug towards me, and smiled.

"You know what else Cicero said?" Maecenas laid his hand on my arm, resisting my effort to shake it off. "He asked, 'What god has given this godlike youth to the Roman people?'"

"So you see," the godlike youth smiled again, "the game is going my way, Mouse. I don't think you have anything to offer me."

Hope all but left me then, but I struggled on. Antony marched against me, forced me into Mutina, where we withstood a terrible siege that winter. His success alarmed Octavius, who persuaded the Senate to declare him a public enemy. In his alarm he made a new overture towards me. I responded as if I trusted him. But trust had died in the early autumn sunshine in the hills above Orvieto. Yet an alliance was constructed, an alliance of shifting interest, nothing more. The consuls-elect, Hirtius and Pansa, marched against Antony, compelling him to raise the siege. My ragged, half-starved soldiers emerged from the city where we had waited for death.

If I had had cavalry, if my poor legions had not been so weakened by their privations, if, if, if . . . Then I would have pursued Antony, and might still have snatched victory. But all I could do was urge Octavius to cut off Antony's jackal, Publius Ventidius, as he marched from Picenum with three veteran legions; but the boy failed, or chose to fail . . .

My last hope was to effect a union with Lucius Munatius Plancus, governor of Gallia Comata. I knew him for a time-server, but he had written to me deploring the state of the Republic and describing Antony as "a brigand". I pushed north over the pass of the Little St Bernard. At every stage of the march deserters slipped away. Food was in short supply, likewise money. A courier came from Cicero, addressing me as the last hope of the Republic in the West. He inveighed against Antony, against Octavius, against Fate. I read his missive as hope tumbled from me like the rocks that clattered down the Alpine hillsides.

I reached Grenoble and found Plancus there. He received me with smiles and soft words. His troops were fat; they looked on my scarecrows with wonder, horror and contempt. Plancus smiled as he insulted my enemies. "Young Caesar was a monster of odious ingratitude and ambition; Antony an unprincipled scoundrel; Lepidus a vain buffoon whose word was as worthless as a Greek whore's."

Or as Plancus' own. How can you rely on a man who will speak well of no one but himself?

On the eighth day trumpets sounded. They heralded the arrival of Caius Asinius Pollio with two legions. Pollio was an old comrade. He had been with me when we crossed the Rubicon, had fought by my side in Spain. When I greeted him, he said:

"I come from Antony."

"Oh," I said, "and Plancus has been waiting your arrival."

"Just so."

"I am sorry," Plancus said, "but I really have no choice but to ally myself to Antony and Octavius."

I tried to argue my case. They would have none of it. When I said that Antony and Octavius had come together in a criminal conspiracy against the Republic, Pollio said:

"That's enough."

I withdrew to my camp, surprised that they permitted me that liberty.

That night, I slipped away, under cover of darkness, wind and rain. Only two centuries would follow me. The rest received my orders with dumb insolence and I was powerless to punish them.

My remnant of a plan was to make a wide circuit through the Alps and then head for Macedonia where Cassius was assembling an army. You know how it ended. Unable to deploy scouts (for I feared they too would desert) we were surprised, encircled, taken. The Gauls, when they learned who I was, looked on me with amazement.

CHAPTER
25

And so night closed upon me.

I have written to both Antony and Octavius, but am reconciled to death. My last wish is to avoid dishonour; therefore I have penned this history of my engagement in the death of Caesar. Should it survive, I am confident that posterity will judge me a true servant of the Republic.

I warned Antony to beware of Octavius. "The boy will be your master," I said, "and you only his accomplice in the destruction of liberty which alone gives meaning to life."

My last flicker of hope is to sow dissension. Accordingly I reminded Octavius that Antony had described him as "a mere boy who owes everything to a name".

If only it were true . . . but the boy is no shadow of Caesar. More careful, more judicious, he will exceed him in tyranny. We thought to save liberty; we leave Rome threatened with a closer confinement, a more degrading slavery.

I have had no word from Longina. I do not even know whether our son lives.

It does not matter how a man ends. What matters is how he has lived, and I have lived honourably.

I have charged Artixes with the safekeeping of this memoir. I do not think he will fail me, though he cannot understand the importance I attach to it.

This morning he ushered in a messenger whom I recognised as one of Lepidus' men. I experienced a surge of hope, which was grotesque: how could a thing like Lepidus offer hope?

His master, he said, had come together with Antony and Octavius. They were convening on an island in the river near Bologna. There they would arrange matters of State. There would be no clemency. All were agreed that Caesar's policy had been mistaken. Instead they would draw up a list of proscribed persons.

So I received my death warrant. I asked Artixes for wine.

"I take it," I said, "that your father has received the same message."

He nodded, unable to speak.

"Tell him," I said, "that I understand and accept my fate."

He looked at me with horror and admiration.

I have said farewell to my few faithful attendants. I have given the most trusted a letter for Longina, assuring her of my love, and thanking her . . .

Even as I wrote it I wondered if she had not already found a new lover. Yet I feel her lips on mine.

Artixes brought me a case containing my own jewelled dagger. He brought also a message from his father. I have till dawn. This is more honourable conduct than I had expected from a barbarian. But then I know he has been impressed by the dignity with which I have borne my misfortunes. There is something in the barbarian soul which responds nobly to nobility.

Death is the extinction of a candle; nothing more.

I do not believe the poets who promise . . . but it is not good to brood on these matters. It serves nothing.

I also wrote again to Octavius, for my mind was full of him:

> Do you recall that dinner at Cicero's where we first met? (Incidentally, I wager that Cicero is included, at Antony's insistence, on your list of those proscribed and that you have washed your hands of his fate; am I right?) On that occasion you said: "A man is but a man; he should not see himself as a tragic figure." I agree.
>
> And do you recall how we talked of the danger that the pursuit of self-interest portended for the Republic?

Think of that now that you are about to be assailed by the temptations which lured Caesar to his death. Recall your friend and lover whose only crime was to care more for the Republic than for himself or Caesar. Reflect that other Brutuses will arise, if virtue and the love of liberty have not been extinguished in Rome.

You will destroy Antony. You will be wiser than Caesar and not assume the appearance of absolute power.

Yet you will possess it.

Will its exercise corrupt and obliterate the boy I loved?

I beg you to care for my wife Longina. As the daughter of Gaius Cassius and the spouse of Decimus Brutus she suffers from connections that may do her harm. Pray see to it that neither she nor our son is afflicted on my account.

It is hard to end, hard to finish all, confessing failure. Yet, Crassus, Pompey, Caesar, the great men of my youth and manhood, all met inglorious death.

Beware the jealous gods, Octavius . . .

Remember me, while the flesh is on you. In time you too will be spilt on air.

The grey morning is touched with rosy fingers. At the door of my hut, I have breathed free air, soft for the mountains. Cocks crow in the valley.

What were Clodia's words?

"The cold grey clutch of death . . ." Something like that. "We cannot play gods," she said.

When we slew Caesar we dared all that a man is fit for.

The dagger with which I stabbed him is to hand.

There is no more to be said.